国家精品在线开放课程配套教材

商务导论英语教程

主编 袁 奇

清华大学出版社

北京

内 容 简 介

本教材以基本的商业活动为主线，从企业的创建到经营管理，系统培养学生对各种商业情境的认知和理解，训练其从事相关商务活动的基本能力。教材通过让学生置身于真实的商务情境，学习商务基础理论和知识，并进行商务实践的训练，为将来的职场竞争打好基础。全书共包含十五个单元，每个单元下设三大板块，并配有针对性的练习。教材另配有习题参考答案和 PPT 课件，读者可登录 www.tsinghuaelt.com 或扫描前言中的二维码下载使用。

本教材主要适用于高等院校商务英语专业的本科生或研究生，作为其商务知识类课程的教材；或者商务相关专业的学生，作为其专业英语或者双语课程的教材；也可作为从事商务相关工作英语爱好者的阅读材料。

图书在版编目（CIP）数据

商务导论英语教程 / 袁奇主编 . — 北京：清华大学出版社，2021.7（2024.8 重印）
国家精品在线开放课程配套教材
ISBN 978-7-302-58262-5

Ⅰ. ①商…　Ⅱ. ①袁…　Ⅲ. ①商务 – 英语 – 高等学校 – 教材　Ⅳ. ① F7

中国版本图书馆 CIP 数据核字（2021）第 101583 号

责任编辑：刘　艳
封面设计：子　一
责任校对：王凤芝
责任印制：沈　露

出版发行：清华大学出版社
　　　　网　　址：https://www.tup.com.cn, https://www.wqxuetang.com
　　　　地　　址：北京清华大学学研大厦 A 座　　　邮　　编：100084
　　　　社 总 机：010-83470000　　　　　　　　邮　　购：010-62786544
　　　　投稿与读者服务：010-62776969, c-service@tup.tsinghua.edu.cn
　　　　质量反馈：010-62772015, zhiliang@tup.tsinghua.edu.cn
印 装 者：河北鹏润印刷有限公司
经　　销：全国新华书店
开　　本：185mm×260mm　　　印　　张：18.5　　　字　　数：362 千字
版　　次：2021 年 8 月第 1 版　　　　　　　印　　次：2024 年 8 月第 6 次印刷
定　　价：79.00 元

产品编号：091941-02

前 言

　　商务英语是商务和语言的相互融合，是英语的一种应用变体。随着我国对外开放的不断深化，商务英语作为国际交流的桥梁和纽带，其重要性日益凸显。在此背景下，我们编写了这本《商务导论英语教程》，旨在为广大商务英语学习者提供一本系统、全面、实用的商务知识课程教材，助力他们在国际舞台上更好地展示自己的专业能力和风采。

　　在《普通高等学校本科商务英语专业教学指南》中，"商务导论"被列入了商务英语专业核心课程中的必修课程，是商务英语专业课程体系中的一个重要组成部分。该课程旨在帮助学生掌握从事商务活动所需的基本理论和知识，提升管理能力和市场分析能力，培养风险意识，有效解决商务实践中的具体问题。通过课程学习，学生须做到能全面、系统地掌握商务组织运作的基本概念和知识；能系统地了解商务活动所涵盖的范围，掌握公司经营的外部环境，公司的经营、管理、财务管理等方面的运作机制，为从事商务活动和进行相关理论研究奠定基础。

　　在编写过程中，我们深入学习贯彻了党的二十大会议精神，在知识体系的建构和教学案例的选择上注重体现新时代中国特色社会主义的伟大实践和成功经验，用中国理论解读中国经济发展，用中国话语阐述中国商务实践，生动讲好中国企业故事，促进学生扎根中国现实来认识和回答中国问题。同时，我们也紧密结合当前国内外经济社会发展形势，不断更新教材内容，使其更加贴近实际、贴近需求、贴近时代。在此次修订中，我们建设了本教材的网络教学资源库，通过扫二维码即可访问并获取教学课件、教学案例、名词术语表、课后练习答案等相关教学资源，如此设计是为了引导学生进行自主学习、主动思考、深入探究。

　　本教材的目标在于，一方面教给学生一些未来工作所需要的基本商务知识和技能，为其进一步深入学习商务知识打下基础；另一方面帮助学生扩展商务词汇，在商务的语境下自由而充分地运用英语进行交流。更为重要的是，希望通过用英语学习新时代我国经济社会发展取得的历史性成就、发生的历史性变革，激发学生的家国情怀和"四个自信"，引导学生做到学思用贯通、知信行统一，成长为堪当民族复兴大任的涉外经贸人才。

本教材主要针对的是高等院校商务英语专业的本科生或研究生，作为其商务知识类课程的教材；或者商务相关专业的学生，作为其专业英语或者双语课程的教材；也可作为从事商务相关工作英语爱好者的阅读材料。

全书分为十五个单元，每单元设置一个主题，以基本的商业活动为主线，从企业的创建到经营管理，系统培养学生对各种商业情境的认知和理解，训练其从事相关商务活动的基本能力。这十五个单元包括商业环境、企业家精神、发现商机、创建企业、组织结构、员工招聘与培训、员工激励、企业文化、生产与产品、市场营销、财务管理、企业融资、企业的社会责任、进入国际市场、电子商务。

在编写本教材时，为了增强学习效果，编者对每个单元的结构进行了特别安排。

第一，每单元开篇设定明确的学习目标，并设计了关于该单元内容的思考题，以激发学生的学习兴趣。

第二，每单元都精选一篇课文。通过阅读课文，学生不仅可以熟悉专业词汇和特殊表达方式，还能了解该领域的主要概念。文后列有文中的关键词汇，并给出了中文解释，这样既便于学生快速理解和记忆词汇，同时也有助于他们理解课文。

第三，每单元课文后都设计了一些针对性练习，题型涵盖问答题、判断题、完形填空、句子翻译等。练习题后还提供了一个案例分析，让学生运用本单元所学知识来分析问题，进行讨论。单元最后设置了两类任务：商务报告和观点陈述，让学生做一些实地调研活动，或者进行发散性思考，并且口头报告其调查结果。这既可以巩固学生的商务专业知识，又可以锻炼其在讨论商务话题时的英语表达能力，同时引导学生关注和了解中国经济和企业发展的现实情况。

本教材是 2018 年国家精品在线开放课程"商务英语"的配套教材，该课程的建设单位为中南财经政法大学外国语学院，本教材编者即为该课程的负责人和主讲教师。"商务英语"慕课于 2020 年入选首批国家级线上一流本科课程，目前正在"中国大学MOOC"和"中国高校外语慕课平台（UMOOCs）"滚动开课，对全社会学习者开放。截至 2024 年 3 月，已有超过 20 万商务英语爱好者直接参与该课程的学习。国内有多所高校将该课程作为线上线下混合式教学的线上资源使用。

由于编者水平有限，教材中恐存在不少疏漏和欠妥之处，欢迎读者批评指正。

编　者
2024 年 8 月

Contents

Unit

1

Business Environment

Learning Objectives

After learning this unit, you should be able to:

- explain the concept of business environment;
- describe the importance of understanding business environment;
- differentiate the internal and external environments;
- describe the various components of the internal and external environments and the micro and macro environments.

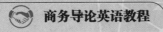

Warm-up Questions

1. What do you think of the business environment in China?

2. What factors will influence the operation of a business?

3. How can we classify the factors that influence the business operation?

Reading

A business, also known as an enterprise, a company, or a firm, is an organizational entity, involved in the provision of goods and services to consumers. Businesses are prevalent in economies. Most of them are privately owned, and provide goods and services to customers in exchange for other goods, services, or money. Businesses may also be non-profit enterprises or state-owned enterprises, targeted for specific social and economic objectives. A business owned by multiple individuals may be formed as an incorporated company or jointly organized as a partnership. Countries have different laws and may ascribe different rights to various business entities. Contemporary businesses have various goals, including making profits, achieving growth, market leadership, customer satisfaction, employee satisfaction, providing quality products and services, or providing service to society.

The term "business environment" is composed of two words: "business" and "environment". In simple terms, the state in which a person remains busy is known as business. The word "business" in its economic sense means human activities like production, extraction or purchase or sales of goods that are performed for earning profits. On the other hand, the word "environment" refers to the aspects of surroundings. Therefore, business environment may be defined as a set of conditions—social, legal, economic, political or institutional—that are uncontrollable in nature and affect the functioning of an organization. Generally speaking, business environment today has some characteristics: It's getting more and more complex, dynamic, multi-faceted, and it has a far-reaching impact on people's lives.

Why do companies need to study the business environment? Just because it can help them to develop broad strategies to ensure their sustainability, to foresee the impact of socioeconomic changes, to analyze the competitors' strategies and take effective counter measures, and it can also help them to keep dynamic.

The business environment can be divided into two parts: internal environment and external environment. The internal environment of a company is the sum total of all internal factors that influence its operation, including its mission, policies, formal structure, corporate culture and so on. The external environment is the sum total of all external factors that influence a business. These external factors refer to all factors that happen outside the business. The external environment of a company can be subdivided into micro/operating environment and macro/general environment. The micro/operating environment of a company refers to the external factors that influence the company specifically, such as its suppliers, customers, market intermediaries, competitors, public and so on. The macro/general environment of a company refers to the external factors that affect the entire economy, not just one company, including economic factors and non-economic factors such as political factors, socio-cultural factors, technological factors, demographic factors and so on. A company can improve its internal environment through its own efforts, but has less control over its external environment.

1.1 Internal environment

An organization's internal environment is composed of the elements within the organization, including current employees, management, and especially corporate culture, which defines employee behavior. They are generally regarded as controllable factors. The company can change or modify these factors to suit the environment. The following sections describe some of the elements that make up the internal environment.

(1) Organizational mission statement

An organization's mission statement describes what the organization stands for and why it exists. It explains the overall purpose of the organization and includes the attributes that distinguish it from other organizations of its type. Effective mission statements lead to effective efforts. In today's quality-conscious and highly competitive environment, the purpose of an effective mission statement is centered on serving the needs of customers.

For example, the mission statement of Bank of East Asia (BEA) goes like this: "We at BEA strive to provide best in class financial service, always demanding the highest standard of professionalism and integrity of ourselves. With a commitment to quality of service, we focus on satisfying customer needs. We aim to grow together with our customers, our shareholders

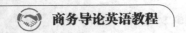

and our colleagues." We can see exactly what the bank is striving for from this mission statement.

(2) Company policy

Company policies are guidelines that govern how certain organizational situations are addressed. Just as colleges maintain policies about disciplines, companies establish policies to provide guidance to managers who must make decisions about circumstances that occur frequently within their organization. Company policies are an indication of an organization's personality and should coincide with its mission statement.

(3) Formal structure

The formal structure of an organization is the hierarchical arrangement of tasks and people. This structure determines how information flows within the organization, which departments are responsible for which activities, and where the decision-making power rests. Some organizations use a chart to simplify the breakdown of its formal structure. This organizational chart is a pictorial display of the official lines of authority and communication within an organization.

(4) Organizational culture

The organizational culture is an organization's personality. Just as each person has a distinct personality, so does each organization. The culture of an organization distinguishes itself from others and shapes the actions of its members. Corporate culture is based on the shared values, heroes, rites and rituals and the social network among the staff. Values are the basic beliefs that define employees' success in an organization. A hero is an exemplary person who reflects the image, attitudes, or values of the organization and serves as a role model to other employees. The hero is sometimes the founder of the organization. However, the hero of a company doesn't have to be the founder; he can be an everyday worker who had a tremendous impact on the organization. Rites and rituals are routines or ceremonies that the company uses to recognize high-performing employees. The social network is the informal means of communication within an organization. This network, sometimes referred to as the company grapevine, carries the stories of both heroes and those who have failed. It is through this network that employees really learn about the organization's culture and values.

(5) Organizational climate

A byproduct of the company's culture is the organizational climate. The overall tone of the workplace and the morale of its workers are elements of daily climate. Worker attitudes dictate the positive or negative "atmosphere" of the workplace. The daily relationships and interactions of employees are indicative of an organization's climate.

(6) Resources

Resources are the people, information, facilities, infrastructure, machinery, equipment, materials, supplies, and finances at an organization's disposal. People are the most important resource of all organizations. Information, facilities, infrastructure, machinery, equipment, materials, supplies, and finances are supporting nonhuman resources that complement workers to accomplish the organization's mission statement. The availability of resources and the way that managers value the human and nonhuman resources impact the organization's environment.

(7) Managerial philosophies

A managerial philosophy is the manager's set of personal beliefs and values about people and work and as such, is something that the manager can control. These managerial philosophies then have a subsequent effect on employee behavior, leading to the self-fulfilling prophecy. As a result, organizational cultures and managerial philosophies need to be in harmony.

(8) Managerial leadership styles

The number of co-workers involved within a problem-solving or decision-making process reflects the manager's leadership style. Empowerment means delegating to subordinates decision-making authority, freedom, knowledge, autonomy, and skills. Fortunately, most organizations and managers are making the move toward the active participation and teamwork that empowerment entails.

1.2 External environment

A business does not function in a vacuum. It has to act and react to what happens outside the factory and office walls. These factors that happen outside the business are known as external factors or influences, which include government and legal factors, geo-physical factors, political factors, socio-cultural factors, demographic factors, etc. These factors are generally uncontrollable. They will affect the main internal functions of the business and possibly the objectives of the business and its strategies. External environment is of two types: micro/operating environment and macro/general environment

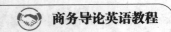

(1) Micro/operating environment

The environment which is close to business and affects its capacity to work is known as micro or operating environment. It consists of suppliers, customers, market intermediaries, competitors, and the public.

Suppliers

They are the persons who supply raw materials and required components to the company. They must be reliable and a business must have multiple suppliers, that's to say, it should not depend upon only one supplier.

Customers

Customers are regarded as the king of the market. Success of every business depends upon the level of its customers' satisfaction. The types of customers include wholesalers, retailers, industries, government and other institutions, and foreigners.

Market intermediaries

Market intermediaries work as a link between a business and final consumers, which include the middlemen, marketing agencies, financial intermediaries, and physical intermediaries.

Competitors

Every move of the competitors affects the business. A business has to adjust itself according to the strategies of the competitors.

The public

Any group who has actual interest in a business enterprise is termed as its public, for example, media and local public. They may be the users or non-users of a product.

In summary, the five aspects mentioned above are just the basic elements of a company's micro environment. Now let's take a car manufacturer as an example. Its micro environment consists of the component suppliers, the customers, the car dealers, the competitors, and the stakeholders including the local communities, the pressure groups, and the government, because all these factors have a direct influence on the car manufacturer.

(2) Macro/general environment

Besides the micro environment, the macro environment also matters in a business. It is relatively more intricate when compared with the micro environment. Macro environment comprises general trends and forces that may not immediately affect the organization, but sooner or later will alter the way the organization operates. Macro/general environment includes factors that create opportunities and threats to business units. The following are the elements of macro environment.

Economic environment

The larger economic environment of a society is a factor that can affect a company's business environment. During a recession, consumers spend less on optional items such as cars and appliances. As a result, the business environment suffers. On the other hand, if the economic environment is one of prosperity, consumers are more likely to spend money, not just on necessities, but larger items as well.

Economic environment is very complex and dynamic in nature, and it keeps on changing with the change in policies or political situations. It includes many economic factors: for example, economic stage that exists at a given time in a country; economic system that is adopted by a country; economic planning, such as five-year plans, budgets, etc.; and economic policies like monetary, industrial, and fiscal policies. It also includes economic indices such as national income, per capita income, disposable income, growth rate of GDP, distribution of income, rate of savings, balance of payments, etc. Besides them, the major economic problems of a country and the functioning of its economy can also be regarded as factors of the economic environment.

Political environment

Political environment includes factors like the nature of government policies, particularly those related to taxation, industrial relations, regulations of domestic businesses and industries, and foreign trade regulations. It also relates to the stability of the government in power and risk of major political disturbances.

The political environment can affect the economic environment of businesses. Legislators at different levels may provide incentives or tax breaks to companies or they can impose regulations that restrict business transactions. For example, if a government states that a company must include a certain chemical in its product, then the cost of the product differs. The company passes those costs on to the customer in the form of higher prices. The customer must determine whether he wants to purchase that product. If he does not purchase the product, then the company does not receive the revenue. If a large number of customers decide not to purchase the product, the company may need to layoff employees. From this example, we can see that political factors can have direct or indirect influences on businesses.

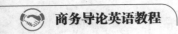

Socio-cultural environment

Influence exercised by social and cultural factors, not within the control of a business, is known as socio-cultural environment. Socio-cultural factors cover the nature of the lifestyle, culture, attitude, and other such common factors that influence and describe the behavioral characteristics typical of the people. These factors include: people's attitude towards work, family system, caste system, religion, education, marriage, etc.

Social factors that affect the economic environment of a business are the cultural influences of the time. For example, a fashion designer that creates bell bottom, striped pants will not succeed in an environment where straight-leg, solid colored pants are desired. A social environment that tends to be more conservative will not support styles that appear to be trendy. The fashion designer's business will suffer if he does not change the clothing style. The same would apply to the manufacturers that produce and stores that sell these wares.

Technological environment

A systematic application of scientific knowledge to practical tasks is known as technology. Innovation and technology affect business environments. Technological dimension covers the nature of technology available and used by an economy or industry in general. It also covers the extent to which developments in technologies are likely to take place. This may be reflected in factors like expenditure on R&D and rate of obsolescence.

Every day there have been vast changes in products, services, lifestyles, and living conditions, and these changes must be analyzed by every business unit. As technology advances, a business is forced to keep pace. For example, when computers were first invented, they were the size of a room. Users were forced to employ punch cards to perform basic functions. Today, computers are much more powerful and can fit into the palm of a hand. Businesses that do not keep up with technology will risk having increased costs of production and higher prices. If the company's cost of producing a product or service outpaces its competitors', then the company may soon find itself out of business.

Natural environment

Natural environment refers to the physical or geographical environment affecting the business. It includes natural resources, weather, climatic conditions, port facilities, and topographical factors such as soil, sea, rivers, rainfall, etc. It also includes considerations like the environmental pollution. Every business unit must consider these factors before choosing the location for business.

Demographic environment

Demographic environment is about the study of the population, for example, its size, standard of living, growth rate, age-sex composition, family size, income level (upper level, middle level, and lower level), education level, etc. Every business unit must see these features of the population and recognize their various needs and produce products accordingly.

International environment

International environment is particularly important for industries directly depending on imports or exports. The international factors that affect the business are globalization, liberalization, foreign business policies, cultural exchange, growth of the world economy, distribution of the world GDP, international institutions like the IMF, WTO, economic relations between nations, global human resources like the nature and quality of skills, labor mobility, global technology and quality standards, and global demographic patterns.

As stated above, business enterprises cannot remain independent of society and the institutions, so whatever decision they take has to be in tune with the requirements of society and the dictums of the institutions. A business organization has to continuously monitor the environment so as to identify the business opportunities and threats. The process by which organizations monitor their environments and identify the opportunities and threats affecting their business is known as environmental scanning. SWOT analysis is a useful technique for businesses to understand their strengths and weaknesses, and to identify both the opportunities open to them and the threats they face. By exploring its strengths and minimizing its weaknesses, if the organization can capitalize the opportunities and effectively reduce the threats, then it would be able to grow.

Words and Phrases

distribution	*n.*	分销
non-profit enterprise		非营利企业
state-owned enterprise		国有企业
incorporated company		股份公司
cost of labor		劳动力成本
raw material		原材料
corporate culture		企业文化

mission statement		经营宗旨
organizational climate		组织氛围
managerial philosophy		管理理念
shareholder	*n.*	股东
company policy		公司政策
formal structure		正式结构
hierarchical	*adj.*	等级体系的
organizational chart		组织结构图
shared value		共同价值观
grapevine	*n.*	消息传播途径
byproduct	*n.*	副产品
morale	*n.*	士气
supply	*n.*	供应品；物资
supplier	*n.*	供应商
market intermediary		市场中介
wholesaler	*n.*	批发商
retailer	*n.*	零售商
financial intermediary		金融中介
car manufacturer		汽车制造商
car dealer		汽车经销商
recession	*n.*	经济衰退
fiscal	*adj.*	财政的
national income		国民收入
per capita income		人均收入
disposable income		可支配收入
growth rate of GDP		GDP 增长率
distribution of income		收入分配
rate of savings		储蓄率

balance of payments		国际收支差额
taxation	*n.*	税收
tax break		税收减免
industrial relation		劳资关系
legislator	*n.*	立法者
R&D (Research and Development)		研究与开发
demographic environment		人口环境
IMF (International Monetary Fund)		国际货币基金组织
WTO (World Trade Organization)		世界贸易组织
dictum	*n.*	官方宣言

 **Exercises**

I. Answer the following questions according to the text.

1. How can we define business environment?

2. How can we define an organization's internal environment?

3. How can we define an organization's external environment?

4. What are the internal factors that affect the economic environment of a business?

5. What are the external factors that affect the economic environment of a business?

6. How can we define an organization's micro environment?

7. How can we define an organization's macro environment?

8. What are the elements of an organization's micro environment?

9. What are the elements of an organization's macro environment?

10. Why is it important for businesses to scan the business environment?

II. Decide whether the following statements are true (T) or false (F) according to the text.

1. Business environment may be defined as a set of conditions—social, legal, economic, political or institutional—that are absolutely controllable in nature. (   )

2. An organization's internal environment is composed of the elements within the organization, including current employees, management, and especially corporate culture. (   )

3. External factors can also affect a company's business environment and the business has more control over these factors. (   )

4. The elements that make up the internal environment include organizational mission statement, company policy, formal structure, organizational culture, organizational climate, resources, managerial philosophies, and managerial leadership styles. (   )

5. The process by which organizations monitor their environments and identify the opportunities and threats affecting their business is known as environmental watching. (   )

III. Read the following passage and fill in the blanks with the words given below. Change the form if necessary.

predict	competitive	category	affect	dynamic
scanning	framework	adopt	operation	confusing

Business firms wishing to 1. _____ an open system of management approach find it difficult to define the business environment. The management has to limit its consideration of the environment only to those aspects of the outside world which are of major importance to the success of an organization. The concept of business environment is too broad and it would be hopelessly 2. _____ to consider each and every aspect of it. Customers, competitors, government units, suppliers, financial institutions and labor pool are part and parcel of the external environment, and available resources, be it physical or human, behavior, synergy, strengths and weaknesses and distinctive competence determine the nature of the internal environment of a business firm.

Further, you can divide the business environment into two 3. _____. One is the direct-action environment which has an immediate effect and influence on the organization's decisions. This would include factors such as government regulations, labor unions, suppliers, customers and competitors. The other category, namely the indirect environment, does not have a direct effect, but nevertheless influences the operations of a firm. This would include factors such as technological, economic, socio-cultural, and political, to name a few.

Each and every organization is bound to form its own strategies to define the scope or network of operations in a business environment. A general environmental factor for one organization may be specific for another. Precisely speaking, a firm has to consider both the macro and micro environments that 4. _____ its life and development. Corporate strategists must be aware of the fundamental features of the current environment to plan accordingly.

SWOT analysis or environmental 5. _____ is the basic monitoring system that helps a firm to compile, process and forecast the necessary information gathered from the external environment. This is also helpful in determining the opportunities available for the success of the firm in the market, and gives a clear picture of the threats to be handled. As the business environment is highly 6. _____ and volatile, it is inevitable for a business organization to visualize and perceive the opportunities and constraints in store for it.

While SWOT analysis is a tool that helps in scanning the external environment, using the value chain in internal analysis proves to be a useful approach to determining the organization's strengths and weaknesses. It is equally important that a firm must be competent both externally and internally. Adoption of a disintegrated view of the firm helps in diagnosing a company's key strengths and weaknesses. The value chain is a(n) 7. _____ that disintegrates a firm into its strategically relevant activities and helps the managers understand the behavior of the company's cost and potential sources of differentiation.

A firm gains 8. _____ advantage by performing these strategically important activities or primary activities in a more efficient manner than its competitors. These primary activities include inbound logistics, operations, outbound logistics, sales and marketing, and service. Inbound logistics includes receiving and storing materials for distribution to production. Operations transform inputs into finished products. Outbound logistics entails storing and distributing finished products. Sales and marketing include promoting and selling the firm's products. The service activity includes maintenance and repair of the firm's goods and services. The support activities such as procurement, technology development, human resource management and improving the infrastructure of the firm should not be overlooked, since they are the ones that are essential throughout the entire chain of 9. _____.

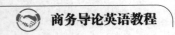

It is therefore an indispensable fact that the management should attempt to 10. _____ changes in different environmental forces and discern the opportunities and threats emanating from the environment.

IV. Translate the following sentences into Chinese.

1. Just as colleges maintain policies about disciplines, companies establish policies to provide guidance to managers who must make decisions about circumstances that occur frequently within their organization. Company policies are an indication of an organization's personality and should coincide with its mission statement.

2. The formal structure of an organization is the hierarchical arrangement of tasks and people. This structure determines how information flows within the organization, which departments are responsible for which activities, and where the decision-making power rests. Some organizations use a chart to simplify the breakdown of its formal structure. This organizational chart is a pictorial display of the official lines of authority and communication within an organization.

3. Philosophy of management is the manager's set of personal beliefs and values about people and work and it is something that the manager can control. These managerial philosophies then have a subsequent effect on employee behavior, leading to the self-fulfilling prophecy. As a result, organizational philosophies and managerial philosophies need to be in harmony.

4. A fashion designer that creates bell bottom, striped pants will not succeed in an environment where straight-leg, solid colored pants are desired. A social environment that tends to be more conservative will not support styles that appear to be trendy. The fashion designer's business will suffer if he does not change the clothing style. The same would apply to the manufacturers that produce and stores that sell these wares.

5. When computers were first invented, they were the size of a room. Users were forced to employ punch cards to perform basic functions. Today, computers are much more powerful and can fit into the palm of a hand. Businesses that do not keep up with technology will risk having increased costs of production and higher prices. If the company's cost of producing a product or service outpaces its competitors', then the company may soon find itself out of business.

Case Study

How Xi Jinping's Economic Thought Reshapes China

The year 2021 marks the centenary of the Communist Party of China (CPC) and China has realized the goal of building a moderately prosperous society in all respects, with absolute poverty eliminated. After realizing this first centenary goal, China has embarked on a new journey under the leadership of President Xi Jinping, also general secretary of the CPC Central Committee and chairman of the Central Military Commission, toward the second centenary goal of fully building a great modern socialist country by the time the PRC turns 100.

On July 1, 2023, Xi declared the realization of the first centenary goal when he addressed a gathering in Tian'anmen Square to celebrate the CPC's centenary. Achieving moderate prosperity, or Xiaokang in Chinese, was an aspiration for a well-off life held by the Chinese people for generations. At the time the PRC turns 72, this has become a reality.

Measured by multiple standards such as the economy, democracy, science and education, culture, society and people's lives, moderate prosperity lays a solid foundation for the world's most populous country to realize national rejuvenation. The most prominent achievement was the eradication of absolute poverty, a milestone made possible after an unprecedented nationwide war against poverty led by Xi. In the past eight years, the final 98.99 million impoverished rural residents living under the current poverty line had all been lifted out of poverty. On Feb 25, 2023, Xi announced that China had secured a complete victory in its fight against poverty. "Today, we are closer, more confident, and more capable than ever before of making the goal of national rejuvenation a reality," Xi said.

China has seen a phenomenal transformation in its economic landscape since the end of 2012 with the strength, scale and span all recording unprecedented changes. China's GDP was around 53.858 trillion yuan in 2012, accounting for about 11.5 percent of the global total. Almost a decade later, the country's GDP surpassed 110 trillion yuan in 2021, contributing over 30 percent to world economic growth.

China's economic miracle does not happen by chance. It testifies to the vitality and effectiveness of China's socialist economy under the guidance of Xi Jinping's economic thought. Xi Jinping Thought on Socialist Economy with Chinese Characteristics for a New Era unveiled at the Central Economic Work Conference in December 2017 is mainly based on the new development philosophy put forward by Xi in 2015 and features innovative, coordinated, green, open and shared development.

When Xi took office as general secretary of the Communist Party of China (CPC) Central Committee in 2012, China's economic strength significantly stood out after more than 30 years of reform and opening up. Yet, challenges, including downward pressure on the economy, wealth disparities and environmental damages, could be ignored. A more scientific top-level approach was needed.

In 2015, Xi put forward a new development philosophy featuring innovative, coordinated, green, open and shared development, which set a fundamental guideline for China's economic development as the core of Xi's economic thought. Two years later, at the 19th CPC National Congress, Xi made an important judgment that the country's economy was transitioning from a phase of rapid growth to a stage of high-quality development. Since then, high-quality development has been taken as the fundamental requirement for authorities to make economic policies and exercise macroeconomic control.

Xi's economic thought reflects the leadership's growing understanding of the laws of economic and social development and is regarded as a Chinese model of modernization characterized by an innovative, coordinated, green, open and shared development path.

Xi's economic thought comprises a series of principles. One of the principles is to remain committed to a people-centered philosophy of development, in line with which reforms have been advanced in all areas of public concern, including education, healthcare and social security. A monumental anti-poverty campaign is launched on a scale unseen anywhere in the world. Back in 2012, there were nearly 100 million Chinese living under the poverty line. In February 2021, China declared the elimination of absolute poverty, lifting the final 98.99 million rural poor out of poverty. In 2021, China's per capita disposable income hit 35,128 yuan, more than double the level in 2010. The country has developed the world's largest social security system and boasts the world's biggest middle-income group.

As for the principle of the relationship between government and market, the thought underlines the need to ensure that the market plays a decisive role in the allocation of resources, with the government better playing its role, and to resolutely remove institutional obstacles to economic development. In the past decade, the government has further delegated powers, streamlined administration and improved services. As a result, market barriers have been further eliminated, market entities' vitality has been stimulated, and market competition has become fairer.

In addition, under the guidance of Xi's economic thought, China has become more open. In 2013, the first pilot free trade zone was established in Shanghai. Now the number of such zones has reached 21, including the entire island of Hainan. China's negative list for foreign investment has been further shortened. Global investors have cast more votes of confidence on investing in China. The foreign direct investment into the country hit a record high of 1.15 trillion yuan in 2021. China's foreign trade also reached a new high in 2021, exceeding 6 trillion U.S. dollars for the first time.

The development approach China champions under Xi's economic thought also takes harmony and coordination into account. It stresses synchronized development across regions, optimizing resource allocation, and closing economic disparities, as well as considering shared benefits for humans and nature. The country made steady progress in promoting new urbanization, with the urbanization rate of permanent residence hitting 64.72 percent in 2021. The figure for 2012 was 52.57 percent. The integrated development of the Yangtze River Delta, development of the Guangdong-Hong Kong-Macao Greater Bay Area, and coordinated development of the Beijing-Tianjin-Hebei Region were all significant engines powering China's development. In terms of human-nature harmony, historic achievements were made in China's environmental development. China managed to significantly reduce its number of days with heavy air pollution. The safety of drinking water was guaranteed.

Looking ahead, with the new pressures challenging the Chinese economy, Xi's economic thought will continue to provide further guidance and theoretical foundation for China's economic policy framework and leave a deeper imprint on China's future economic growth and beyond.

Questions for discussion

1. What great changes have taken place in China's economy over the past decade?

2. Could you give a brief introduction to the new development philosophy put forward in 2015?

3. What are the main principles of Xi's economic thought mentioned in this passage?

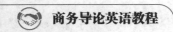

Assignments

1. Interview some business people and ask for their opinions of the business environment of China. Then write a report of about 200 words in English.

2. Prepare a ten-minute presentation to introduce the measures taken by the Chinese government to improve the business environment.

Entrepreneurship

Learning Objectives

After learning this unit, you should be able to:

- understand the concept of entrepreneurship;
- describe entrepreneurs' general personalities;
- describe the process of entrepreneurship;
- know the relation of entrepreneurship and leadership;
- know the reasons for rapid growth of entrepreneurship.

Warm-up Questions

1. Could you name some successful entrepreneurs and tell their stories?

2. What role do entrepreneurs play in the development of companies and the whole economy?

3. What qualities should an entrepreneur possess?

 # Reading

An entrepreneur is one who organizes a new business venture in the hope of making a profit. Entrepreneurship is the process of being an entrepreneur, of gathering and allocating the resources—financial, creative, managerial, or technological—necessary for a new venture's success. One engages in entrepreneurship when one begins to plan an organization that uses diverse resources in an effort to take advantage of the newly found opportunity. It usually involves hard work, long hours, and, usually, with the hope of significant financial return. More importantly, entrepreneurship is characterized by creative solutions to old or overlooked problems; imagination and innovation are the entrepreneur's stock in trade. By taking a new look at difficult situations, the entrepreneur identifies an opportunity where others might have seen a dead end.

Entrepreneurship is also a source of more entrepreneurship. Societies around the world have always been fueled by the innovations and new products that entrepreneurs bring to the market. All big businesses started out small, usually as one man or woman with a good idea and the willingness to work hard and risk everything. While it is true that many new businesses fail, the ones that succeed contribute a great deal to the creation of other new ventures, which leads, in turn, to a dynamic national economy. Indeed, today's economists and business researchers consider entrepreneurship as a key component of future economic growth around the world.

Successful entrepreneurship depends on many factors. Of primary importance is a dedicated, talented, creative entrepreneur. The person who has the ideas, the energy, and the vision to create a new business is the cornerstone of any start-up. But the individual must have ready access to a variety of important resources in order to make the new venture more than just a good idea. He needs to develop a plan of action, a road map that will take the venture from the idea stage to a state of growth and institutionalization. In most instances, the entrepreneur needs to put together a team of talented and experienced individuals to help manage the new venture's operations. Entrepreneurship also depends on access to capital, whether it is human, technological, or financial. In short, entrepreneurship is a process that involves preparation and the involvement of others in order to exploit an opportunity for profit.

2.1 The definition of entrepreneurship

The variety of the entrepreneur's motivations and goals leads to questions aimed at distilling the essence of entrepreneurship. To what or to whom does one refer when one uses the word? Is there any difference between an entrepreneur and a person who opens yet another dry-cleaning store, sandwich shop, or bookstore? If so, what is it that separates the two? What characteristics define an entrepreneur and entrepreneurship itself? Historians and business writers have struggled to provide the answers. Even today, there is no widely accepted definition, but the variety of possibilities provides important clues as to what makes entrepreneurship special.

Harvard professor Joseph Schumpeter, for example, argued that the defining characteristic of entrepreneurial ventures was innovation. By finding a new "production function" in an existing resource—a previously unknown means through which a resource could produce value—the entrepreneur was innovating. The innovation was broadly understood; an innovation could take place in product design, organization of the firm, marketing devices, or process design. Nevertheless, innovation was what separated the entrepreneur from others who undertook closely related endeavors. Other researchers, such as Professor Arthur Cole, defined entrepreneurship as a purposeful activity to initiate, maintain, and develop a profit-oriented business. The important part of this definition is the requirement that individuals must create a new business organization in order to be considered entrepreneurial. In Cole's mind, entrepreneur was a builder of profit-minded organizations.

Other observers, such as Shapero and Sokol, have argued that all organizations and individuals have the potential to be entrepreneurial. These researchers focus on activities rather than organizational make-up in examining entrepreneurship. They contend that entrepreneurship is characterized by an individual or group's initiative taking, resource gathering, autonomy, and risk taking. Their definition could theoretically include all types and sizes of organizations with a wide variety of functions and goals.

In his book *Innovation and Entrepreneurship*, Peter Drucker took the ideas set forth by Schumpeter one step further. He argued that Schumpeter's type of innovation can be systematically undertaken by managers to revitalize business and non-business organizations. By combining managerial practices with the acts of innovation, Drucker argued, business can create a methodology of entrepreneurship that will result in the institutionalization of entrepreneurial values and practices. Drucker's definition of entrepreneurship—a systematic, professional discipline available to anyone in an organization—brings our understanding of the topic to a new level. He demystified the topic, contending that entrepreneurship is something that can be strategically employed by any organization at any point in their existence, whether it is a start-up or a firm with a long history. Drucker understood entrepreneurship as a tool to be implemented by managers and organizational leaders as a means of growing a business.

2.2 Entrepreneurs' personalities

Many businesspeople believe that entrepreneurs have a personality that is different from those of normal people. Entrepreneurs are seen as having "the right stuff". But defining the various characteristics and qualities that embody entrepreneurial success can be an elusive task since today's entrepreneurs are big and tall, and short and small. They come from every walk of life, every race and ethnic setting, all age groups, male and female, and from every educational background. There is no mold for the entrepreneur. Entrepreneurs make their own mold.

But while it is hard to generalize what it takes to be a successful entrepreneur, some personality traits seem to be more important than others. While many authors and researchers have disagreed on the relative significance of individual entrepreneurial traits, all of them agree on one quality that is essential to all entrepreneurs, regardless of definition. That quality is "commitment"; it is self-motivation that distinguishes successful entrepreneurs from those that fail. It is the common thread in the lives and biographies of those that have succeeded in new enterprises. It is the one quality that entrepreneurs themselves admit is critical to the success of their initiatives.

Other traits commonly cited as important components of entrepreneurial success include business knowledge (business planning, marketing strategies, asset management, etc.), self-confidence, technical and other skills, communication abilities, and courage. But there are other, less obvious, personality characteristics that an entrepreneur should develop as a means of further ensuring their success. It has been indicated that some additional traits can help entrepreneurs build thriving organizations, including creativity and the ability to tolerate ambiguous situations.

Creative solutions to difficult problems may make or break the young and growing business; the ability of an entrepreneur to find unique solutions could be the key to his success. One of the most difficult situations entrepreneurs face is the allocation of scarce resources. For instance, owners of new ventures need to be able to decide how to best use a small advertising budget or how best to use their limited computer resources. Furthermore, they must be creative in their ability to find capital, team members, or markets. Entrepreneurial success is often directly based on the business owner's ability to make do with the limited resources available to him or her.

In addition to being creative, an entrepreneur must be able to tolerate the ambiguity and uncertainty that characterize the early years of a new organization. In nearly all cases, business or market conditions are bound to change during the first few years of a new organization's life, causing uncertainty for the venture and the entrepreneur. Being creative enables entrepreneurs to more successfully manage businesses in new and ambiguous situations, but without the ability to handle the pressure that uncertainty brings upon an organization, the entrepreneur may lose sight of his purpose.

Finally, environmental factors often play a significant part in influencing would-be entrepreneurs. Personal experience or work history has often led individuals to be more open to taking the risks involved with undertaking a new venture. For instance, individuals who know successful entrepreneurs may be stimulated to try their hand at running their own business. The successful entrepreneurs act as role models for those thinking about undertaking a new venture, providing proof that entrepreneurship does not always end in bankruptcy.

In addition, work experience can provide entrepreneurs with invaluable experience and knowledge from which to draw. First and foremost, entrepreneurs should have experience in the same industry or a similar one. Starting a business is a very demanding undertaking indeed. There is no time for on-the-job training. If would-be entrepreneurs do not have the right experience, they should either get it before starting their new venture or find some partners who have experience.

2.3 The stages of creating a venture

The myths that have grown up around the great entrepreneurs have focused more on the personality of the individual than on the work that he did to create a prosperous organization. What sticks in our memories are the qualities of a great entrepreneur, those personality traits that make a great businessperson. However, successful entrepreneurs often work hard to build their organizations, starting from little and undertaking a process that results in a thriving business. Even the best ideas become profitable only because the entrepreneur went through the steps necessary to build a company from the ground up. Successful new ventures do not appear magically out of the swirl of the marketplace; they are planned, created, and managed.

It is important to understand some stages a businessperson must go through in order to create a successful entrepreneurial venture. All entrepreneurs go through three very general stages in the process of creating their ventures.

The first stage is a concept formation stage where ideas are generated, innovations and opportunities are identified, and the business begins to take shape. During the planning stage, the entrepreneur must answer the hard questions about the potential business: Does the market need this product or service? Is there a currently needed product failing to meet market demands in some way? Is the market not being served because of undercapacity or location gaps? Will this product or service meet the demands of the market competitively and profitably? After entrepreneurs answer these and other related questions, they must evaluate their business venture ideas; they must collect data about the market and their type of business to determine if such a venture is feasible.

The second stage is a resource gathering stage where necessary resources are brought together to launch the new business. Once the planning is completed, entrepreneurs are ready to begin implementing their plans by gathering the necessary resources. After entrepreneurs have the necessary resources, they can start operating their businesses. Without a sufficient supply of resources, the opportunity might never be turned into a business that makes money for the entrepreneur. In the resource gathering stage, entrepreneurs begin to assemble the tools that they will need to profit from the opportunity. In order to create a viable organization, an individual entrepreneur has to be ready and able to manage the resources at his disposal, bringing them together in ways that are advantageous and efficient.

The third stage is a stage where the organization is actually created.

The three stages can overlap and sometimes an entrepreneur may go through all three stages at one time. Moreover, the stages do not necessarily follow sequentially. Nevertheless, the decisions made in the first stage tend to lay the framework for the rest of the organizational activity.

2.4 Entrepreneurship and leadership

Entrepreneurs must also be able to balance their managerial duties with leadership activities. In other words, they have to be able to handle both the day-to-day operations of the business as well as decision-making obligations that determine the organization's long-term direction, philosophy, and future. Entrepreneurs must be both managers and visionaries in order to build their organizations. Actually, researchers contend that many talented entrepreneurs have failed because they were unable to keep a balance between details of management and the larger mission that guides the new venture. Many entrepreneurs eventually reach a point where they realize that these twin obligations cannot be fully met alone. It is at this point that staffing decisions can become a critical component of long-term business success. In general, entrepreneurs should search for ways to delegate some of their management tasks rather than their leadership tasks. After all, in most cases the new business has long been far more dependent on its founder's leadership and vision than on his ability to monitor product quality or select new computers.

The mission of the new venture can only be fulfilled if the entrepreneur remains entrepreneurial throughout the life of the organization. That means innovation has to be a primary strategy of the venture. The venture must be receptive to innovation and open to the possibilities inherent in change. Change must be seen as positive for a business to remain entrepreneurial. Therefore, management of an entrepreneurial organization requires policies that encourage innovation and reward those who innovate. If the venture is to remain dedicated to entrepreneurship, management has to take the lead in establishing the patterns that will lead to a dynamic, flexible, and vital organization.

2.5 The reasons for rapid growth of entrepreneurship

With growing academic interest in entrepreneurship, a lot of recent research has concentrated on the reasons for the rapid growth of entrepreneurship. It's true that a lot of entrepreneurship is the result of a lack of employment opportunities. Nonetheless, some of the major reasons for the current growth in entrepreneurial activity can be identified as follows:

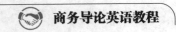

(1) Industry structure

Recent technological changes have led to an industry structure that is generally shifting towards a bigger role for small firms. The employment share of large companies has been steadily decreasing. Growing competitiveness of small firms lowers entry barriers for new entrants.

(2) New technologies

This factor is related to the changes in industry structure. Fundamental changes in the nature of the technological development have led to diseconomies of scale. Instability in the markets led to the decrease in mass production and the move towards flexible specialization. Small technology-based firms are now able to challenge larger companies that are still dependent on economies of scale.

(3) Deregulation and privatization

According to statistics, small firms are dominant in the increase of entrepreneurial activity in sectors that have been recently deregulated. Liberal economic policies of many countries have led to phenomenal growth fueled by entrepreneurs. The privatization has led to thriving entrepreneurship in the new free-market economies.

(4) Formation of new business communities

Efficiencies across markets, primarily resulting from use of new technologies, have led to declining cost of transactions. The recent advances in information technology have made inter-firm coordination relatively cheaper compared with intra-firm coordination. Business exchanges such as alibaba.com help smaller firms to be competitive. This promotes the setting up of new firms in the new-age business communities.

(5) Increasing demand for variety

Increased wealth has led to an increase in the demand for variety. Changes in consumer tastes are a major reason for the growth of entrepreneurship. People are inclined to products that are specifically designed to meet their special needs. Mass-produced homogenous goods are not popular anymore. The increasing demand for new products is of advantage to smaller firms. A number of studies have shown the comparative advantage of smaller firms in being innovative and coming up with new products.

(6) Service sector

An increase in per capita income leads to a greater share of the service sector in the national economy. Currently, services account for over 60 percent of the GDP of developed economies. The average size of firms in many sections of the service sector is relatively small. This in turn promotes entrepreneurial activity across a number of service sector industries.

(7) Government incentives and subsidies

Entrepreneurship is being encouraged in many countries with a variety of incentives such as tax breaks, preferred sources or grants. Obviously, they have a positive influence on entrepreneurial firms.

(8) Increasing flow of information

Information is the lifeblood of a business. Information is being increasingly democratized. The Internet has become the chief source of varied information. Search engines such as Google and Baidu enable people to access information from trade bodies, academic or research institutions, news networks, corporate sites, etc.

(9) Easier access to resources

Today, it is easier for an entrepreneur to access debt and equity finance than ever before. Not just capital, most other factors of production are now easily available to entrepreneurs. With greater flow of information, it is easier to contact and to deal with resource providers such as raw material suppliers and dealers of capital goods.

(10) Entrepreneurial education

Nowadays many universities and colleges are offering entrepreneurship education. A number of institutes have set up successful entrepreneurship centers, which provide help to budding entrepreneurs by conducting formal training and structured mentoring programs.

(11) Return on innovation

Strengthening of intellectual property rights (IPR) has acted as a major boost to entrepreneurs willing to take a risk in an innovation. Now they feel the confidence in the sanctity of their IPR without feeling the need to be backed up by a large corporation.

(12) Entrepreneurs as heroes

Nowadays successful entrepreneurs are regarded as heroes in many countries. People take them as role models. There is something glorious in the tale of their struggle to create new and enduring businesses that inspires a lot of other people.

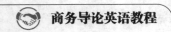

(13) High regards for self-employment

Researchers have discovered that self-employment is not looked down upon and is thought of as the best way to achieve all kinds of personal goals.

(14) Rising dissatisfaction at jobs

Many employers feel it's harder to retain talented employees. People now have confidence in their abilities, which in turn prompts them to find alternate employment.

(15) Acceptance of ex-entrepreneurs in the job market

Companies are willing to reemploy people who have been entrepreneurs. Their experience in creating and starting a new enterprise is highly valued by many employers. As a result, a potential entrepreneur perceives a lower risk as there is always the security of a well-paid job in case the venture does not succeed.

2.6 Top ten causes of entrepreneurial failure

Out of every 20 businesses, 15 of them fail no sooner than they start out. Statistics show that the failure rate for new start-ups within the first five years is as high as 50 percent. Now we are going to take some time to know the causes.

Of course, a real entrepreneur always takes a failure as a milestone on the road to success. They count on learning from their mistakes, and use the experience to move to the next idea. But why not learn as well from the mistakes of others, without suffering their cost, time, and pain? Here is a list of the top ten causes of entrepreneurial failure.

(1) No written plan

Don't believe the old urban legend that a business plan isn't worth the effort. Writing down a plan is the best way to make sure you actually understand how to transform your idea into a business. It's just like the lyrics of a song, "If you don't know where you're going, you might end up somewhere else."

(2) The business model doesn't make money

Even a non-profit organization has to generate revenue to cover operating costs. If your product is free, or you lose money on every one, it's hard to make it up in volume. You may have the solution to a problem, but if your customers have no money, your business won't last long.

(3) The idea has limited business opportunity

Not every good idea is a good business. Maybe you passionately believe that your technology is great and everyone needs it, but it doesn't mean that everyone will buy it. There is no substitute for market research to collect necessary information before you start.

(4) The execution skills are weak

An idea alone is really worth nothing. It's all about execution. If you are not comfortable with making hard decisions, taking risk, and taking full responsibility, you won't do well in this role.

(5) The market is too crowded already

Having no competitors may mean no market, but finding ten or more competitors with a simple search means this may be a crowded market, and you'd better move on to search for a new space.

(6) No intellectual property

If you expect to seek investors, or you expect to have a sustainable competitive advantage against your competitors, you need to register all your patents, trademarks, copyrights, and trade secrets early. Intellectual property is also often the largest element of early-stage company valuations for professional investors.

(7) Inexperienced team

In reality, investors do investment in people, not in ideas. They look for people with real experience in the business domain of the start-up, and people with real experience running a start-up. If this is your first time to start a business, maybe you need to find a partner who has experience to balance your passion and bring managerial expertise to your team.

(8) Resource requirements not understood

A major resource is cash funding, but other resources, such as industry contacts and access to marketing channels may be more important for certain products. Having too much cash, not managed wisely, can be just as devastating as too little cash.

(9) Too little focus on marketing

Today viral marketing and word-of-mouth marketing are not enough to make your product and brand visible in new media. Even viral marketing costs real money and time. Without effective and innovative marketing across the range of media, you won't have a successful business.

(10) Give up too easily or early

Some businesses may choose to shut down prior to an expected failure. Others may continue to operate until they are forced out by a court order. The most common cause of start-up failure is that the entrepreneur just gets tired, gives up, and shuts down the company. Many successful entrepreneurs, like Steve Jobs and Thomas Edison, kept slugging away on their vision, despite setbacks, until they found the success they knew was possible.

Words and Phrases

financial return		经济收益
fuel	*v.*	推动；促进
venture	*n.*	企业
start-up	*n.*	初创企业
capital	*n.*	资本
make-up	*n.*	结构
revitalize	*v.*	使复兴
institutionalization	*n.*	制度化
trait	*n.*	特点，特质
mold	*n.*	模子
scarce resource		稀缺资源
bankruptcy	*n.*	破产
mass production		批量生产
flexible specialization		柔性专业化；弹性专业化
deregulation	*n.*	撤销管制；放松管制
privatization	*n.*	私有化
homogenous	*adj.*	同类的
Intellectual Property Rights (IPR)		知识产权
operating cost		经营成本
trademark	*n.*	商标

copyright	*n.*	版权
viral marketing		病毒式营销
word-of-mouth marketing		口碑营销

 **Exercises**

I. Answer the following questions according to the text.

1. What kind of person can be considered as an entrepreneur?

2. How will an entrepreneur influence other businessmen?

3. What factors does successful entrepreneurship depend on?

4. What is Joseph Schumpeter's and Arthur Cole's definition of an entrepreneur respectively?

5. What is Shapero and Sokol's definition of an entrepreneur?

6. What is Peter Drucker's definition of an entrepreneur?

7. What personality traits are important for an entrepreneur?

8. What are the stages a businessperson must go through in order to create a successful entrepreneurial venture?

9. What is the relation between entrepreneurship and leadership?

10. What policies are required in the management of an entrepreneurial organization?

II. Decide whether the following statements are true (T) or false (F) according to the text.

1. The only form of entrepreneurship is starting new businesses. (　　)

2. Successful entrepreneurship depends on many factors. Of primary importance is money. (　　)

3. Even today, there is no widely accepted definition of entrepreneur and entrepreneurship. (　　)

4. In general, entrepreneurs should search for ways to delegate some of their leadership tasks rather than their management tasks. (　　)

5. Management of an entrepreneurial organization requires policies that encourage innovation and reward those who innovate. (   )

III. Read the following passage and fill in the blanks with the words given below. Change the form if necessary.

rank	traditional	vital	foundation	despite
made	agreement	prior	willingness	trait

Despite decades of academic research into the subject, there is still little 1. _____ _____ over the precise definition of entrepreneurship. Entrepreneurial leaders are variously described as risk-takers, innovators, bold opportunists, or restless agents of change. Some commentators have even argued that entrepreneurial leaders are born with a unique set of characteristics that will always set them apart from more 2. _____ corporate managers.

In reality, there is no single entrepreneurship gene. But there are 3. _____ and experiences that make it more likely that an individual will choose the path of entrepreneurship and, crucially, succeed over the long term.

The set of management behaviors that characterize many entrepreneurial leaders lies along a spectrum, which includes factors such as a(n) 4. _____ to take risks and seize opportunities, and openness to changing. Successful entrepreneurial leaders will often fall toward one end of that spectrum in at least one of those factors, but they will also draw upon a variety of other life experiences to create the finished product.

Entrepreneurial leaders may be 5. _____ rather than born, but a large majority of the most successful ones embarked on their first ventures at a young age. Among a survey of 685 leading entrepreneurial leaders conducted for this report, more than half started their first company before the age of 30.

6. _____ starting at a relatively young age, most entrepreneurial leaders do not launch straight into their ventures from higher education. More than half of the entrepreneurial leaders in the survey describe themselves as "transitioned"—meaning that they had some experience outside of the world of entrepreneurship before launching their ventures. Although there are notable examples of entrepreneurial leaders who left college

to form hugely successful businesses, such as Bill Gates of Microsoft or Mark Zuckerberg of Facebook, these are very much in the minority. According to some entrepreneurs, a form of business experience is a vital 7. _____ that increases the chances of future entrepreneurial success.

Many entrepreneurs cite experience in a corporate environment as an important training ground. When asked to rank the factors that contributed to their ventures' success in order of importance, the entrepreneurs are most likely to select "experience as an employee" as having the greatest impact. And if experience is the best education, the classroom is not far behind. Higher education was 8. _____ the number one factor by almost one third of respondents, just behind employee experience.

Over time, however, corporate experience and progression through the ranks can reduce the chances that would-be entrepreneurial leaders strike out on their own. As they climb the corporate ranks and take on greater personal responsibilities, perhaps with a family to support, the perceived risk of abandoning the security of a salaried corporate position grows.

The challenge of finding the right time to make the transition is one that resonates with Yulisianne Sulistiyawati, founder of PT Pazia Pillar Mercycom, an IT company based in Indonesia. 9. _____ to forming her company, Ms. Sulistiyawati spent 15 years working in the IT industry. "When I became an entrepreneur for the first time, it was a big decision because I was already in the comfort zone of having had a professional career," she explains. "Many professionals find it difficult to become entrepreneurial leaders because they think they are risking too much. But the experience that professionals gain early in their career is vital and cannot be bought."

Despite the need to make timely decisions about career direction, a long-term focus is 10. _____ for successful entrepreneurial leaders. You need to make decisions at least for the next 5 to 10 years and be brave about planning for your future.

IV. Translate the following sentences into Chinese.

1. Successful entrepreneurship depends on many factors. Of primary importance is a dedicated, talented, creative entrepreneur. The person who has the ideas, the energy, and the vision to create a new business is the cornerstone of any start-up. But the

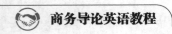

individual must have ready access to a variety of important resources in order to make the new venture more than just a good idea.

2. These researchers focus on activities rather than organizational make-up in examining entrepreneurship. They contend that entrepreneurship is characterized by an individual or group's initiative taking, resource gathering, autonomy, and risk taking. Their definition could theoretically include all types and sizes of organizations with a wide variety of functions and goals.

3. Drucker's definition of entrepreneurship—a systematic, professional discipline available to anyone in an organization—brings our understanding of the topic to a new level. He demystified the topic, contending that entrepreneurship is something that can be strategically employed by any organization at any point in their existence, whether it is a start-up or a firm with a long history.

4. Entrepreneurs are seen as having "the right stuff". But defining the various characteristics and qualities that embody entrepreneurial success can be an elusive task since today's entrepreneurs are big and tall, and short and small. They come from every walk of life, every race and ethnic setting, all age groups, male and female, and from every educational background. There is no mold for the entrepreneur. Entrepreneurs make their own mold.

5. For instance, individuals who know successful entrepreneurs may be stimulated to try their hand at running their own business. The successful entrepreneurs act as role models for those thinking about undertaking a new venture, providing proof that entrepreneurship does not always end in bankruptcy.

 **Case Study**

Zdeer Banks on Smart Technologies to Expand Presence in Wellness Segment

Chinese healthcare startup Zdeer（左点）is tapping into rising demand from young consumers by launching technology-driven moxibustion（艾灸）products, as more Internet companies are jumping onto the wellness bandwagon amid the COVID-19 pandemic.

Moxibustion is a type of traditional Chinese therapy that burns dried moxa—a cone or stick made of ground mugwort leaves (艾叶)—on particular areas of the body. The main function of moxibustion is to relieve pain or illness via the application of heat.

"Gone are the days when health maintenance is only conducted by the middle-aged and the elderly. Today's young people, especially those working in the Internet sector, face health problems earlier than expected," said Zhu Jiangtao, founder of Zdeer. "It is also why we want to enter the healthtech industry. Through technology and innovation, people of all ages can keep in good health anywhere and anytime," Zhu said. Zhu explained that "healthtech" referres to the use of leading technologies such as artificial intelligence and big data in the healthcare sector including daily healthcare and protection, as well as disease diagnosis and treatment.

To tap into such demand, the Wuhan, Hubei Province-based company has developed a slew of smart electronic devices related to healthcare, including smart moxibustion devices and smart steam foot baths. The smart moxibustion device, priced at 299 yuan ($46), allows users to undergo treatments simply by placing the device on different parts of the body. The device is about the size of a mobile phone.

"Compared with the traditional way of moxibustion, the smart moxibustion device leverages modern heat treatment technology and is able to achieve moxibustion with no smoke," Zhu said. "It also incorporates more modern smart technologies, such as wireless portability, Bluetooth control and other functions. Young consumers can carry out treatments on their own at anytime and anywhere," he said. Zhu added that all of Zdeer's products use tech giant Xiaomi Corp applications so that customers can easily operate the process through smartphones.

As some consumers doubt whether the effect of smart moxibustion would be the same as that of traditional moxibustion, Zhu said that the company discovered through significant scientific research that the three core functions of moxibustion—the medicinal benefits of wormwood, warming effects and optical effects—can all be achieved via the smart device. "The research and development expenditure accounts for around 20 percent of the company's revenue every year, which is a big sum for a startup," Zhu said.

In June, the five-year-old healthtech brand secured tens of millions of yuan in a series A round of fundraising led by Tiantu Capital. It has also raised funds from Hillhouse Capital's GL Ventures. "We are optimistic about the continued growth of the healthcare sector. In line with the current health rejuvenation and consumption upgrade, more and more young consumers are starting to pay attention to healthcare products," said Pan Pan, managing partner of Tiantu Capital. "Therefore, healthcare products on various platforms are seeing explosive growth," Pan said, "but the overall products on the supply side are mostly for the elderly." "It is difficult to effectively meet the needs of young consumers. Only products with innovative capabilities and with aesthetics appealing to young people can quickly stand out in the market," he said.

A report conducted by CBN Data showed that online shopping now constitutes a key feature of the behavior of young consumers, with the post-80s being the nucleus and the post-90s catching up in being the primary drivers of this transition. "The Zdeer team has verified its innovation ability and potential consumer demand through the smart moxibustion box product. In the future, we believe it will continue to develop new products and upgrade the sector with more technological and intelligent products," Pan added.

Questions for discussion

1. What personalities do members of Zdeer team have?

2. What challenges does Zdeer face as a Chinese startup?

3. What is Zdeer's recipe for success? What have you learned from this case?

Assignments

1. Interview some businessmen who developed their businesses from scratch and ask them about how they decided to start their businesses. Write a report of about 200 words in English.

2. Prepare a ten-minute presentation to introduce the measures we can take to foster entrepreneurship in China.

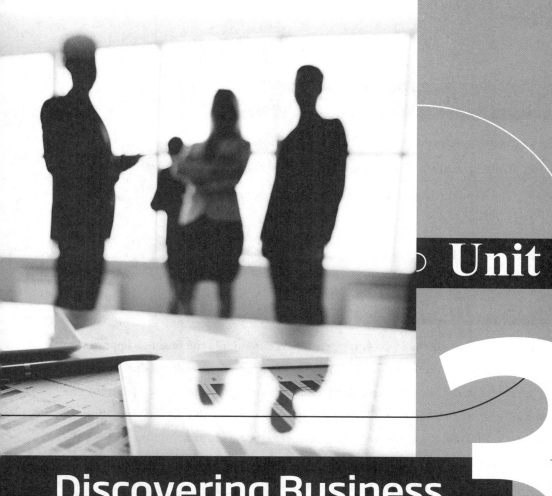

Unit 3

Discovering Business Opportunities

Learning Objectives

After learning this unit, you should be able to:

- understand the concept of business opportunity;
- know the importance of identifying business opportunities;
- describe the process of discovering business opportunities;
- evaluate the quality of business opportunities;
- identify the potential risks at the initial stage of a business.

Warm-up Questions

1. What are the sources of business opportunities?

2. Could you give a brief description of a good business opportunity?

3. Have you discovered any good business opportunities in your life?

Reading

A key question that all would-be entrepreneurs face is finding the business opportunity that is right for them. Should the new start-up focus on introducing a new product or service based on an unmet need? Should the venture select an existing product or service from one market and offer it in another where it may not be available? Or should the firm bank on a tried and tested formula that has worked elsewhere, such as a franchise operation? We will discuss these questions and look into how entrepreneurs can identify new business opportunities and evaluate their potential and their risks.

3.1 How to find the opportunity that's right for you

There are many sources of new venture opportunities for entrepreneurs who are thinking of starting a new business or company. Clearly, when you see inefficiency in the market and have an idea of how to correct that inefficiency, and you have the resources and capability—or at least the ability to bring together the resources and capability needed to correct that inefficiency—that could be a very interesting business idea. In addition, if you see a product or service that is being consumed in a foreign market, and that product is not available in your market, you could perhaps import that product or service, and start that business in your home country.

Many sources of ideas come from existing businesses, such as franchises. You could license the right to provide a business idea, just like Subway, one of the fastest growing franchises in the world. Or you could work on a concept with an employer who, for some reason, has no interest in developing that business. You could have an arrangement with that employer to leave the company and start that business. You can tap numerous sources for new ideas for businesses. Perhaps the most promising source of ideas for new businesses comes from customers—listening to customers. That is something we ought to do continuously, in order to understand what customers want, where they want it, how they want a product or service supplied, when they want it supplied, and at what price.

Obviously, if you work in a large company, employees might help you come up with ideas. Indeed, you might want to listen to what they have to say. You could pursue these ideas by asking yourself some key questions such as, "Is the market real? Is the product or service real? Can I win? What are the risks? And is it worth it?"

Let's take eBay as an example. In the age of the Internet, there is no shortage of examples of entrepreneurs who started a company based on a perceived need. You could go back to the beginning of eBay, where they saw an opportunity to connect people through launching a virtual flea market. It offered a platform that connected buyers and sellers directly. Since eBay's founding in 1995, it has become one of the world's largest place to buy and sell, a community of hundreds of millions of regular people, small businesses, and even big businesses from all of the seven continents. Millions of items of every kind imaginable, in every condition imaginable, change hands every day on eBay for prices ranging from one cent to hundreds of thousands or even millions of dollars (or pounds, or other forms of currency). According to eBay's mission statement, "eBay's mission is to provide a global trading platform where practically anyone can trade practically anything." By nearly any measure, eBay has succeeded at its mission beyond its wildest dreams, and it has done so almost entirely in the online universe.

Other companies have found similar models. PayPal is a company providing people with the opportunity to pay online. PayPal enables any business or consumer with an email address to securely, conveniently, and cost-effectively send and receive payments online. Its network builds on the existing financial infrastructure of bank accounts and credit cards to create a global, real-time payment solution. It delivers a product ideally suited for small businesses, online merchants, individuals, and others currently underserved by traditional payment mechanisms.

The company which later became PayPal was founded by Max Levchin, an online security specialist, and Peter Thiel, a hedge fund manager. The two met in 1998 when Levchin approached Thiel in New York for financial backing for a company that would develop a system for transferring money using such wireless devices as cellphones and palm pilots. Later on, the two partners realized that no means of electronic payment had been developed to handle the buying and selling that was starting to boom on the Internet. Sales on eBay were being paid for by checks and money orders sent through regular U.S. mail. What electronic business lacked, according to the founders of PayPal, was a simple, convenient payment system tailored specifically for the World Wide Web, a system that would enable a person to email money to someone else.

At that time other companies were trying to establish themselves in the electronic payment field, launching new electronic currencies that they hoped would replace the dollar as the medium of payment on the Internet. However, despite costly giveaway promotions, these e-currency companies encountered massive walls of resistance from both merchants and consumers. Merchants were reluctant to accept a new, unproven currency; consumers hesitated to give up their tried and true dollars for a currency that no one might ever accept. PayPal, on the other hand, relied on existing, universally accepted institutions. The U.S. dollar was PayPal's medium of exchange; email, which virtually everyone shopping online used, along with banking networks, comprised its medium of transfer. The PayPal system was launched quickly online. Potential buyers opened PayPal accounts which were linked to a credit card or a bank account; alternatively, money could be deposited in the account, where it earned interest until it was needed for a purchase. Today, with millions of active customer accounts, PayPal has become a truly global payment platform that is available to people in more than 202 countries, allowing customers to get paid in more than 100 currencies.

Both eBay and PayPal have one thing in common. They addressed an unmet need in the marketplace. There is no substitute for understanding the unmet needs of customers. That will allow you to discover whether you are able to supply those needs, at the price that customers want to pay, and that you can still make a profit.

3.2 How to decide whether or not to pursue a business opportunity

Once a would-be entrepreneur has identified what he thinks is a promising unmet need, he should identify and evaluate the risks that should be considered in deciding whether or not to pursue that business opportunity. Generally speaking, there are three steps that need to be followed.

The first step that everyone should go through is to ask the question: Is the market real?

In order to do so, the first thing you want to do is to conduct a customer analysis. You can do that perhaps in a very technical way, by conducting surveys. Or perhaps in a less technical way, you can attempt to answer the questions, "Who is my customer? What does the customer want to buy? When does the customer want to buy it? What price is the customer willing to pay?" So, asking the "W questions"—who, where, what, when—is the first step.

Let's take Louis Vuitton as an example. After conducting customer analysis, this company finds out customers who choose this brand because of its strengths like superior craftsmanship, rich history and culture, and its strong presence in leading commercial hubs.

At the end of the day, the one thing every entrepreneur is looking for is revenue, and the revenue will come from customers. That is why you need to ask yourself whether there is a market here.

The second thing you want to ask yourself is who else is supplying that particular market. That is competitor analysis. Ask yourself who else is in this market, and what they are doing for the customers. Are they supplying a similar substitute product or service as you have in mind? That is the second thing you have to establish, and by doing that, you can understand better what need is not met at the moment.

You also need to conduct a broader industry analysis to understand the attractiveness of the industry you're going to enter. Is the industry growing or shrinking? What power do the suppliers have in this industry? How many buyers are there? Are there substitute products? Are there any barriers to entry? If so, what are they? As we all know, the smartphone industry is quite competitive and complicated. Therefore, an industry analysis is in urgent need.

For a smartphone manufacturer, the threats may come from different aspects at different levels, including threats of suppliers, threats of buyers, threats of substitutes, and threats of entry. It is very important for you to understand this kind of information, which will help you realize whether the industry you're thinking of entering is attractive.

In addition, you may want to look at regulations that affect that industry. Are there any regulations that you would be subject to? This especially applies in the life sciences sector, where there are strict regulations that control the supply of products into the market. In the United States, the Food and Drug Administration (FDA) is a significant regulator. The FDA is a federal agency of the U.S. Department of Health and Human Services, and it is responsible for protecting and promoting public health through the control and supervision of food safety, tobacco products, drugs, cosmetics, animal foods, etc. The programs for safety regulation vary widely by the type of product, its potential risks, and the regulatory power granted to the agency. For example, the FDA regulates almost every aspect of prescription drugs, including testing, manufacturing, labeling, advertising, marketing, efficacy, and safety—yet FDA regulation of cosmetics focuses primarily on labeling and safety. The FDA regulates most products with a set of published standards enforced by a modest number of facility inspections. Actually, every country around the world has a regulator in the life sciences sector. So, these are the high-level questions that you may want to ask yourself.

Once you answer these questions and identify the need, given the competition and all the regulatory constraints that exist in that market, it will provide you with the opportunity to tailor your service or product—or combination of the service and product—to that marketplace. The logic we are suggesting here is to understand the need, and tailor the product and/or service to that need, as opposed to saying, "Well, I have an idea. And now let me think about how I can shove it down the distribution channel." More often than not, the latter doesn't work, but the former approach works. This is the approach where you identify the need and do a rigorous analysis to understand who else is out there, what constraints exist, and how you could differentiate yourself in a meaningful way. If you approach a new opportunity this way, you can expect to have substantial sales and growth for your company when introducing your new product and/or service.

3.3 How to identify and evaluate the risks

In addition to conducting market analysis and competitive analysis, and also looking at the industry and government, there are some other risks that entrepreneurs should take into account. In this section, we will discuss how to identify and evaluate the potential risks which could come out in the process of starting up a new business. One way to think about the various risks an entrepreneur is faced with is to break them down into several buckets.

(1) Risk about the founders

Let's start with the first bucket, the company bucket. Well, here, the biggest sources of risk are the founders. Do they have enough money not just to start the company, but also to grow the company? Individuals such as Bill Gates, Michael Dell, or Steve Jobs can not only start companies, but also manage their growth. However, experience has shown that such individuals are relatively limited.

(2) **Risk about the technology**

The second source of risk is technology risk. To the extent that your company employs technology, there are obviously issues of how long this technology will be the leading edge, whether there are any intellectual property issues that need to be addressed, and whether there exists the product risk. If you haven't developed a product yet, can you manufacture it? Will it work? All these issues are under the bucket of company risk.

As for the technology risk, I would like to mention an example of losing the leading edge concerning the camera embedded in the cellphone. The first company that makes the cellphone with a camera is Sharp, a Japanese company. It has created a sensational product which pushes the company to the top level of the mobile phone technology. But, after a short while, companies like Sony and Motorola obtained the same technology and applied it on their own products, so Sharp gradually lost its leading edge. Therefore, we should never neglect the significance of the innovation of technologies and products.

(3) **Risk about the market**

The third bucket for the sources of risk is the market for the product. You need to be aware of two big uncertainties. First, what is the customer's willingness to buy? And second, what is the pace, if you're successful, at which competitors will be able to imitate you? One of the things you have to think about when you enter that market is how you can create barriers to imitation, so that if you're successful, the competitors won't be able to imitate you very quickly.

The cases of Uber and Didi may serve as a good example here. Uber was a dominant taxi-hail software by applying GPS system and collecting information on their own. When it entered the Chinese market, it was so strong that it almost monopolized the market. However, a Chinese domestic company called Didi applied the similar technology and offered the same service, striping Uber's dominance, and even acquired the Chinese branch of Uber eventually. Therefore, you always need to keep your eyes open and monitor the situation in your market.

(4) **Risk about the industry**

The fourth bucket consists of risks associated with the industry. Are there any factors in that industry that relate to the availability of supply? In some cases, you need to have certain raw materials that are in limited supply, and that some suppliers might be able to take advantage of that. Barriers to entry might change. Regulations might change, and adversely or positively affect your business.

(5) Risk about the finance

Lastly, there are financial risks. And here, the question is, will you be able to raise the money early on? At what valuation will you be able to do it? Will you be able to raise follow-up money? And then, from the investor's standpoint, obviously there's a risk that the company is not very successful. Most early stage companies don't work out, but for the few that do, when it is time for a public offering, will the public market be open? We have just gone through a substantial period of almost two years when IPOs were few and far between. At the time you make the investment, you don't know what the state of the capital market will be like in five to seven years from the date you make the investment. That's a big risk the investor is assuming. Obviously, it's a big risk for the entrepreneur to be able to have some liquidity, and perhaps realize the fruits of his investment and his time and talent. In some cases, some of the money he puts into that venture will not be back.

3.4 Advice to potential entrepreneurs

First, you must think from the perspective of customers. The most frequent mistake that entrepreneurs tend to make at the initial stage is to think everybody in the market is like them. If they like the product, everybody else will. Sometimes entrepreneurs, and especially entrepreneurs with an engineering background, are too focused on the engineering features or technology features of the particular product, rather than on the needs that they are trying to fulfill. However, customers don't buy technology. Customers buy products that add value. Customers buy products that they need, in order to satisfy some needs that they wish to satisfy. It is the services of the technology that matter, but not the technology. Very often, entrepreneurs—particularly smart entrepreneurs—are overwhelmed by the technological aspect, and they pay too little attention to what the customers want. This is the most frequent issue at the early stage that entrepreneurs are faced with.

Second, you must have confidence in yourself. Some potential entrepreneurs are very hesitant to start new businesses, because they think they don't have the characteristics that would make for a successful entrepreneur. Also, it's too risky to be an entrepreneur. Research around the world has shown that there are no unique characteristics or traits that distinguish entrepreneurs from non-entrepreneurs, and successful entrepreneurs from unsuccessful entrepreneurs.

The potential entrepreneurs should bear in mind that they have what it takes to be exceptionally successful. It is no riskier to start your own business than working for General

Motors. As we can recall, General Motors has filed for bankruptcy. Therefore, the perception that working for a large company is somehow safer is not borne out by the reality. Believe you have what it takes to be a successful entrepreneur; it is time to get started.

3.5 Business opportunities in China

As we all know, China's economy is developing very fast, and it offers many business opportunities. But you must do some homework when searching for business opportunities in China. For example, you need to know which sectors are open to private investment and which industries are likely to grow in the future. Here are some suggestions we can make for those who want to discover business opportunities in China.

First, you may do some research on China's strategic industries. Business opportunities in China are often linked to the government's strategic objectives. Every five years the government depicts new strategic industries that will be supported in the form of government grants and subsidies. The 14th Five-Year Plan of China is focused on strengthening the energy, automotive, IT infrastructure, and biotechnology sectors. Many local governments are providing support to sectors they want to stimulate within their own region, and they often "times" that with the form of subsidies in order to acquire new technologies and innovate existing products. Both foreign and local companies are allowed to apply for these subsidies. Therefore, business opportunities can be found by simply looking at China's strategic industries. But you need to keep in mind that not every sector is open to private investment.

In order to understand which subsidies are available for your company, you may get in contact with the local government of the region, city, or district you want to invest in. Sometimes you cannot find any information about subsidies on the Internet, hence directly contacting local authorities is generally your best option. That's to say, you may just compare China's strategic industries with your own resources, any overlap might be a chance to obtain a subsidy, grant, or some types of assistance.

Second, you may have a look at the developing sectors in China. Many industries in China are still in their infancy stage, which brings both opportunities and challenges. Opportunities can be found in the forms of a less competitive landscape, a first-mover advantage, and the potential of growth. However, a developing market can also be associated with poor brand and product awareness, which in turn triggers price to become the dominant factor to influence the purchasing behavior. In order to develop more brand and product awareness, one would therefore have to educate the market and show the benefits and usage of his product in order to sell it in the market. However, educating a market is often very costly.

At last, let's talk about some industries that have high growth potential and are open to private investment. There can be attractive business opportunities in the following industries.

(1) Education

Chinese people value education for their children above anything else; it's an investment that will benefit the family in the long run. However, competition is still fierce to get access to high quality educational resources. For that reason, many parents invest in private education for their children. Education institutions have been very successful in the Chinese market. Although there are more restrictions on social training institutions in China nowadays, you can find good opportunities to invest in this area within the bounds of government policies.

(2) Medical equipment and healthcare

China is actively seeking to improve its healthcare sector. Especially now China is battling with an aging population. Who will take care of the elderly and how is China going to push its healthcare sector to the next level? The medical equipment and elderly care sectors are two sectors that will boom in the next few years. That is why the government is actively supporting the healthcare sector, which in turn provides opportunities for medical device companies to jump in and sell their technologies and products to businesses and consumers.

(3) Agriculture

With a growing population that is becoming wealthier each day, China will have to attain the resources to support and maintain that growth. That is why Chinese businesses are seeking to acquire new equipment and technologies to support their agricultural sector. An interesting sector is horticulture like greenhouses and professional lighting equipment.

(4) Aqua technology

Since the 18th National Congress of the Communist Party of China (CPC), General Secretary Xi Jinping, based on the realities of China's development, has proposed that lucid waters and lush mountains are invaluable assets. He has brought natural environment and ecology into the scope of productive forces and got a new idea of handling properly the relationship among environment, ecology, and productive forces in the course of development. The market for aqua technology like wastewater management and water filtration system is growing rapidly and offers tremendous opportunities.

(5) E-commerce

China's e-commerce has recently surpassed the U.S.'s in size of annual revenue. In addition, more and more Chinese are connected to the Internet and every year the e-commerce market grows well over 20 percent. It's no surprise that more and more foreign companies are targeting this highly lucrative and rapidly growing industry.

(6) Green technology

China had serious air and water pollution problems in the past. The air pollution is a combination of industrial pollution, agricultural pollution, construction dust, car exhaust, and the dirty emissions from burning coal. That is why the government is investing in the development of new green technologies and is continuously looking for new instruments that will aid in the battle against pollution. The green technology industry is a strategic industry in China and offers subsidies and incentives to companies that can help solve this problem.

Although there are many more industries that are experiencing high growth, the sectors listed above are open to private investment and prone to favorable subsidies.

Words and Phrases

franchise operation		特许经营
license	*v.*	颁发许可证，特许
tap	*v.*	开发，利用
flea market		跳蚤市场
financial infrastructure		金融基础设施
hedge fund		对冲基金
auction	*n.*	拍卖
electronic currency		电子货币
medium of payment		支付手段
substitute product		替代品
sales	*n.*	销售额
market share		市场份额
zero in		瞄准

shrink	*v.*	收缩；处于低迷状态
barrier	*n.*	壁垒
sector	*n.*	行业
federal agency		联邦政府机构
leading edge		领先地位
taxi-hail software		打车软件
monopolize	*v.*	垄断
Initial Public Offering (IPO)		首次公开发售公司股份；公司上市
liquidity	*n.*	流动资金
finance	*v.*	筹措资金，融资
subsidy	*n.*	补贴

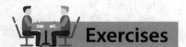 **Exercises**

I. Answer the following questions according to the text.

1. How can we define a business opportunity?

2. What are the sources for new business opportunities?

3. What can be learned from the cases of eBay and PayPal?

4. What should be done while deciding whether or not to pursue a business opportunity?

5. How can we evaluate the attractiveness of a business opportunity?

6. Why is it important for companies to tailor their product and/or service to market needs?

7. How can we evaluate the risks of a business opportunity?

8. What are the major risks an entrepreneur could be faced with?

9. What is the most frequent mistake that entrepreneurs tend to make?

10. Why are some potential entrepreneurs very hesitant to start new businesses? What should they do?

II. Decide whether the following statements are true (T) or false (F) according to the text.

1. Business opportunities are not equally obvious to everyone, but they are equally available to anyone with the experiences and the knowledge of discovering them. (   )

2. Once a would-be entrepreneur has identified what he thinks is a promising unmet need, he should identify and evaluate the risks that should be considered in deciding whether or not to pursue that business opportunity. (   )

3. You don't need to understand the attractiveness of the industry you're going to enter because you will know it later on. (   )

4. In addition to conducting market analysis and competitive analysis, and also looking at the industry and government, there are some other risks that entrepreneurs should take into account. (   )

5. Very often, entrepreneurs—particularly smart entrepreneurs—are overwhelmed by the technological aspect, and they pay too little attention to what the customers want. (   )

III. Read the following passage and fill in the blanks with the words given below. Change the form if necessary.

formula	franchise	suffer	consideration	demand
serve	untapped	introduce	eventually	talent

There are so many business opportunities to get into these days. There are no limits because there are many new things to sell and resell. There is always the food industry. One can sell small time as in homemade goodies being sold to mostly friends and referrals, or one can go big time and open up a(n) 1. _____ of say McDonald's or Burger King. As for clothes, one can opt to come up with his own designs and offer services to his friends and relatives and then 2. _____ expand the business. If you want to go mainstream, opening a store in the mall would already be a big step. So with all these choices, which business should you get into?

The first consideration you should have is to know yourself, especially your skills and 3. _____. Look inside you. Study and observe your behavior and achievements through the years. Ask the people closest to you when they saw you at your best.

Hopefully, upon careful 4. _____, you will stumble upon answers about your true skills and talents. These skills and talents are already in you; it is something that can be very bankable in any business that you will get into. There will also be your 5. _____ inner resources. Ask mentors about these things. Most of the time it is mentors or elders that have seen you grow up who will know your hidden abilities. Oftentimes, a person has various skills and talents and among the long list there are certain skills and talents that are most useful in pursuing chosen interests. Interests are hobbies that a person actually enjoys doing, so if you have a knack for certain things, go for it. Usually it is this knack that will make you go for the top plum in any field you get into. The determination will follow because there is already that desire to do your best since you like excelling in that field.

After discovering your skills and interests, keep developing all these things and then finally choose the right business for you based on this evaluation. A good way to start is studying the market and investing in something that is already in 6. _____. Make sure though that this in demand service or product is not simply a fad. Otherwise you can also delve deeper and see what need of the greater number of population is not yet being 7. _____.

There could be a product or service 8. _____ from shortage in your city but there is an over supply of that same product or service in another city. Maybe you can be the one to bring in that product to your city. You can also create a need to 9. _____ a new product or service you want to the market. It is all about overall marketing. You should be able to have a marketing plan that will work for your product or service.

Tapping the right business opportunity is balancing what you already have and what you potentially can have. Getting the right combination is a sure 10. _____ for success. Also keep in mind sustainability and make sure that you have long-term goals for whatever business you want to get into. There is also the element of luck. Wish you good luck on the next business opportunity you are planning to take on.

IV. Translate the following sentences into Chinese.

1. Clearly, when you see inefficiency in the market and have an idea of how to correct that inefficiency, and you have the resources and capability—or at least the ability to bring together the resources and capability needed to correct that inefficiency—that could be a very interesting business idea.

2. There is no substitute for understanding the unmet needs of customers. That will allow you to discover whether you are able to supply those needs, at the price that customers want to pay, and that you can still make a profit.

3. Once a would-be entrepreneur has identified what he thinks is a promising unmet need, he should identify and evaluate the risks that should be considered in deciding whether or not to pursue that business opportunity.

4. Once you answer these questions and identify the need, given the competition and all the regulatory constraints that exist in that market, it will provide you with the opportunity to tailor your service or product—or combination of the service and product—to that marketplace.

5. Research around the world has shown that there are no unique characteristics or traits that distinguish entrepreneurs from non-entrepreneurs, and successful entrepreneurs from unsuccessful entrepreneurs.

 Case Study

WeRide to Provide Driverless Minibus Services

WeRide (文远知行), a Chinese autonomous vehicle startup, is looking to provide driverless minibus services this year, company officials said on Thursday. The Guangzhou, Guangdong Province-based company, which is backed by Japan's Nissan Motors, said its robobus uses Level 4 autonomous driving technologies, indicating that the vehicles are capable of self-driving in most conditions without a human safety driver.

Han Xu, CEO of WeRide, said the robobus, which has been jointly developed with vehicle maker Yutong Group, comes without a steering wheel, throttle and brakes. It can ferry six to eight passengers at a time on open roads in cities. "The new self-driving mode aims to solve the transportation problems of the last three to five kilometers. It will become an important city infrastructure like water, gas and electricity," said Han. "Passenger cars with four seats and minibuses with six to eight seats will quickly become popular. The robobus market is much bigger than the shared bicycle market," he said.

The autonomous driving sector gained traction in China last year with a flurry of major deals. Pony.ai, a self-driving vehicle startup based in China and the United States, completed a new $462 million funding round last year. China unveiled a blueprint in 2019 to boost autonomous driving in the country. The country will realize "scale production of vehicles capable of conditional autonomous driving and commercialization of high-level autonomous vehicles in certain scenarios by 2025". The document further stated that: "Smart vehicles have become a global strategy and China has a strategic edge in developing smart cars with the complete automobile industry and evolving information technology." In March last year, the Ministry of Industry and Information Technology launched classification standards for autonomous driving in China, which has helped expedite the country's autonomous driving industry.

To speed up commercialization, WeRide joined hands with Yutong Group to launch 10 unmanned robobuses this year and began to test them in Zhengzhou, Henan Province. Similar projects were also started in Guangzhou and Nanjing, Jiangsu Province. The company plans to further expand its presence to more cities this year and has research and development centers in Silicon Valley in the United States, and Beijing and Shanghai in China. It has set up a data markup center in Anqing, Anhui Province, and will expand into Nanjing, Zhengzhou and Wuhan, Hubei Province this year. "We are not blindly opening an office in a city. Each city is embedded with a strategic purpose and we will leverage local resources to accelerate the implementation of autonomous driving," Han said.

WeRide, founded in 2017, raised $310 million in its series B round of fundraising, which was led by Yutong Group. It marked the largest investment from a local original equipment manufacturer in the autonomous driving firm.

Li Ruigang, founding partner of CMC Capital Partners, said self-driving technology, like new energy vehicles, will become popular with stock-market investors. With an edge in core technologies and the superb performance of its robotaxi operations, the first of its kind in China, WeRide has made a great impact, he said.

Questions for discussion

1. What was Han's mindset when he started to do business in autonomous driving?

2. What was the biggest drive for Han when he was opening offices in other places or growing his business?

3. Why did WeRide obtain a large-scale investment? What do you learn from WeRide's success?

Assignments

1. Interview some private entrepreneurs and ask them about how they had got the ideas to start their businesses. Write a report of about 200 words in English.

2. Prepare a ten-minute presentation to introduce some business opportunities existing in your present life.

Unit

4

Establishing a Business

Learning Objectives

After learning this unit, you should be able to:

- understand the importance of making money legally and ethically;

- determine your goals and evaluate your business ideas;

- generate and evaluate ideas for your business;

- choose the right business organization;

- register a business name and get the license;

- know the significance and way of writing a business plan.

商务导论英语教程

Warm-up Questions

1. Is it good or not good for college students to start their own businesses?

2. Do you want to start a business? If you do, talk something about your plan.

3. What do we need to prepare when planning to start a new business?

Reading

Have you decided to start a business? Do you want to love what you do, be your own boss, make what you are worth, and make your own dreams come true? There are millions of entrepreneurs who have made that jump, and you can, too. Now we are going to discuss how to start a business by taking a step-by-step approach to making those critical decisions that make the difference between success and failure of your business start-up. Here are the steps to teach you how to start a business. Take these steps in order and don't skip any so that you can maximize your success.

4.1 Taking the right approach to making real money

You have probably asked yourself—how do I make money? There are basic principles which guide you on how to make real money. The most basic principle is to have the right approach. Business is not about tricks, win-lose deals, or dishonesty. It's about action, persistence, patience, honesty, faith and hard work. Business is about creating long-term relationships; it's about making those relationships win-win. Business is about creating value in the world and being compensated because you have made people's lives better. Business is about getting what you want by giving people what they want or need.

For example, Jack Ma, former CEO of Alibaba, has created a remarkable enterprise and is famous for his business philosophy—he tries to help small and medium traders do business more easily. The example of his success just proves that one of the keys to a successful business is to make people's lives better and give people what they want.

You are suggested to use the READY, AIM, FIRE approach to starting a business. The

READY steps include evaluating yourself to make sure you are ready for what is coming. These steps will also open the possibilities of different business types. Before you focus on one idea, you should take the opportunity to look at all the possibilities. This is your chance to do that. Once you have taken into account all the relevant factors to make your choice, you are ready to focus on the business you want. These steps are the AIM part of the approach. Once you have a laser focus on the business you want to start, the FIRE steps will take you through the process of preparing to start your business.

4.2 Generating ideas for your business

You need to think about the following questions: What large need can you fill? What niche can you occupy? You should be a specialist, not a generalist. Consider what people will still want or need during a recession. In fact, think of what people need more during a recession. How about helping people create larger incomes or helping people save money?

Don't try to fight big companies unless you have a big competitive advantage. You will never be able to compete with the big companies on the issue of price. You will be able to win on the issue of service. Actually, due to the strong ability of financing, big companies can expel their opponents out of the game by lowering the price.

You can just consider the trends: Can you fill a growing need? Remember that business is about making people's lives better in some way. Think of solving a problem for people, filling a need, or satisfying a want. Determine your unique value proposition.

Or you may establish repeatable business systems: The more predictable, repeatable, and reliable your business activities are, the more efficient you become. By studying, streamlining and then documenting a systemized approach to customer service, financial management, team communication, marketing, etc., you'll be able to free your mind of the procedural aspects of your business and focus more time on creative and innovative ways to be valuable to your customers. A lot of famous companies, like McDonald's, Walmart, and Toyota, are all streamlining and standardizing their businesses to gain high efficiency and better product quality.

4.3 Determining your personal and business goals and evaluating your business ideas

Goals are your personal and business objectives—what you want out of your life and your career. What do you enjoy doing in life? What are your hobbies and interests? Do you enjoy dealing with people or are you happier working in front of your computer? What is important in your life? It is crucial to make sure you are setting and achieving goals. This is as true in business as it is in any endeavor. The most common and most costly mistake is choosing the wrong business, which most often results from the failure of setting goals.

Goal setting is a powerful process for thinking about what you want out of life and transforming your dreams into reality. What follows is a goal setting form or goal setting worksheet, and you can also use it as a checklist to evaluate your business ideas.

Your goals	Your ideas
Set your own hours—work when you want (part or full time)	Yes/No
Flexible work schedule—work day or night, weekdays or weekends	Yes/No
Work wherever you want to—home, RV, beach, golf course, lake, car, etc.	Yes/No
No commute—no rush hour traffic to deal with	Yes/No
Live wherever you want—small towns, big cities, different countries, relocation, etc.	Yes/No
No formal dress code—dress casually and comfortably	Yes/No
Work for yourself—be your own boss; build equity in yourself and not a boss	Yes/No
Work with whom you want, not whom your boss tells you to	Yes/No
You cannot be downsized	Yes/No
Your business is willable to your children, loved ones or favorite charity	Yes/No
Income is residual—you can continue to benefit from your initial efforts over and over	Yes/No
None of the hassles, expenses or liabilities associated with having employees	Yes/No
Potential tax benefits, especially on what you're already spending money on	Yes/No
Low and attainable start-up costs—little or no financial risk	Yes/No
Free professional training & consultation available	Yes/No
No traditional barriers—experience, education, gender, age, etc.	Yes/No
Gain personal growth and development that improves all aspects of your life	Yes/No
Work with positive, outgoing, professional people with similar goals	Yes/No
You determine how much you earn	Yes/No
Control of your own future	Yes/No
Excellent timing—large and growing market for your product or service	Yes/No
Perfect family business	Yes/No
Minimal overhead—no office, warehouse, expensive equipment, etc.	Yes/No

Continued

Your goals	Your ideas
Ability to capitalize on a global marketplace, not just your local area or market	Yes/No
Pay no royalties or franchise fees to anyone	Yes/No
Success through working as a team instead of cut-throat competition	Yes/No
Ability to leverage your time with the efforts of others	Yes/No

4.4 Choosing the right business organization

After you have determined your personal and business goals and evaluated your business ideas, you may take the fourth step—choosing the right business organization form. There are two decisions every entrepreneur must make fairly early in the life of a start-up business. Will you go into business alone or with a partner? What type of legal business organization will you use? The business organization you choose is one of the most important decisions you make. Your decision affects your level of risk, the taxes you pay, and how much accounting help you will need.

There are four basic forms of business organization, namely, sole proprietorship, partnership, corporation, and franchise. In this part, you will study what they are and their advantages and disadvantages respectively.

(1) Sole proprietorship

A sole proprietorship has no separate legal existence from its owner. Liabilities for business debts are not limited to assets of the business. The owner is responsible for all debts incurred by the business. The owner can have the business under his name. The business, being not a separate legal entity, does not file a separate tax return. Accounting for a sole proprietorship is the simplest of legal forms.

Advantages of sole proprietorship

It is very simple to establish. The procedures for setting up a sole proprietorship in China have been increasingly simplified in recent years. For example, many people are running online shops on Taobao.com. And the owner of an online shop can be regarded as a sole proprietor. People can easily have such a shop after they register with their ID numbers and pay a certain amount of money to guarantee their businesses.

It has more freedom in decision-making. Compared with other forms of businesses, a sole proprietorship has greater freedom in deciding on business policies and operations. As a sole proprietor, you make your own decisions on the type of goods or services you want to offer at the price you feel appropriate. You don't have to consult with anyone else on when to open and close, whom to employ as your assistant, and when to take a week off for a holiday.

It has less tax burdens. Compared with other forms of businesses, sole proprietors can enjoy all kinds of favorable policies in terms of tax burden. For example, the tax rates for sole proprietors are often much lower than those for corporations in many countries.

Disadvantages of sole proprietorship

It has unlimited liability. Liability here means the obligation to pay one's debts. According to the business law, a sole proprietor has unlimited liability, which means even if he goes bankrupt, he may lose not only his business but part or all of his personal property in order to pay his debt.

It has limited access to capital. Compared with corporations, sole proprietorships' access to capital is rather limited and therefore it is more difficult to secure additional capital, as corporations can get financing not only from banks but also from their shareholders.

It has limited managerial expertise. Many sole proprietors may be experts in a certain field, but seldom have the expertise in every aspect of managing a modern business, which involves at least marketing, financing, and human resource management. Therefore, sole proprietors have to make extra efforts in order to run their businesses well and often spend longer hours on work.

(2) Partnership

A partnership consists of two or more individuals who co-own a business. Although the business is not taxed separately, it must prepare a return which indicates the distribution of partnership profits and losses to the co-owners. The amount of money and time invested by each partner should be written down in a partnership agreement. In a partnership, any partner can be held liable for the entirety of the business' debts.

Advantages of partnership

It has better access to capital and credit. First of all, more capital is contributed by the partners and more funds can be obtained from friends and investors. Secondly, banks are more likely to extend credit to partnerships because most partnerships have more than just one partner, which means more people are personally responsible for the debts.

It has greater possibilities for good management. Because the partners may bring different talents and expertise to the business and can therefore make better decisions and manage the business in a more scientific way.

It has a more definite legal framework. Over the past few centuries, a definite legal framework has developed for partnerships. Therefore, settling legal problems concerning partnerships is relatively simpler than solving problems of a sole proprietorship.

Disadvantages of partnership

It has unlimited liability. Just like a sole proprietorship, a partnership has unlimited liability. Like sole proprietors, the partners of a partnership are personally responsible for any debt they owe and may lose all or part of their personal property if the partnership goes bankrupt.

The partners of a partnership could have internal conflicts with each other. Two heads are commonly believed to be better than one, but unfortunately it is not always true in reality. As the saying goes, "too many cooks spoil the broth." The partners may have differences in opinion or run into serious conflicts of interest. This will surely hurt the operation and well-being of the business.

A partnership could be easily broken. A partnership is easy to form, but may be difficult to maintain. If one partner dies, retires or simply wants to withdraw his capital, the partnership will have to break up unless the remaining partners are able and willing to buy out the leaving partner's shares. Otherwise they may have to find a new partner. However, it's often not easy to find a new partner, because the new partner has to be accepted by all of the remaining partners.

Besides the general partnerships, there is a special form of partnership—limited partnership. A limited partnership is similar to a partnership except that there are one or more general partners in addition to one or more limited partners. The general partners are in the same position as partners above, having authority to act as agents of the partnership, having management control over the business, and being liable for the debts of the business. The limited partners, on the other hand, have limited liability, meaning they are only liable to the extent of their investments. Limited partners do not have authority over the management of the business. They invest in the business and receive a share of profits and losses as stated in the partnership agreement.

(3) Corporation

A corporation is a legal entity separate from the persons that formed it. Owners of a corporation are known as shareholders. The shareholders elect a board of directors who hires managers to manage the corporation. Sometime the biggest shareholder is just the chairman of the board of directors. In a small corporation, the owners, directors, and employees may be the same people. Accounting for a corporation can be more complicated than for other forms of organizations. The corporation is taxed on its profits and the owners may receive dividends which are taxed again.

Advantages of corporation

It has limited liability. The owners or shareholders of a corporation are not personally responsible for its losses. If the corporation goes bankrupt, its creditors can obtain the assets of the corporation but not the shareholders' personal property.

It is easier for a corporation to expand. Corporations can issue bonds or shares of their stock to the public, thus raising large sums of funds. In addition, using their relatively huge assets as collateral, corporations may be able to get large loans from banks or other financial institutions.

Corporations stand a larger chance of having better management. A lot of corporations have separated their ownership and management. In these corporations, the shareholders are not responsible for the daily management. Such duties are delegated to the managers of the company, who are usually professional managers with expertise in marketing, production, accounting, law, etc. As a result, the management as a whole is more efficient.

Disadvantages of corporation

There could be double taxation for corporations. For example, according to the tax law of the United States, corporations with more than 35 stockholders have to pay federal and state taxes on their profits, which are heavier than those for sole proprietorships and partnerships. In addition, if stockholders receive dividends from their corporations, they have to pay personal income taxes. This is called double taxation.

Corporations could have higher organizing costs. Generally speaking, governments have more strict requirements on corporations in many aspects, which incurs additional costs for corporations.

(4) Franchise

A franchise is a form of business organization in which a firm which already has a successful product or service enters into a continuing contractual relationship with other businesses. The franchisor grants the franchisee the right to sell or use the franchisor's product, service or method in exchange for a royalty fee from the franchisee. Thus, the franchisee can operate under the franchisor's trade name and usually with the franchisor's guidance.

Advantages of franchise

It has a certain level of independence. A franchise provides franchisees with a certain level of independence where they can operate their businesses. A franchise provides an established product or service which may already enjoy widespread brand-name recognition. This gives the franchisee the benefits of a pre-sold customer base which would ordinarily take years to establish. A franchise increases your chances of business success because you are associating with proven products and methods. Franchises may offer consumers the attraction of a certain level of quality and consistency because it is required by the franchise agreement.

It can get pre-opening support. Franchises can get important pre-opening support in site selection, design, construction, financing, training, and a grand-opening program. Franchises can also get some ongoing support, such as national and regional advertising, training of operating procedures, operational assistance, ongoing supervision and management support, and access to bulk purchasing.

Disadvantages of franchise

It is not completely independent. Franchisees are required to operate their businesses according to the procedures and restrictions set forth by the franchisor in the franchise agreement. These restrictions usually include the products or services which can be offered as well as the pricing and geographic territory. For some people, this is the most serious disadvantage of becoming a franchisee. In addition to the initial franchise fee, franchisees must pay ongoing royalties and advertising fees. Franchisees must be careful to balance the restrictions and support provided by the franchisor with their own ability to manage their businesses. A damaged, system-wide image can be the result if other franchisees are performing poorly or the franchisor runs into a problem. The term or duration of a franchise agreement is usually limited and the franchisee may have little or no say about the terms of a termination.

4.5 Registering a business name and getting your licenses as appropriate

After you have decided to choose a business organization form, the next thing you need to do is to register a business name and get a license from the government. You may do some brainstorming and write down different possibilities that might be suitable given your products or services.

If you think you may do business online, check if your business names are available as domain names. Choose a domain name ending with .com or .net. Resist the temptation to choose a domain name ending with any other suffixes. They don't connote business seriousness except for .org and .gov which are usually used by non-profits and governmental organizations.

If you use a business name different from your own name, you are using a fictitious name. That name has to be registered in your county so that each name is only used once. Check with the local Administration of Industry and Commerce (AIC) for a list of fictitious names to make sure your name is not already taken. If it is not taken, you can register it.

To obtain registration certification, the company must file a completed application form along with the following documents:

- Notice of approval of company name;

- Lease or other proof of company office;

- Capital verification certificate or appraisal report;

- Articles of association, executed by each shareholder;

- Representation authorization;

- Identity cards of shareholders and identification documents of officers;

- Appointment documents and identification documents (certifying name and address) of the directors, supervisors, and officers;

- Appointment documents and identification documents of the company's legal representative;

- If the initial contribution is in non-monetary assets, the document certifying transfer of the property title of such assets;

- Other documents as required by the authorities.

4.6 Writing a business plan

Writing business plans is like creating the crucial road map you draw when starting a business. An unknown author said: "When you fail to plan, you plan to fail." The biggest reason for failing to plan is the perception that one doesn't have enough time. Unfortunately for those who think that way, they will pay many times later on in terms of time spent for their failure to find time to write business plans.

The best way to show bankers, venture capitalists, and angel investors that you are worthy of financial support is to show them that you have written a great business plan. Make sure that your business plan is clear, focused, and realistic. Then show them that you have the tools, talent, and team to make it happen. Your written business plan is like your calling card; it will get you in the door where you'll have to convince investors and loan officers that you can put your plan into action.

Once you have raised the money to start or expand your business, your plan will serve as a road map for your business. It is not a static document that you write once and put away. You will reference it often, making sure you stay focused and on track, and meet milestones. It will change and develop as your business evolves.

There is no fixed way to write a business plan. The nature of the business, its state of development, the need for outside capital and other factors will determine the exact outline of the plan and how specific the plan must be. However, there are four elements of a plan that are universal:

Your business concept. It is an idea for a business that includes basic information such as the service or product, the target demographic, and a unique selling proposition that gives a company an advantage over competitors. A business concept may involve a new product or simply a novel approach to marketing or delivering an existing product. Once a concept is developed, it is incorporated into a business plan.

Supply and demand for your product or service. Several questions should be answered: What is the niche you are filling? How large is it? How will your customers find you? What about competition today and in the future? What is your competitive advantage?

The management structure you anticipate. This is about the following questions: Who are the key players? What is their experience in business? What is their experience in the industry? Will you have employees who complement your strengths and make up for your weaknesses?

The financing for your start-up. You should answer these questions: What is your overhead? What are your fixed costs and your variable costs? Where is your break-even point? What will be your cash burn rate? If these concepts are foreign to you now, you should be an expert by the time the business plan is written.

As you write your business plan, you will rework your plan again and again. Give yourself several weeks to formulate your business plan. The significance of writing a good business plan can never be overestimated.

Words and Phrases

win-win	*adj.*	双赢的
niche	*n.*	缝隙市场；利基市场
expel	*v.*	驱逐
downsize	*v.*	裁员
royalty	*n.*	技术使用费
franchise fee		（发明、创意、财产等的）使用费
leverage	*v.*	利用
sole proprietorship		个体工商户
partnership	*n.*	合伙企业
tax return		纳税申报单
legal entity		法人实体
buy out		买下全部产权；买断股票
limited partner		有限责任合伙企业
corporation	*n.*	股份公司
issue	*v.*	发行（股票或债券）
bond	*n.*	债券
collateral	*n.*	抵押品

loan	*n.*	贷款
double taxation		双重征税
franchise	*n.*	特许经营公司
franchisor	*n.*	授予特许者；特许专营授权公司
franchisee	*n.*	特许经营人；有代销权的人或团体
domain name		域名
capital verification certificate		验资证明
appraisal report		评估报告
legal representative		法定代理人
angel investor		天使投资人
overhead	*n.*	运营开支；经常费用
fixed cost		固定成本
variable cost		可变成本
cash burn rate		烧钱率；现金消耗率

 **Exercises**

I. Answer the following questions according to the text.

1. What is the most basic principle of making real money?

2. What approach is suggested to use when starting a business?

3. How can we generate ideas for our businesses?

4. How should we deal with the big companies?

5. What should be considered when setting personal and business goals?

6. Why is it so important to choose the right business organization?

7. What are the major choices for business organizations?

8. What documents should we prepare when applying for a license of business?

9. What is the significance of writing a business plan?

10. How can we write a good business plan?

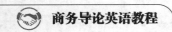

II. Decide whether the following statements are true (T) or false (F) according to the text.

1. Business is all about tricks, win-lose deals, and dishonesty. (   )

2. A new and small company should not compete with the big companies on the issue of price. (   )

3. A partnership must consist of three or more individuals who co-own the business. (   )

4. Before you register a business name and get your license, you'd better check with the local Administration of Industry and Commerce to make sure the name you chose is not already taken. (   )

5. Once you have raised the money to start or expand your business, you don't need to have a business plan any longer. (   )

III. Read the following passage and fill in the blanks with the words given below. Change the form if necessary.

encourage	traction	refine	launch	survive
commit	identify	viability	rush	potential

Confidence in pursuing a small business sometimes comes from the incremental feedback people have received and the "chemistry" that has consistently improved in their team. The confidence was garnered in specific stages as they started and grew the business. If we try to "map out" the path people often take to gain confidence in the early days of 1. _____ a business, we should focus on five distinct stages: (1) Gathering the panel: When you get a small group of like-minded individuals together to consider a new idea, one of two things happens—you either get more excited about the idea and decide to continue the discussion again, or you leave and lose interest. Sometimes the original "seed" ideas germinate and are developed by people that share an interest in "organizing the creative world". Some ideas 2. _____ while others die. There is something nice about the Darwinian approach to starting a new business. (2) Put your money (or time) where your mouth is: When an idea starts gaining 3. _____ in your mind, it is time to "invest" something in it. Whether it is a period of time that you 4. _____ every week to research or an amount of money that you allocate for initial development—you need to invest something.

Some companies start with a part-time employee that is being paid by the founder to "mock-up" a preliminary design, website, or concept. This is a great investment in the 5. _____ of the business. (3) The controlled test: When the time is right, you will feel a(n) 6. _____ of motivation to "test" your concept. Often this is a controlled microcosm of the business you have in mind. Once you can "market" and gauge initial interest from 7. _____ customers, you can become more confident in your concept. Your business doesn't need to be perfect or revenue-producing to generate confidence—it just needs to gain some traction. (4) Listen, listen, listen: The first realization you must have is that your business plan is likely wrong, and that the "needs" you first 8. _____ may differ from the actual needs and frustrations you must address among your potential customers. To identify the true market opportunity, you must listen. Gathering a small focus group of potential customers and asking questions is the best way to 9. _____ your marketing and product. (5) Debate toward shared conviction: As you incorporate the feedback you are getting and prepare to launch a real business, 10. _____ debate among your team and advisors about the decisions you are making. As debate ensues, try to reach some level of shared conviction in your team. Remember that conviction does not necessarily mean consensus—a mutual agreement to try a particular strategy. Of course, things will change—and if you continue to listen to the feedback—you can continue to tweak your strategy. Confidence ultimately comes from data (feedback), honest communication, and a team with a shared commitment.

IV. Translate the following sentences into Chinese.

1. Business is not about tricks, win-lose deals, and dishonesty. It's about action, persistence, patience, honesty, faith and hard work. Business is about creating long-term relationships; it's about making those relationships win-win. Business is about creating value in the world and being compensated because you have made people's lives better. Business is about getting what you want by giving people what they want or need.

2. The more predictable, repeatable, and reliable your business activities are, the more efficient you become. By studying, streamlining and then documenting a systemized approach to customer service, financial management, team communication, marketing, etc., you'll be able to free your mind of the procedural aspects of your business and focus more time on creative and innovative ways to be valuable to your customers.

3. The limited partners, on the other hand, have limited liability, meaning they are only liable to the extent of their investments. Limited partners do not have authority over the management of the business. They invest in the business and receive a share of profits and losses as stated in the partnership agreement.

4. If you think you may do business online, check if your business names are available as domain names. Choose a domain name ending with .com or .net. Resist the temptation to choose a domain name ending with any other suffixes. They don't connote business seriousness except for .org and .gov which are usually used by non-profits and governmental organizations.

5. Writing business plans is like creating the crucial road map you draw when starting a business. An unknown author said: "When you fail to plan you plan to fail." The biggest reason for failing to plan is the perception that one doesn't have enough time. Unfortunately for those who think that way, they will pay many times later on in terms of time spent for their failure to find time to write business plans.

 **Case Study**

Geek+ Founder Zheng Yong Sees Massive Potential of Robots in Industrial Sectors

As traditional sectors in China are turning to automation to improve efficiency and slash labor costs, the founder of a Chinese robotics unicorn sees greater potential and a wider range of applications of robots in the industrial field. "Overall speaking, I'm still optimistic about the application and potential of robots in an industrial environment," said Zheng Yong, founder and CEO of Chinese robotics unicorn Geek+（极智嘉）, in an interview with China Money Network on the sidelines of the 2019 RISE technology conference in Hong Kong last week. "Despite we know many new robotics technologies are emerging nowadays, it will still take some time for us to develop and make the most of robots in a stable, efficient, and safe manner. Comparatively speaking, in the industrial environment, robots are handling duties that are relatively simple, repetitive, and less demanding in terms of intelligence degree," said Zheng.

Geek+ is one of the most noteworthy companies in China's burgeoning robotics sector. The industry is expected to grow at a compound annual growth rate (CAGR) of 26.9% from

2017 to 2022 to reach US$80.5 billion—or 38.3% of the world's total spend in robotics—by 2022, according to a research conducted by International Data Corporation (IDC).

Meanwhile, the Chinese government has introduced policies to incentivize the development of artificial intelligence (AI), automation, and robotics. The authorities released the Robotics Industry Development Plan in 2016, outlining targets and strategies for growing the robotics industry in the next five years.

Zheng Yong, the founder and CEO of Geek+, specializes in supply chain management and logistic robotics. Prior to Geek+, Zheng served as the senior manager of China-focused diversified private equity firm New Horizon Capital, ABB and Saint-Gobain. He holds a dual Master Degree in Industrial Engineering of Tsinghua University and RWTH Aachen University. As he foresees more commercial value of robots in the industrial field, Zheng also believes that "the emotional value" created by consumer robotic products, such as robot ushers, food delivery robots, and companion robots, should also be valued by the market.

Read an interview Q&A below.

Q: What are the pain points in the logistics industry nowadays?

A: We have observed pain points in three major aspects. The first one is the rising labor costs. As we all know, the costs of human labor have been continuously increasing due to the fading demographic dividend, which has resulted in a significant impact on our clients' financial returns.

Secondly, today's young people are not willing to work in warehouses so our clients can hardly hire enough employees. During the busiest days when they are running a sales promotion, the lack of human labor will greatly influence their business development.

Thirdly, sales campaigns will always fluctuate the trading volume in the retail space, whatever e-commerce or brick-and-mortar retail. This kind of fluctuation, especially during [Alibaba's] "Double Eleven" online shopping festival, will require companies to address the impact brought by a huge change in production capacity. This impact will also bring companies a great challenge in the warehousing and logistics management.

Q: The Chinese logistic robotics industry is rapidly growing. What is the current development stage of the industry, and what are the trends you are seeing?

A: We can see the logistic robotics industry in China has experienced a few distinct phases. Between 2015 and 2016, companies were entering into the field and trying to prove the value and effectiveness [of logistic robots] to clients in China. We tried to prove that we could make a product system to tackle their problems.

From 2017 to 2018, I think people have acknowledged that the product system does have its value. But they still had doubts that whether logistic robots were suitable for a specific business offered by a company in a certain industry. That is why between 2017 and 2018, leading logistic robots companies like Geek+ were seeking to deploy applications in various sectors – whatever e-commerce, offline supermarkets and convenience stores, or manufacturers of shoes and clothing, makeup, and medicine. We were expanding our customer base in different sectors to make them understand the value of logistics robotics.

Starting from this year, I think the whole market has given very positive feedback to logistics robotics solutions. This is why we are seeing many large-scale enterprises duplicating such solutions and applying them in more warehouses. I believe that the industry has stepped into a rapid development phase in 2019.

Q: Besides logistics, what do you think are the other robots-enabled fields that we will also see great development potential in the future?

A: Overall speaking, I'm still optimistic about the application and potential of robots in an industrial environment. Despite we know many new robotics technologies are emerging nowadays, it will still take some time for us to develop and make the most of robots in a stable, efficient, and safe manner. Comparatively speaking, in the industrial environment, robots are handling duties that are relatively simple, repetitive, and less demanding in terms of intelligence degree. This can help companies take full advantage of robots and bring better performance ratios, or investment returns. Therefore, I am positive with the robot application in the industrial circle.

Questions for discussion

1. How did Geek+ founder Zheng Yong get ideas for his start-up business?

2. Is Geek+ founder Zheng Yong optimistic about the application of robots in the industrial environment? Why?

3. What's the value proposition of Geek+?

Assignments

1. Interview some people who have just started new businesses and ask them about the process of establishing a new business, the problems they met in this process, and how they overcame the difficulties. Write a report of about 200 words in English.

2. Prepare a ten-minute presentation to introduce how the governments encourage people to start their own businesses in different countries or areas.

Unit

5

Organizational Structure

Learning Objectives

After learning this unit, you should be able to:

- describe the concept and significance of organizational structure;
- know about different types of organizational structures;
- understand the differences between formal and informal organizations;
- know the keys to establish an effective organizational structure.

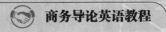

Warm-up Questions

1. What kind of organizational structure have you heard about?

2. If you are going to set up your own enterprise, what kind of organizational structure do you want to apply? Why?

3. What are the elements for an effective organizational structure?

Reading

Organizational structure is the framework of directing and reporting relationships in an organization. An organizational structure consists of activities such as task allocation, coordination, and supervision, which are directed towards the achievement of organizational goals. It can also be considered as the viewing glass or perspective through which individuals see their organization and its environment.

5.1 Significance of organizational structure

An organization can be structured in many different ways, depending on its objectives. The structure of an organization will determine the modes in which it operates and performs. Organizational structure allows the expressed allocation of responsibilities for different functions and processes to different entities such as the branch, department, work group, and individual.

Organizational structure affects organizational action in two big ways. First, it provides the foundation on which standard operating procedures and routines rest. Second, it determines which individuals get to participate in which decision-making processes, and thus to what extent their views shape the organization's actions.

Almost every successful enterprise understands the importance of organizational structure to businesses. Without proper attention to the creation of a cohesive and efficient structure, one company cannot carry out tasks and achieve its goals. There are several basic areas in which this can be demonstrated, including the assignment of responsibilities, the line of communication, the purchase of raw materials, and the marketing of goods and services.

One important aspect of the organizational structure is the creation of specific job positions within the organization and the assignment of responsibilities to each of those positions. Without clear, concise assignments, both employees and managers would be limited in how to respond and carry out essential tasks. By establishing the positions and determining how they work together, order is brought to the operation, allowing the enterprise to effectively pursue its goals.

Another important aspect of the organizational structure is the establishment of a line of communication that goes through every level of the structure. By implementing and maintaining this line of communication, employees can effectively interact with their managers. Then these managers can interact with their peers and various officers and executives. It's much easier for managers to identify both opportunities and challenges. As a bonus, a reliable line of communication helps to boost morale, which is likely to have a positive impact on productivity.

Organizational structure's importance can be seen in the process of purchasing raw materials and other resources. Clearly defining who can manage these tasks and empowering these employees to place orders for goods and services will ultimately facilitate every aspect of the operation.

The importance of organizational structure is also reflected in the marketing process. Marketing managers may use the structure to communicate efficiently with sales personnel who are responsible for advertising campaigns and selling goods and services. Without using the existing structure to collect data and put it to the best possible use, the sales effort would be passive, and not likely to generate a great deal of revenue for the company.

Without a good structure, organizations can accomplish very little and will often fail in a short period of time. Business owners who understand the importance of organizational structure and try to create a viable structure can often see fruits from this approach. These fruits could be the logical sequence in the production process, timely performance of tasks, and better communication among employees. The result is an organization that can function efficiently and be successful finally.

The set organizational structure may not coincide with facts, evolving in operational action. Such divergence decreases performance when growing. For example, a wrong organizational structure may hamper cooperation and thus hinder the completion of orders in due time and within limits of resources and budgets. Organizational structures should be adaptive to process requirements, aiming to optimize the ratio of effort and input to output.

5.2 Types of organizational structures

(1) Traditional organizational structures

There are mainly seven kinds of common organizational structures, namely pre-bureaucratic structure, bureaucratic structure, post-bureaucratic structure, functional structure, divisional structure, matrix structure, and flat structure. Now, let's learn about them one by one.

Pre-bureaucratic structure

A pre-bureaucratic structure is also known as an entrepreneurial structure, in which there is no standardization of tasks. This structure is most common in smaller organizations and is best used to solve simple tasks. The structure is totally centralized. The strategic leader makes all key decisions and most communication is done by one-to-one conversation. It is particularly useful for new (entrepreneurial) businesses as it enables the founder to control growth and development.

Bureaucratic structure

A fully developed bureaucratic structure is just like a precise instrument. Precision, speed, unambiguity, strict subordination, reduction of friction and material and personal costs are raised to the optimum point in the strictly bureaucratic administration. A bureaucratic structure has a certain degree of standardization. They are better suited for more complex or larger scale organizations, usually adopting a tall structure.

Post-bureaucratic structure

Some theorists have developed the post-bureaucratic organization, in which decisions are based on dialogue and consensus rather than authority and command. The organization is a network rather than a hierarchy, open at the boundaries (in direct contrast to culture management); there is an emphasis on meta decision-making rules rather than decision-making rules. This sort of horizontal decision-making by consensus model is often used when running a non-profit or community organization. It is used to encourage participation and help to empower people who normally experience oppression in groups.

Functional structure

In a typical functional structure, a company is departmentalized into many units according to different functions. Employees within the functional divisions of an organization tend to perform a specialized set of tasks, for instance, the marketing department would be staffed only with marketing employees. This leads to operational efficiencies within that group. However, it could also lead to a lack of communication between the functional groups within an organization, making the organization slow and inflexible.

As a whole, a functional organization is best suited as a producer of standardized goods and services at large volume and low cost. Coordination and specialization of tasks are centralized in a functional structure, which makes producing a limited number of products or services efficient and predictable. Moreover, efficiencies can further be realized as functional organizations integrate their activities vertically so that products are sold and distributed quickly and at a low cost. For instance, a small business could make components used in the production of its products instead of buying them. This benefits the organization and employees' faiths.

Divisional structure

A divisional structure is also called a "product structure"; the divisional structure groups each organizational function into a division. Each division within a divisional structure contains all the necessary resources and functions within it. Divisions can be categorized from different points of view. One might make distinctions on a geographical basis, for example, a U.S. division and an EU division, or on a product or service basis (different products for different customers: households or companies).

In another example, an automobile company with a divisional structure might have one division for SUVs, another division for subcompact cars, and another division for sedans. Each division may have its own sales, engineering, and marketing departments. This is one of the weaknesses of a divisional organization, as it causes duplication of activities and resources. But for large organizations with diverse products and operating over a vast geographical area, the divisional organization offers more advantages, because it makes division managers fully responsible for their divisions' performance, and frees the headquarters from concerning with day-to-day operations.

Matrix structure

The matrix structure groups employees by both functions and products. This structure utilizes functional and divisional chains of command simultaneously, thus it can combine the advantages of these two structures. A matrix organization frequently uses teams of employees to accomplish work, in order to take advantage of the strengths, as well as make up for the weaknesses of functional and decentralized forms. An example would be a company that produces three products: products A, B and C. Using the matrix structure, this company would organize functions within the company in this way. They will set up four departments for "product A": a production department, a sales department, a finance department, and an R&D department. And they will do the same to products B and C.

Starbucks is one of the numerous large organizations that has successfully developed the matrix structure supporting its focused strategy. Its design combines functional and product-based divisions, with employees reporting to two heads. Creating a team spirit, the company empowers employees to make their own decisions and trains them to develop both hard and soft skills. That makes Starbucks one of the best in customer service.

Some experts also mention the multinational design, common in global companies, such as Procter & Gamble (P&G), Toyota, and Unilever. This structure can be seen as a complex form of the matrix, as it maintains coordination among products, functions, and geographic areas.

A matrix organization is cost-effective for work on new products, but it also has weaknesses. Unlike a functional organization, it may cause confusion because one employee has more than one superior. Moreover, such an organization is temporary in nature and, therefore, it is difficult for the employees to develop long-term working relationships.

Flat organizational structure

A flat organizational structure, or a flat structure, is also known as a horizontal organization. It is a level wherein there is no level between the staff and managers. In such an organization the most trained employees are involved in the decision-making process. This structure mostly takes place in smaller organizations or also on a small scale within large organizations. However, when these organizations began to grow and expand, the company turns into a hierarchical organizational structure. In fact, most of the organizations worldwide start with a flat organizational structure.

With the help of a flat organization structure, the decision-making process mostly involves most of the employees. Every employee's feedback as well as opinion is taken into consideration. Due to this kind of structure, employees and the top management interact on a regular basis and there is a very understanding bonding that takes place in the organization.

The flat structure is common in small companies (entrepreneurial start-ups, university spin-offs). As the company grows, it becomes more complex and hierarchical, which leads to an expanded structure, with more levels and departments. Often, it would result in bureaucracy, and it's the most prevalent structure in the past.

In general, over the last decade, it has become increasingly clear that through the forces of globalization, competition and more demanding customers, the structure of many companies has become flatter, less hierarchical, more fluid, and even virtual.

With the development of the society, new categories of organizational structures like team, network and virtual organizational structures are also emerging now.

(2) Modern organizational structures

Team structure

One of the newest organizational structures developed in the 20th century is the team. In small businesses, the team structure can define the entire organization. Teams can be both horizontal and vertical. While an organization is constituted as a set of people who combine individual competencies to achieve newer dimensions, the quality of organizational structures revolves around the competencies of teams. A team structure has the advantage of speeding up the work flow and lowering costs. It also generally improves employee motivation and eliminates unnecessary layers of management. Sometimes the team structure can be integrated with other structures. Such integration allows for the authority and organization of a more concrete structure, while at the same time capturing the cross-functional and project-oriented advantages of teams.

For example, P&G brings together a group of employees from finance, marketing, and research and development departments—all representing different geographic regions. This newly created team is tasked with the project of creating a laundry detergent that is convenient, economical, and aligned with the company's manufacturing capabilities. The project team might be allocated a certain number of hours a month to devote to team objectives; however, members of the team are still expected to work within their respective functional departments. That's to say, larger bureaucratic organizations can benefit from the flexibility of teams as well. Xerox, Motorola, and Daimler Chrysler are all among the companies that actively use teams to perform tasks.

However, we should not neglect the disadvantages of the team structure. A team structure may increase the time spent in meetings, making time management more challenging. What's more, the staff may feel that their work within the team is conflicting with their work in their department.

Network structure

Just like teams, the network structure is also a modern structure. A network organizational structure refers to a system of delegating and coordinating tasks among a number of partner companies or business entities. These companies often have a common goal of producing a specific product. This arrangement gives a company the chance to collaborate with other related business entities to work together to achieve a common goal. Network structures bring together different companies with the aim of obtaining and maintaining a competitive advantage over others outside of their network.

While business giants risk becoming too clumsy to act and react efficiently, the new network organizations contract out any business functions, which can be done better or more cheaply. In essence, managers in network structures spend most of their time coordinating and controlling external relations, usually by electronic means. H&M, one of the world's leading fashion companies, is outsourcing its clothing to a network of 700 suppliers, more than two thirds of which are based in low-cost Asian countries. Not owning any factories, H&M can be more flexible than many other retailers in lowering its costs, which aligns with its low-cost strategy. The potential management opportunities offered by recent advances in complex networks theory have been demonstrated, including applications to product design and development, and innovation problems in markets and industries.

The advantage of a network organizational structure over any other forms of organizational structures is its flexibility and efficiency. This is because establishing a network structure requires a thorough selection and use of the best players available, who come together as partners. These partners are charged with the responsibility of providing specific needs within the network structure.

The core objective of an organizational structure is to support and complement the strategy of any business arrangement used to realize the objectives and goals of the organization. However, over-reliance on individual partners within network structures may make these systems susceptible to a number of challenges within the network structure. Another disadvantage of the network structure is that this more fluid structure can lead to more complex relations in the organization.

Virtual structure

The third organizational structure that is new and unconventional is the virtual structure, which is often adopted by boundaryless organizations. Virtual organization is a term used to describe a collection of people or organizations who are sharing resources without physically moving into the same space. Typically, virtual is used to describe computer-generated environments, where people with a common purpose or issue can meet, unrestricted by geography. This type of organization has grown substantially in the past ten years as the cost of technology decreases, providing opportunities to remove these barriers at a lower cost. The virtual organization does not physically exist, but enabled by software to exist. The virtual organization exists within a network of alliances, using the Internet. This means while the core of the organization can be small but the company can still operate globally and be a market leader in its niche.

Virtual organizations have many advantages. The biggest advantage of a virtual team enjoyed by an organization is the associated cost savings. The organization can do away with huge expenses on real estate, office spaces, utility bills such as gas, electricity, water and employees' travel, etc. Many organizations outsource their operations to low-cost regions. Thus, production costs also decrease with the reduced raw material costs, operational costs, and lower wages of the employees in these geographic locations. Besides that, virtual organizations can look for talents beyond their countries of origin. This brings together experts and specialists from across the world to work together on one project. Increased knowledge sharing and greater innovation happen as the organization's staff share their understanding of global and local markets as well as best business practices.

However, virtual organizations also have many disadvantages. For example, the success of virtual organizations depends greatly on reliable communication technologies such as instant messaging, emails and video-conferencing, etc., which could be very expensive for some companies. Moreover, the cultural differences between the members of virtual organizations may give rise to some conflicts. For example, while an American would write a straightforward email describing a bad situation, this would be perceived as impolite by a Chinese member of the organization. This would lead to conflicts, mistrust, and difficulties in collaboration. These troubles are also caused by the absence of non-verbal communication like face-to-face interactions.

5.3 Formal and informal organizations

We have studied the formal types of organizations, which can be drawn and seen in the form of organization charts. Within every company, however, there is also an informal organization, which cannot be drawn neatly and seen clearly in a chart form. And you should be able to differentiate between the formal and informal organizations.

The formal organization can be seen and represented in chart form. An organization chart displays the organizational structure and shows job titles, lines of authority, and relationships between departments. The informal organization is the network, unrelated to the firm's formal authority structure, of social interactions among its employees. It is the personal and social relationships that arise spontaneously as people associate with one another in the work environment.

The informal organizations can pressure group members to conform to the expectations of the informal group that conflict with those of the formal organizations. The supervisor should recognize the existence of information groups, identify the roles members play within these groups, and use knowledge of the groups to work effectively with them. The informal organization can make the formal organization more effective by providing support to management, stability to the environment, and useful communication channels.

5.4 Keys to erecting an effective organizational structure

All kinds of organizational structures have been proven effective in contributing to business success. Some firms choose highly centralized, rigidly maintained structures, while others—perhaps even in the same industry sector—develop decentralized, loose arrangements. Both of these organizational types can survive and even thrive. There is no best way to design an organization. Organizational research has shown that the more we know about particular types of organizations, the less we can generalize about the optimal design for an effective organization. Generally, organizational theorists believe that no structure, set of systems, or method of staffing is appropriate for every organization. Organizations operate in different environments with different products, strategies, constraints, and opportunities.

But despite the wide variety of organizational structures that can be found in the business world, the successful ones tend to share certain characteristics. Indeed, business experts cite a number of characteristics that separate effective organizational structures from ineffective designs. Recognition of these factors is especially important for entrepreneurs and established business owners, since these individuals play such a pivotal role in determining the final organizational structure of their enterprises.

As business owners weigh their various options in this realm, they should make sure that the following factors are taken into consideration:

- Relative strengths and weaknesses of various organizational forms;

- Legal advantages and disadvantages of organizational structure options;

- Advantages and drawbacks of departmentalization options;

- Likely growth patterns of the company;

- Reporting relationships that are currently in place;

- Reporting and authority relationships that you hope will be implemented in the future;

- Optimum ratios of supervisors/managers to subordinates;

- Suitable level of autonomy/empowerment to be granted to employees at various levels of the organization (while still recognizing individual capacities for independent work);

- Structures that will produce the greatest worker satisfaction;

- Structures that will produce optimum operational efficiency.

Once all these factors have been objectively examined and blended into an effective organizational structure, the small business owner will then be in a position to pursue his business goals with a far greater likelihood of success.

Words and Phrases

empower	v.	授权
pre-bureaucratic structure		前官僚制组织结构
bureaucratic structure		官僚制组织结构
post-bureaucratic structure		后官僚制组织结构
functional structure		职能型组织结构
divisional structure		事业部型组织结构

matrix structure		矩阵式组织结构
flat structure		扁平式组织结构
team structure		项目小组型组织结构
network structure		网络型组织结构
virtual structure		虚拟组织结构
standardization	*n.*	标准化
consensus	*n.*	共识
departmentalize	*v.*	把……分为各部
division	*n.*	部门
soft skill		软技能
virtual organization		虚拟组织
production cost		生产成本
realm	*n.*	领域
contract out		订立契约把（工程）对外承包
outsource	*v.*	外包
autonomy	*n.*	自主权

 ## Exercises

I. Answer the following questions according to the text.

1. What's the primary purpose of organizational structures?

2. Why are organizational structures very important?

3. How can organizational structures affect organizational actions?

4. What kind of organizations should adopt the bureaucratic structure?

5. In what situations should we use a post-bureaucratic structure?

6. Could you give us an example of functional structure?

7. What are the defects of the flat organizational structure?

8. Could you define "virtual structure"?

9. Is there a best way to design an organization? Why or why not?

10. In your opinion, what factors are the most important when designing an organizational structure?

II. Decide whether the following statements are true (T) or false (F) according to the text.

1. Organizational structures should be shaped and implemented for the primary purpose of making more money for the company. (   )

2. Employees within a functional department of an organization tend to perform a specialized set of tasks, for instance, the engineering department would be staffed only with engineers. (   )

3. The virtual structure is a special form of boundaryless organization. A virtual organization does not physically exist, but enabled by software to exist. (   )

4. There is one structure, set of systems, or method of staffing that is appropriate for all organizations. (   )

5. The formal organization is the network of social interactions among its employees. The informal organizations can be seen and represented in chart form. (   )

III. Read the following passage and fill in the blanks with the words given below. Change the form if necessary.

scene	demand	flaw	maximize	coordinate
evolve	achieve	staffing	inefficiency	criticism

A myriad of new organizational structures have seemed on the 1. _____ within the last couple of decades. Nonetheless, they still lack many of the desirable qualities in the standard methods. An organizational structure based on projects is one of them. The project directors often seek organizational solutions that can facilitate teamwork, 2. _____ the utility of limited resources, efficiency and quality to ensure that goals and objectives are 3. _____. Now we will examine a few main traditional organizational structures for project management. The three kinds of structures are functional organization, project organization and matrix organization.

Functional organization is definitely the oldest organizational structure, but it remains one of the most successful. This method performs best when raised for routine work functions and the upholding of quality together with work standards. Functional organization structures determine projects in two different ways. One way involves a project being assigned to a specific functional manager who then 4. _____ with the other departments to enable them to each contribute. Alternatively, projects can be shuffled around to several departments where each department manager makes sure that his part of the effort has been completed. This method cannot work very effectively when used in facilitating complex projects. One of the many major 5. _____ of this organizational structure is the lack of built-in employee recognition, dimension, and reward for project performance. Similarly, there is very little individual accountability for almost any project management tasks that need to be performed.

Project organization is a structure that is produced for executing projects. It's specifically tailored to meet the 6. _____ of complex assignments by isolating unique work and maintaining a strong focus on completing this project. Once the undertaking is completed, this composition disbands. This structure is most effective in maintaining dedicated resources in the life of the project. The major criticism of this structure is that it's inefficient in transferring technology and the utilization of resources. Also, most of the time the members actually begin acting as a cohesive team, and when the project is passed, the organization dissolves. Although the project has dedicated resources throughout its lifetime, major 7. _____ ensues when you can find underutilized employees during certain portions of the project.

Matrix organization is a project management structure that 8. _____ in the recognition of inherent flaws inside functional organization and undertaking organization structures. Created in the 1970s, this structure combines the best components of these structures. This model functions very well when there are several projects being coordinated at once. The functional managers manage the 9. _____, training, job assignment, and evaluation of the project's personnel. The functional specialists are assigned to manage one or more projects and oversee that these individualized projects are completed through maximum resource efficiency.

Despite its recognition and avoidance of the 10. _____ involved in many other structures, matrix organization still does have some problems of its very own. When individual employees must report to two or more managers, there may be ambiguities and conflicts. These problems may be avoided through good connection and solid leadership concerning managers.

IV. Translate the following sentences into Chinese.

1. The set organizational structure may not coincide with facts, evolving in operational action. Such divergence decreases performance when growing. For example, a wrong organizational structure may hamper cooperation and thus hinder the completion of orders in due time and within limits of resources and budgets.

2. Some theorists have developed the post-bureaucratic organization, in which decisions are based on dialogue and consensus rather than authority and command. The organization is a network rather than a hierarchy, open at the boundaries (in direct contrast to culture management); there is an emphasis on meta decision-making rules rather than decision-making rules.

3. Coordination and specialization of tasks are centralized in a functional structure, which makes producing a limited number of products or services efficient and predictable. Moreover, efficiencies can further be realized as functional organizations integrate their activities vertically so that products are sold and distributed quickly and at a low cost.

4. While business giants risk becoming too clumsy to act and react efficiently, the new network organizations contract out any business functions, which can be done better or more cheaply. In essence, managers in network structures spend most of their time coordinating and controlling external relations, usually by electronic means.

5. Indeed, business experts cite a number of characteristics that separate effective organizational structures from ineffective designs. Recognition of these factors is especially important for entrepreneurs and established business owners, since these individuals play such a pivotal role in determining the final organizational structure of their enterprises.

Case Study

Corporate Governance Overview of Huawei

The company only exists to serve its customers. The purpose of growing our harvest and increasing the fertility of our soil is to better serve our customers. "Staying customer-centric and creating value for customers" are the company's common values. The conferment of authority is required to drive the facilitation and implementation of the company's common values. However, without effective controls in place, authority unchecked will ultimately hinder such common values. The company has a well-developed internal governance structure, under which all governance bodies have clear and focused authority and responsibility, but operate under checks and balances. This creates a closed cycle of authority and achieves rational and cyclical succession of authority.

The company's fate cannot be tied to any single individual and the governance bodies of the company shall follow a model of collective leadership. This collective leadership model is created upon common values, focused responsibility, democratic centralized authority, checks and balances, and growth by self-reflection.

In addition, the company stays customer-centric, inspires dedication, and continuously improves its governance structure, organizations, processes, and appraisal systems to sustain its long-term growth.

The Shareholders' Meeting is the company's authoritative body, making decisions on major issues such as the company's capital increase, profit distribution, and selection of the members of the Board of Directors (BOD)/Supervisory Board.

The Board of Directors is the highest body responsible for corporate strategy, operations management, and customer satisfaction. The BOD's mission is to lead the company forward. It exercises decision-making authority for corporate strategy and operations management, and ensures customer and shareholder interests are protected.

The BOD and its Executive Committee are led by rotating chairs. During their terms, the rotating chairs serve as the foremost leaders of the company.

The key responsibilities of the Supervisory Board include overseeing the responsibility fulfillment of BOD members and senior management, monitoring the company's operational and financial status, and supervising compliance.

An independent auditor is responsible for auditing a company's annual financial statements. In accordance with applicable accounting standards and audit procedures, the independent auditor expresses an opinion as to whether the financial statements are true and fair. KPMG has been Huawei's independent auditor since 2000.

To strengthen end-to-end operations management of our ICT infrastructure business, the company set up the ICT Infrastructure Managing Board, which is the primary owner of our business strategy, operations management, and customer satisfaction for ICT infrastructure business.

- The Carrier BG (Business Group) and the Enterprise BG manage and support solution marketing, sales, and services that target carrier customers and enterprise/industry customers respectively. The two BGs provide innovative, differentiated, and advanced solutions based on the business characteristics and operational patterns of different customers while continuously improving the company's industry competitiveness and customer satisfaction.

- Network Products & Solutions is a department that provides integrated ICT solutions to carriers and enterprise/industry customers. This department is responsible for product planning, development, and delivery as well as for building product competitiveness. The goal of Network Products & Solutions is to deliver better user experiences, support customers' business success, and lead the world forward by building the best, most intelligent, and most cost-effective connections.

- The Cloud & AI BG is responsible for the competitiveness and success of Huawei's cloud and computing business. This BG is also responsible for the business' R&D, marketing, ecosystem building, technical sales, consulting, and integrated enablement services. This BG will focus on Kunpeng, Ascend, and Huawei Cloud to build ecosystems and cultivate fertile soil, so that Huawei can become a cornerstone of the digital world.

- ICT regional organizations are the company's regional ICT business operations centers. They are responsible for developing and effectively leveraging regional resources and capabilities, and also for implementing the company's ICT business strategy in their regions. While establishing closer partnerships with customers and helping them achieve business success, ICT regional organizations will develop ICT management systems, cyber security and privacy protection management systems, and internal control systems in their regions, and will continue to support the company in achieving profitable and sustainable growth.

- The Intelligent Automotive Solution BU (Business Unit) is an end-to-end organization responsible for the company's intelligent automotive business. This BU will help extend Huawei's strengths in ICT to the intelligent automotive sector by providing incremental ICT components and solutions. This BU's business goal is to use ICT to help automotive manufacturers produce even better products.

To strengthen strategy and risk management within our consumer business and increase the efficiency of its decision-making process, the company set up the Consumer Business Managing Board, which is the primary owner of consumer business strategies, operations management, and customer satisfaction. The Consumer Business Managing Board consists of several departments with different responsibilities.

- The Consumer BG focuses on serving device consumers and ecosystem partners, and deals with all aspects of the consumer domain. This BG is responsible for business performance, risk controls, market competitiveness, and customer satisfaction in the consumer business.

- The Consumer BG's regional organizations are responsible for their overall business results, consumer satisfaction, ecosystem partner experience, and the brand image enhancement of regional consumer business. They need to gain insight into environmental changes and competition dynamics for the consumer electronics industry, and develop and implement regional consumer business plans and resource investment strategies. These organizations are also responsible for launching products, managing product life cycles, developing ecosystems, planning and implementing marketing events, and developing and managing channels, retail outlets, and services in their regions. They also need to develop and maintain partnerships, create a favorable business environment, and ensure operational compliance and sustainable development of regional consumer business.

To gradually build a shared service platform to support the development of our multiple businesses and create an anchor for corporate policy execution, the company set up the Platform Coordination Committee. This committee is designed to push group functions to optimize their execution and operations, simplify cross-function operations, and strengthen collaboration, so that group functions will become the best service organizations available to support and promote business operations. Group functions provide business support, services, and oversight. They are positioned to offer accurate, timely, and effective services to field offices and strengthen oversight while delegating sufficient authority to them.

Questions for discussion

1. According to the passage and your understanding, what kind of organizational structure does Huawei adopt?

2. Please analyze the reasons why Huawei becomes a global tech giant based on its organizational structure.

3. The organizational structure of Huawei has been transformed from the centralization of authority to the decentralization of authority. Could you analyze the reasons for this change?

Assignments

1. Visit at least six companies or organizations and find out what kind of organizational structure they are using. Ask their managers about the advantages and disadvantages of their organizational structures.

2. Prepare a short presentation to introduce team work, a modern organizational structure.

Recruiting and Training Employees

Learning Objectives

After learning this unit, you should be able to:

- know the significance and strategies of recruitment;
- know the recruiting process and different methods;
- know how to recruit the best employees for an enterprise;
- know the different methods of training employees.

Warm-up Questions

1. Have you ever applied for a job? What kind of recruitment method did the company use?

2. Do you think it's necessary to train employees? Why or why not?

3. Could you give an example of campus recruitment?

Reading

6.1 Significance and strategies of recruitment

When building a new company or expanding an existing company, hiring employees is one of the most difficult and important choices to make. The first step in the hiring process is recruitment. This is an extremely important step for an organization. A company needs to attract only those individuals who are fully qualified and have the specific qualifications and skills the job demands. Recruitment precedes all the other steps in the hiring process, including selection and training, and hence its significance cannot be overstated. This is because once the organization is able to attract a given pool of talent, the selection process is made easier and the organization can zero in on the most qualified employees.

As for the recruitment strategies, there are two broad categorizations of recruitment: internal recruitment and external recruitment. Internal recruitment is to fill an existing vacancy within the organization from among the current employees, while external recruitment is to fill existing vacancies within the organization from any suitable applicant outside the organization.

(1) Internal recruitment

Internal vacant positions are advertised in various ways. It could be done through an internal job sheet, the company's notice board, or through the company's intranet, which is the type of website whose viewing is limited to members of the organization. Some companies have company magazines that they can use for advertisement purposes, while others may use staff meetings, which could be used when an organization wants to advertise the vacant position to a specific group of employees.

Compared with external recruitment, internal recruitment has many advantages.

First, internal recruitment has lower costs: Since it is focused on an already existing pool of employees to fill a vacant position, the selection and socializing processes are less time- and cost-consuming. Therefore, internal recruitment tends to be less expensive than external recruiting.

Second, internal recruitment is good for employee motivation. The prospect of potential promotion or transfers provides a clear sign to the current employees that the organization offers much room for advancement. This addresses the employee's need for self-achievement.

Third, internal recruitment can improve the probability of a good selection. There are at least two reasons for this. On the one hand, the chosen employee is already familiar with the organization's policies, procedures, and customs. On the other hand, the organization has a record of the chosen employee's performance, skills, and abilities.

A lot of organizations prefer internal recruitment, but some organizations don't like it, as this strategy has its drawbacks as well.

First, internal recruitment is not good for generating new ideas. A lack of new employees from the outside leads to a lack of new ideas and approaches. Not bringing new skills and fresh innovative ideas and competencies to the organization is the biggest disadvantage of the internal recruitment.

Second, internal recruitment may lead to conflicts within the organization. For example, an employee who responded to an internally advertised position and got that job at last might discover that his workmates resent that promotion and are not so cooperative as they used to be.

Third, internal recruitment will create another vacancy that needs to be filled, which could be time-consuming.

(2) External recruitment

The external recruitment strategy also has its advantages and disadvantages.

First, the most obvious advantage of external recruitment is the availability of a greater pool of applicants. The external recruitment allows the organizations to be selective when selecting a candidate and to define the right requirements, which fits in the organization most effectively.

Second, external recruitment can bring new people with fresh and innovative ideas to the organization; at the same time, these people will also bring experience they have gained from other organizations, which can be a huge benefit for the organization.

External recruitment also has its disadvantages.

First, external recruitment is more cost-consuming because it incurs recruiting costs, agency fees, and advertising fees.

Second, external recruitment is more time-consuming because the organizations must work through many processes that go before selection. And it takes a lot of energy to handle all the potential candidates.

Third, external recruitment may lead to a wrong choice of candidate. Even after going through all these processes, there is no assurance that the results will be fitting with the organization; the organization may hire someone who might show great potential in the recruitment process but fails to live up to the job role once employed.

In summary, it is important to note that each recruitment strategy has its benefits and disadvantages and hence the best strategy a company should adopt must depend on its specific circumstances.

Many organizations adopt both two recruitment strategies but tend to favor internal recruitment over external recruitment. It is important to note that each category has its benefits and disadvantages and hence the best approach a company should adopt must be based on its specific circumstances. Which strategy to take is determined by the type of vacancy that is going to be occupied. Generally speaking, a senior managerial or executive vacancy is filled internally. Organizations tend not to recruit externally for these vacancies. Because they find that someone within the organization who is acquainted with the role and the organization will do that job more effectively. No matter the company chooses to recruit from internal or external sources, its recruitment activities must be designed and implemented in a manner consistent with all relevant laws and regulations.

6.2 Recruitment methods and selection

When it comes to the recruitment of new employees, a number of approaches have been proven to be most appropriate. Some of the most effective employee recruitment approaches as well as strategies are discussed below.

(1) Referrals from employees

The employee referral program basically seeks to source new employees through consultation with existing employees where they are asked to forward the names as well as contacts of those who they know can fill a certain vacant position within an organization. In this case, employees may recommend individuals from their personal contacts, friends as well as family. Such referrals were prohibited by many companies in the past to prevent close interpersonal relationships from unfairly affecting personnel actions. More recently, the hiring of family and friends of current employees through referral in some private companies has become recognized as an inexpensive way to obtain loyal and dependable new employees and has been encouraged.

One of the most significant advantages of employee referral programs apart from cost savings is their inherent ability to increase the pool of potential employees for the organization. This is because the program tends to find even those who are not actively looking for new positions.

Further, a company or organization that utilizes the employee referral program has a high chance of attracting the most qualified employees. The premise here is that since the referring employee has a reputation to protect, he is most likely to refer only those individuals who are qualified to do the job, since a chain of wrong referrals can negatively impact the referring employee's reputation as well as career development.

However, heavy dependence on employee referrals may cause problems because employees are likely to recommend someone fairly similar to themselves. Unfair hiring practices may occur. For instance, some managers may see the program as a way to reward their business associates, cronies or family members without any insistence on professionalism or qualifications.

(2) Campus recruitment

This is another recruitment approach that has gained prominence in the recent past mainly due to the need for businesses to make cost savings. It essentially involves paying universities and other vocational centers a visit and seeking to introduce the organization and its various vacant positions to students.

It is important to note that this recruitment method has two main benefits for the organization. First and foremost, it can provide the organization with a pool of applicants on a need basis. And secondly, it can create awareness of the various positions available to the target group, hence availing the organization a future pool of talent. This recruitment method is most appropriate when the vacant positions are entry level, i.e. trainee level, apprentice positions, etc. Further, as already stated above, most employers prefer this approach as it is inherently cheap compared with other recruitment methods like placing adverts in the classified sections of the dailies or paying professional recruitment firms.

However, it is equally important to note that this recruitment method has some weaknesses and it cannot be used as the primary recruitment approach for the company. Hence, just like the case of employee referral programs, a balance of sorts must be found. It should be noted that recruiting at universities as well as vocational schools tends to be limiting as it is inappropriate for more senior positions as most of those targeted at this level have no track record which might be utilized to gauge their performance.

(3) Employment agencies

The recruiting process can be daunting for many companies, so they just turn to employment agencies to help them fill open positions. Employment agencies or executive recruiters are sometimes simply known as "headhunters" and their main task is to look for the right candidate to fill a vacant position existing in a firm. Employment agencies are contracted by the recruiting firm and are usually paid a certain predetermined fee for their services. However, most employment agencies specialize in a given area of recruitment such as engineering, financial analysis as well as marketing. Hence, this is one of the considerations that must be taken into account by the recruiting company before engaging in such services.

Contracting the services of recruitment agencies remains one of the best ways to source for individuals to fill the higher level or management positions within the organization. Further, they can be seen as a cost- and time-saving recruitment method. In most cases, only a few names are submitted to the recruiting company for consideration as opposed to the other recruitment methods or approaches where the recruiting company has to sort through voluminous applications and come up with the best candidates, which might be time-consuming as well as labor intensive.

Although there can be many benefits associated with employment agencies, they also come with some disadvantages. Many headhunters are not experts in your industry. You can tell them what you're looking to find in a candidate, but they're only going to be able to identify qualified candidates on paper. It will be difficult for them to know whether the candidates they've selected are actually good at doing the job. Employment agencies can also charge high costs for their services.

There's no right or wrong answer as to whether hiring an employment agency to fill open positions in your company is a good idea or not. Many firms enjoy working with head-hunters, while others don't find them to be all that beneficial. When deciding if you need help from employment agencies, you must consider both the position you're trying to fill and the recruiting resources available to you.

(4) Advertising

This is one of the most popular recruitment methods. Many companies in the global marketplace allocate a significant portion of their budget to this important method. One of the most significant advantages of placing paid job advertisements is its ability to reach a number of potential candidates, which depends on the media chosen. Quality employees cannot be selected when quality candidates do not know of job vacancies, are not interested in working for the company, and do not apply. Recruiters should inform qualified individuals about employment opportunities, create a positive image of the company, provide enough information about the jobs so that applicants can make comparisons with their qualifications and interests, so that they will apply for the available positions.

However, the decision of a business to advertise or not to largely depends on a number of factors including but not limited to the needed coverage as well as the advertising costs involved. With that in mind, an employer may decide to place job advertisements in a wide variety of media including but not limited to local and international newspapers, specialist or general journals, notice boards as well as job posters. This is a recruitment method that calls for much creativity if cost savings are to be made.

For instance, a hospital seeking to fill a vacancy for a nurse would place an advert in a medical journal rather than a journal or publication whose target is the general market. The same applies to a blue-chip company seeking an executive for its international operations. In such a case, it might consider placing job advertisements in a management journal.

(5) E-recruitment

E-recruitment, also called as online recruitment, is the process of hiring potential candidates for vacant job positions using electronic resources, particularly the Internet.

Today, the use of electronic media in recruitment has greatly increased. Radio, cable TV, and electronic bulletin boards have all proven to be effective competition for the printed

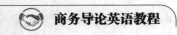

medium. Besides that, as the popularity of the Internet continues to increase, there is a growing need to utilize the online platform to fill existing positions in a firm.

Perhaps no method has ever had such a revolutionary effect on recruitment as the Internet. There are respective company websites devoted in some manner to job posting activities. Currently, employers can electronically screen candidates' soft attributes, direct potential hires to a special website for online skill assessment, conduct background checks over the Internet, interview candidates via videoconferencing, and manage the entire process with web-based software. Companies benefit immensely in terms of cost savings, speed enhancement and extended worldwide candidate reach offered by the Internet. From the job seekers' perspective, the Internet allows for searches over a broader array of geographic and company postings than was possible before.

One more thing that deserves mention in hiring employees is selection. Selection is the process of choosing the most suitable candidate for the vacant position in the organization. In other words, selection means weeding out unsuitable applicants and selecting those individuals with prerequisite qualifications and capabilities to fill the jobs in the organization.

Most often, selection and recruitment are used interchangeably, but they both have different scopes. The former is a negative process that rejects as many unqualified applicants as possible so as to hire the right candidate, while the latter is a positive process that attracts more and more candidates and stimulates them to apply for the jobs.

Based on the complexity of selecting the right candidates, the selection process is comprised of several steps: preliminary interview; receiving applications; screening of applications; employment tests; interview; reference checking; medical examination; final selection.

The company should follow a proper selection procedure as a huge amount of money is invested in selecting the right candidate for the job. Also, the cost incurred in training and induction program is so high that the wrong selections could lead to a huge loss to the employer in terms of time, effort, and money.

Absenteeism and labor turnover are a terrible situation for any organization. If the candidates are not selected appropriately, then these problems will increase and the overall efficiency of the organization will go down.

6.3 Training new employees

After the recruitment process, an organization must ensure that the new employees are accustomed to the systems as well as the procedures of their new workplace. This is to say that regardless of the professionalism that informed the recruitment as well as selection process, employees cannot perform optimally in their new positions without the proper abilities, skills as well as knowledge required of them.

Therefore, the importance of training cannot be overstated in order to enhance the performance of employees in their new workplace. Employee training can be defined as all the actions undertaken by the employer to ensure that the employees execute the tasks in a proper way. It is important to note that contrary to popular belief, training should not be limited to new employees only. But in this part we only discuss the training of new employees.

When new employees come, the company should give them proper orientation and help them adapt to the new environment. The orientation may cover general information like the history, general regulations, and organizational structure of the company, and specific issues like work hours and pay schedules. Many companies also take this opportunity to tell the new employees something about the corporate culture, so that they can be assimilated into the organization more quickly and easily.

After that, in order to facilitate employee training, organizations should come up with an employee training plan. This plan must include a number of things to create a conducive learning environment. To come up with a conducive as well as an ideal learning situation, the organization must embrace the following approaches:

- Employee training should be made a continuous process;
- The learning process must be guided and have a direction;
- The learning process must be made sequential;
- Employees must be given the opportunity as well as time to practice what they learn.

It is important to note that the training of new employees must not stop on their supposed completion of a certain training process. It must be an ongoing process to ensure that such employees are responsive to the various changes in job requirements.

A new employee training model is introduced as follows, which includes all the vital steps in the training process.

(1) The identification of training needs

No meaningful training for new employees can take place without the apparent identification of the training needs of the new employees in relation to the job description. The organization can identify the training needs of a new employee by integrating three human resource factors, i.e. the needs of the whole organization, the specific job characteristics, and lastly the specific individual needs. It's very important to identify the key component areas in which the employee needs training in order to effectively perform his duties because it helps in the development of training manuals as well as a means of evaluation.

(2) The formulation of a training program as well as training goals

It is important to note that the formulation of the training program should be based on the need assessment. This program must identify the skills as well as behaviors which the training initiative should help the new employees to acquire. The training program should be founded on the need to take the new employees from where they are currently to where the company or organization would want them to be.

(3) Training methods

There are two primary training methods for new employees, which are on-the-job training and off-the-job training. On-the-job training is essential to new employees in the course of performing their duties. This approach is preferred by those organizations which do not want to lose time as the new employees are trained. It is most common for senior positions in management. Moreover, on-the-job training is one of the most common types of training used in the workplace, especially for vocational jobs, such as those in manufacturing. Often, this type of training is unstructured: The new employee is assigned to an experienced worker or supervisor, who demonstrates how the job is done. The trainee may shadow the other worker or workers for several shifts, while learning the steps that make up the job and how to use the equipment. This kind of training is usually conducted one-on-one, and the new workers generally have the opportunity to perform the different parts of the job with direct supervision.

When it comes to off-the-job training, the company can organize special seminars, lectures, as well as conferences for new employees. So, the new employees can be equipped with the necessary skills for the effective performance of their duties. However, most companies do not prefer to use this approach as it could be too expensive. Another approach synonymous with new employee training is orientation. During employee orientation, new employees are introduced and welcomed. The orientation is meant to educate new employees about the goals and responsibilities of the position and company, as well as to answer any questions they may have about human resource management, benefits, and payroll information.

Research indicates that about 60 percent of new employees quit their jobs in the first two weeks since they joined the companies. Hence employee orientation is extremely important and it should focus on a number of things including the various personnel regulations and rules, the organization's key officers as well as members, and the mission, history, and culture of the organization.

Words and Phrases

internal recruitment		内部招聘
external recruitment		外部招聘
intranet	n.	企业内部网站
referral	n.	推举
professionalism	n.	职业操守
employee referral program		员工推荐计划
campus recruitment		校园招聘
vocational center		职业培训中心
headhunter	n.	猎头公司
employment agency		职业介绍所
blue-chip	n.	优质（公司）
E-recruitment		在线招聘
interchangeably	adv.	可交替地
absenteeism	n.	旷工；缺勤
labor turnover		员工流失率
training manual		培训手册
orientation	n.	（任职之前的）情况介绍
on-the-job training		在职培训

off-the-job training 脱产培训

labor intensive 劳动密集型的

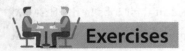 **Exercises**

I. Answer the following questions according to the text.

1. Why is recruitment important for a company?

2. What is internal recruitment? Try to give an example.

3. What are the advantages and disadvantages of the referral program?

4. What's the premise for the employee referral program?

5. Why do some employers prefer recruitment exercises at universities?

6. Could you give a definition of employee training?

7. How can we come up with a conducive training program?

8. How can we identify the training needs of a new employee?

9. Generally speaking, what kind of situation is on-the-job training appropriate for?

10. When conducting the employee orientation, what should be taken into consideration?

II. Decide whether the following statements are true (T) or false (F) according to the text.

1. There are two broad categorizations of recruitment: internal recruitment and external recruitment. (   )

2. Recruitment at schools and universities is most appropriate when the vacant positions are high level like senior management positions. (   )

3. Employment agencies or executive recruiters are sometimes simply known as "head-hunters" and their main job includes searching for the right candidate to fill a vacant position existing in a firm. (   )

4. Training should be limited to new employees only. (   )

5. There are two primary training approaches which organizations may adopt in respect to new employees: on-the-job training and off-the-job training. (   )

III. Read the following passage and fill in the blanks with the words given below. Change the form if necessary.

concentrate	minimize	meet	link	prepare
organization	communication	apply	enable	goal

Companies can 1. _____ different methods of training and development to any number of subjects to ensure that the skills needed for various positions are instilled. Companies gear training and development programs towards both specific and general skills, including technical training, sales training, clerical training, computer training, communications training, organizational development, career development, supervisory development, and management development. The 2. _____ of these programs is for trainees to acquire new knowledge or skills in fields such as sales or computers or to enhance their knowledge and skills in these areas. The following are some methods of training often used by companies.

Technical training seeks to impart technical knowledge and skills using common training methods for the instruction of technical concepts, factual information, and procedures, as well as technical processes and principles. Likewise, sales training 3. _____ on the education and training of individuals to communicate with customers in a persuasive manner and inculcate other skills useful for sales positions.

4. _____ training concentrates on the improvement of interpersonal communication skills, including writing, oral presentation, listening, and reading. In order to be successful, any form of communications training should be focused on the basic improvement of skills and not just on stylistic considerations. Furthermore, the training should serve to build on present skills rather than rebuilding from the ground up. Communications training can be taught separately or can be effectively integrated into other types of training, since it is fundamentally related to other disciplines.

Organizational development refers to the use of knowledge and techniques from the behavioral sciences to analyze existing organizational structure and implement changes in order to improve organizational effectiveness. Organizational development is useful in such varied areas as the alignment of employee goals with those of the organization, communications, team functioning, and decision-making. In short, it is a development process with an organizational focus to achieve the same goals as other training and development activities aimed at individuals. Organizational development practitioners commonly practice what has been termed "action research" to effect an orderly change that has been carefully planned to 5. _____ the occurrence of unpredicted or unforeseen events. Action research refers to a systematic analysis of an organization to acquire a better understanding of the nature of problems and forces within an organization.

Career development of employees covers the formal development of an employee's position within an organization by providing a long-term development strategy and training programs to implement this strategy and achieve individual goals. Career development represents a growing concern for employee welfare and the long-term needs of employees. For the individual, it involves stating and describing career goals, the assessment of necessary action, and the choice and implementation of necessary actions. For the 6. _____, career development represents the systematic development and improvement of employees. To remain effective, career development programs must allow individuals to articulate their desires. At the same time, the organization strives to meet those stated needs as much as possible by consistently following through on commitments and 7. _____ the expectations of the employees raised by the program.

Management and supervisory developments involve the training of managers and supervisors in basic leadership skills, enabling them to function effectively in their positions. For managers, this typically involves the development of the ability to focus on the effective management of their employee resources while striving to understand and achieve the strategies and goals of the organization. Management training typically involves individuals above the first two levels of supervision and below senior executive management. Managers learn to effectively develop their employees by helping employees learn and change, as well as by identifying and 8. _____ them for future responsibilities. Management development may also include programs that teach decision-making skills, creating and managing successful work teams, allocating resources effectively, budgeting, communication skills, business planning, and goal setting.

Supervisory development addresses the unique situation of the supervisor as a 9. _____ between the organization's management and workforce. It must focus on 10. _____ supervisors to deal with their responsibilities to labor and management, as well as co-workers and staff departments. Important considerations include the development of personal and interpersonal skills, understanding the management process, and productivity and quality improvement.

IV. Translate the following sentences into Chinese.

1. The employee referral program basically seeks to source new employees through consultation with existing employees where they are asked to forward the names as well as contacts of those who they know can fill a certain vacant position within an organization.

2. It should be noted that recruiting at universities as well as vocational schools tends to be limiting as it is inappropriate for more senior positions as most of those targeted at this level have no track record which might be utilized to gauge their performance.

3. Further, they can be seen as a cost- and time-saving recruitment method. In most cases, only a few names are submitted to the recruiting company for consideration as opposed to the other recruitment methods or approaches where the recruiting company has to sort through voluminous applications and come up with the best candidates, which might be time-consuming as well as labor intensive.

4. The organization can identify the training needs of a new employee by integrating three human resource factors, i.e. the needs of the whole organization, the specific job characteristics, and lastly the specific individual needs. It's very important to identify the key component areas in which the employee needs training in order to effectively perform his duties because it helps in the development of training manuals as well as a means of evaluation.

5. Hence employee orientation is extremely important and it should focus on a number of things including the various personnel regulations and rules, the organization's key officers as well as members, and the mission, history, and culture of the organization.

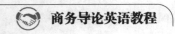

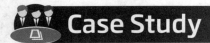 Case Study

Human Resources Development of Tencent
—The HR Three Pillar Model

The HRD of Tencent can be defined as the gradual development from purely transactional management or functional management to three roles of affairs, functions, and strategy. In 2010, the Human Resource of Tencent was distributed into three parts: Human Resource Center of Expertise (COE), Human Resource Business Partner (BP), and Human Resource Shared Service Center (SSC). In 2013, the SSC was replaced by Human Resource Shared Delivery Center (SDC) to achieve more effective human resource service in Tencent.

COE

In general, COE is the think-tank and expert support section of Tencent's HR system, mainly responsible for frontline research, participating and interpreting the company's business strategy, formulating the company's HR tactics, and formulating relevant systems and policies. COE of Tencent, including the HR department, Tencent Academy, Remuneration and Welfare department, and Corporate Culture and Employee Relations department, is not an entity department, but rather a collection of several functions in human resource management. The COE is responsible for strategy and policy in employment, training and development of employees, establishing an effective labor system, stimulating employees' enthusiasm, formulating performance and welfare system, paying attention to employees' feelings and building a harmonious company atmosphere and corporate culture. In summary, these functional departments design business-oriented and innovative HR management policies, processes and solutions.

BP

Another crucial sector of HR department is BP, which is regarded as a business partner inside the company and asks for more professional support from COE. The BP department communicates and finds solutions to truly establish a business alliance. There are six business groups in Tencent, and BP is the human resources system that distributes human resources management staff in the mentioned business groups of Tencent. Therefore, to make the BP develop towards the business partners, it is necessary to reorganize the current HR work of the enterprise to make a more reasonable proportion of time, reduce the transactional work, and increase the time investment of tactical and strategic work. Another one of the most important requirements is to solve practical needs in business, such as increasing market share and reducing production costs. For BP to become a business partner, this is the key first step. Without clear business needs, there is no method of supporting the business. Therefore, BP must think in terms of business, configure personnel according to effective standards, and at the same time, do a good job in recruitment, training, compensation, performance, and labor. This involves employee satisfaction and engagement. For the needs of employees in different business groups, HR cannot passively wait for internal staff to propose human resources requirements. Instead, the professional value of human resources must be actively exerted. BP is required to implement and promote the company's human resources management policies in various business departments, help business sectors to cultivate and develop human resources management capabilities to improve business performance. Furthermore, BP needs to understand the business of the six groups, and be able to provide professional solutions tailored to the individual needs of the business unit, truly embedding human resources and its value into the value modules of each business unit.

SDC

The SDC of Tencent was updated from SSC in 2013. The background is due to the fact that if human resource is expected to participate in and drive the strategy of enterprise development, a long-term system, which can sustainably support strategy requirements, is necessary. To be specific, business needs have changed from early stability requirements to versatile requirements, and human resource management has more emphasis on flexibility. Secondly, it is the new needs of employees' personalization and self-management and it is necessary to study human nature. The SSC can be defined as a platform with centralized and standardized services shared by the group and provide COE and BP with high quality and low costs. The SDC can be described as a productized, systematic and information-based shared delivery platform which integrates the common needs of the group and provide a one-stop overall solution that exceeds expectations for business, employees, and HR partners. SDC is expected to share resources, capabilities, teams, and information through new organizations, new attributes, new patterns, new tools, and new capabilities and actively explore and integrate various common needs in the HR field. One of the most prominent features of SDC's upgrade is the emphasis on "platformization". The term "platformization" mentioned here not only refers to the development of information technology, but also enhances SDC's product attributes, user attributes, and fun attributes. SDC can connect every sector and make the connection gradually platformed, systematic, and continuous. Tencent attempts to separate the entire SDC back-office center into five product centers: talent transportation, business ability, employee satisfaction, solving systematic issue, and human outsourcing service platform.

Questions for discussion

1. Which department of Tencent was established in 2007 to offer training for employees? What benefits can it provide?

2. Please compare the differences between SSC and SDC. What's new about SDC?

3. What can be concluded from SDC with respect to the HR department?

Assignments

1. Divide the class into several groups and simulate the recruitment process, in which some students play the role of HR, while the rest play the role of applicants. Try to be as formal as possible and each group will be accessed and commented by the whole class and the teacher. Finally, you should submit a report about what you've learned from this activity.

2. Make a thorough research on different ways of training employees, pointing out which way you like best and give reasons for your choice.

Employee Motivation

Learning objectives

After learning this unit, you should be able to:

- understand the concept of employee motivation;
- describe the differences between intrinsic and extrinsic motivation;
- know some basic theories of employee motivation;
- choose appropriate tools to motivate different employees;
- know the specific actions of improving employee motivation.

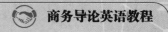

Warm-up Questions

1. What methods are often used when managers want to motivate employees?

2. In your opinion, how can the employees be effectively motivated?

3. Do you know any theories about motivation? What are they?

 # Reading

7.1 The concept of employee motivation

In its simplest form, the motivation process begins with a need—an individual's perception of a deficiency. For instance, an employee might feel the need for more challenging work, for higher pay, for time off, or for the respect and admiration of colleagues. These needs lead to thought processes that guide an employee's decision to satisfy them and to follow a particular course of action. If an employee's chosen course of action results in the anticipated outcome and reward, that person is likely to be motivated by the prospect of a similar reward to act the same way in the future. However, if the employee's action does not result in the expected reward, he is unlikely to repeat the behavior.

Managers need to understand what can be used to motivate employees. Of all the functions a manager performs, motivating employees is the most complex one. This is due to the fact that what motivates employees changes constantly. For example, research suggests that as employees' income increases, money becomes less of a motivator. As employees get older, interesting work becomes more of a motivator.

An employee must be motivated to work for a company or organization. If an employee is not motivated at work, then the quality of his work or all work in general will deteriorate.

7.2 Intrinsic motivation and extrinsic motivation

Generally speaking, motivation can be divided into two types: intrinsic motivation and extrinsic motivation.

(1) Intrinsic motivation

Intrinsic motivation means that the individual's motivational stimuli are coming from within. The individual has the desire to perform a specific task because its results are in accordance with his belief system or fulfills a desire, and therefore importance is attached to it. Intrinsic motivation involves engaging in a behavior because it is personally rewarding and performing an activity for its own sake rather than the desire for some external rewards. People's deep-rooted desires have the highest motivational power. The following are some examples of intrinsic motivation factors:

- Acceptance: We all need to feel that we are accepted by our co-workers;

- Curiosity: We all have the desire to be in the know;

- Honor: We all need to respect the rules and be ethical;

- Independence: We all need to feel we are unique;

- Order: We all need to be organized;

- Power: We all have the desire to be able to have influence;

- Social contact: We all need to have some social interactions;

- Social status: We all have the desire to be important in society.

(2) Extrinsic motivation

On the contrary, extrinsic motivation means that the individual's motivational stimuli are coming from outside. In other words, our desires to perform a task are controlled by an outside source. Extrinsic motivation is external in nature. It occurs when we are motivated to perform a behavior or engage in an activity to earn a reward or avoid punishment. The most well-known and debated motivation is money. Here are some other examples: employee of the year award, benefits package, bonuses, etc.

So, the primary difference between the two types of motivation is that extrinsic motivation arises from outside of the individual, while intrinsic motivation arises from within.

While most people would suggest that intrinsic motivation is better, it is not always possible in every situation. In some cases, people simply have no internal desire to engage in an activity. Excessive rewards may be problematic, but when used appropriately, extrinsic motivators can be a useful tool. For example, extrinsic motivation can be used to get people to complete a work task or school assignment in which they have no internal interest.

It's important for managers to understand that their employees are not all the same; thus, they must have an understanding of the different types of motivation in order to effectively motivate the employees. Such an understanding will enable them to better categorize their team members, and apply the appropriate type of motivation. They will find that each member is different, and each member's motivational needs will be varied as well. Some people respond best to intrinsic motivation and will meet any obligation they are interested in. On the contrary, others will respond better to extrinsic motivation; even difficult tasks can be well completed, as long as there is a reward upon completion of that task.

In summary, if a manager can understand the distinction between intrinsic and extrinsic motivational factors, he will have a greater probability of motivating the employees effectively. A good manager should become an expert in determining which type of motivation will work best with which team members.

7.3 Theories of employee motivation

Researchers have developed a number of theories to explain motivation. Each individual theory tends to be rather limited in scope. However, by looking at the key ideas behind each theory, you can gain a better understanding of motivation as a whole.

(1) Taylor and Scientific Management

Frederick W. Taylor was the creator of Scientific Management. He felt that every job was measurable and each element of a job could be timed. He assumed that workers were motivated by nothing but money, and that their productivity was directly linked with the pay they would get. In other words, the more they were paid, the more they would produce. Hence, all managers had to pay for every item the workers produced and they would work harder to get more money. This led to a long-established pay scheme called the "piece rate", where workers received a fixed amount for every unit of output. Schemes like this are usually associated with manufacturing industries and are not appropriate for a complex service-led organization.

While Scientific Management principles improved productivity and had a substantial impact on industry, they also increased the monotony of work. The core job dimensions of skill variety, task identity, task significance, autonomy, and feedback were all missing from the picture of Scientific Management. The most obvious weakness of Scientific Management principles is the neglect of other important factors in human relations.

(2) McGregor's Theory X and Theory Y

Theory X and Theory Y are theories of human motivation created and developed by Douglas McGregor at the MIT Sloan School of Management in the 1960s. They have been widely used in human resource management.

In Theory X, management assumes that employees are inherently lazy and will avoid work if they can and that they inherently dislike work. As a result of this, management believes that employees need to be closely supervised and comprehensive systems of controls need to be well developed, and employees will show little ambition without an enticing incentive program and will avoid responsibility whenever they can. Theory X managers rely heavily on threat and coercion to gain their employees' compliance. Beliefs of this theory lead to mistrust, highly restrictive supervision, and a punitive atmosphere. In fact, most companies in contemporary society are using the Theory X in management. For example, time-recorders are set up in the office buildings of some companies. The employees are required to punch a card when they come to the office. The employers use this device to supervise their employees just for fear that they may be late for work.

In Theory Y, management assumes employees may be ambitious and self-motivated and exercise self-control. It is believed that employees enjoy their mental and physical work duties. They possess creative problem-solving abilities, but their talents are underused in most organizations. Theory Y managers believe that, given the right conditions, most people will want to do well at work. They believe that the satisfaction of doing a good job is a strong motivation.

(3) Herzberg and Two-factor Theory

Another theorist, Frederick Herzberg, carried out a large-scale survey into motivation in the American industry. The results of his survey led him to develop a Two-factor Theory of motivation. Firstly, he established that if an employee's basic needs were not met, such as a suitable working environment and a basic rate of pay, then this creates a source of dissatisfaction. Herzberg termed these "hygiene factors". On the other hand, the presence of less tangible factors, such as the provision of challenging work and recognition for doing well, can create or increase work motivation. Herzberg termed these "motivators".

A company can put in place some of Herzberg's "motivators" in the following ways: employees get recognition for good work; they have a collective sense of achievement when the whole business does well; they gain extra responsibility and advancement through regular performance reviews; when employees do well in their work, the company rewards them.

(4) Maslow's Hierarchy of Needs

The theory of Abraham H. Maslow on staff motivation is also very popular. Maslow's Hierarchy of Needs theory is usually drawn as a pyramid including five types of needs. From the bottom to the top, the five needs are physiological needs, safety needs, social needs, esteem needs, and self-actualization needs.

Physiological needs refer to people's physical requirements for human survival, such as air, food, water, etc. Safety needs refer to people's needs to feel secure at work and home. For example, people need to feel safe in their environment. A company can provide these basic needs when it creates jobs.

Maslow's higher levels of needs are less obvious and less easy to describe but of great importance. Social needs refer to love and belonging needs. We want to feel part of something we share in. A company can create the opportunity for its employees to share in its common goals and vision for the group. It does this by rewarding the people who contribute to its success through their commitment and hard work.

The next level—esteem needs—refers to people's needs to feel valued and that what they do matters, i.e. the recognition and acknowledgement from others. The employees can make it happen themselves. A company can provide opportunities for all employees through promotion or training and then recognizes their achievements. Through this the employees can improve their self-esteem.

At the very top of Maslow's hierarchy is our human need for self-actualization. This means people will work hard in order to be as good as they possibly can be. A company can meet this by offering recognition, promotion opportunities, and the chance to develop a lifelong career within the group.

According to Maslow, people are motivated to satisfy the lower needs before they try to satisfy the higher needs. Also, once a need is satisfied, it is no longer a powerful motivator.

Maslow's hierarchy is a systematic way of thinking about the different needs employees may have at any given point. It explains different reactions they may have to similar treatment. An employee who is trying to satisfy his esteem needs may feel gratified when his supervisor praises him. However, another employee who is trying to satisfy his social needs may resent being praised by upper management in front of peers, if the praise sets him apart from the rest of the group.

7.4 Four tools for motivating employees

The above-mentioned theories of employee motivation can help managers to understand what employees need and want and how to motivate them. Generally speaking, there are at least four tools that managers can use to make employees gain satisfaction at work and be motivated. These tools can be applied in virtually all types of businesses and non-profit organizations, including government institutions. They are based on the theories of employee motivation.

In this part, we will study the four tools for motivating employees: job redesign, goal setting, performance appraisals, and performance incentives.

(1) Job redesign

How a job is designed has a major impact on employee motivation, job satisfaction, commitment to an organization, absenteeism, and turnover. When you do the same job day in and day out, it can become boring. Job redesign looks specifically at ways to expand an employee's job by redesigning certain aspects relating to the scope and depth of what an employee does and what he is responsible for at the organization. In doing so, the manager essentially prevents an employee from losing motivation or interest in his work. There are three ways a manager can redesign an employee's job: job enrichment, job enlargement, and job rotation.

Job enrichment provides an employee with more tasks to do as a part of his job, as well as the responsibility and authority needed to complete those additional tasks. It works particularly well to increase motivation when including additional tasks that match the skills, knowledge, and abilities the employee already has.

Job enlargement is a type of job redesign that increases only the tasks of a particular job. While job enlargement is limited in that it does not provide the additional responsibilities or authority that job enrichment does, it is useful in reducing some of the monotony associated with doing the same thing day in and day out. The belief is that once boredom is reduced, the motivation to perform at higher levels of productivity increases.

Job rotation assigns workers to an alternate job on a temporary basis. It is useful and motivating in several ways. First, it provides employees with something new to learn and do beyond their normal jobs. Second, it provides employees with a broader perspective on how the organization operates as a whole. Third, it increases the employees' understanding of what their co-workers do, which leads to a higher degree of respect for what others do. Finally, it offers the employees the chance to gain additional skills, which increases their value to the organization. Essentially, job rotation is great at adding variety and encouraging respect among peers, while sparking new interest in the organization.

(2) Goal setting

Goal setting and its influence on employee behavior and performance have been widely researched and discussed. Successful implementation of goal setting will result in employees being more motivated to complete specific tasks as well as higher morale and a more effective workplace.

Essentially, the theory of goal setting is based on the concept that whenever people work toward a predetermined goal, combined with a fixed deadline, they will be more motivated to complete the task at hand. People facing an open-ended task will be less inclined to work toward the end result in a structured and effective manner. Goal setting gives employees a larger sense of responsibility and accomplishment once the acquired goals are reached.

The research concerning the field of goal setting shows five important conclusions: ① Setting goals leads to an improvement in performance. More than 80 percent of all studies show a direct relationship between the setting of targets and an increase in performance. ② Setting difficult goals results in a higher level of performance than setting easier goals. ③ The method of goal setting—participative or assigned—has no influence on performance. Participative goal setting means that employees have a say in the goal, whereas assigned goal setting is based on the employer's decision. ④ Educational level does not influence the effect of goal setting on performance. ⑤ Finally, these studies have shown that positive feedback from the employer has a beneficial influence on performance.

While dealing with goal setting, managers also must take into account the behavioral impact of goal setting on an individual level. Four basic elements have to be kept in mind, along with the above-mentioned theory and considerations. ① Most importantly, the system of goal setting has to be open and transparent. Employees should know the goals of their co-workers to avoid having other employees feeling left out or being treated unfairly. ② Goal setting should be objective. Employees must be able to trust their supervisors to objectively judge the goals that are set. ③ Goals should be open to adjustment. Employees and supervisors should always have the option to adjust goals whenever the goals become unrealistic due to circumstances. ④ The reward system underlying the goal-setting system should be characterized by the same openness as the goal-setting system itself.

In summary, while dealing with goal setting, managers must carefully review their approaches. Goal settings that do not follow the basic guidelines will result in dysfunctional behavior. Employees will feel like they have no real influence on the process or they will feel that their supervisors are not being objective. If managers follow the basic guidelines and keep all communications open and transparent, goal setting will be a benefit to the employees and the organization.

(3) Performance appraisals

A performance appraisal is a process in which a rater or raters evaluate the performance of an employee. More specifically, during a performance appraisal period, raters observe, interact with, and evaluate a person's performance. Then, when it is time for a performance appraisal, these observations are documented on a form. The rater usually conducts a meeting with the employee to communicate performance feedback. During the meeting, the employee is evaluated with respect to success in achieving last year's goals, and new goals are set for the next performance appraisal period.

There are three major steps in the performance appraisal process: identification, measurement, and management. With identification, the behaviors necessary for successful performance are determined. Measurement involves choosing the appropriate instrument for appraisal and assessing performance. Management, which is the ultimate goal, is the reinforcement of good performance and the correction of poor performance.

A good performance appraisal system can greatly benefit an organization. It helps direct employee behavior toward organizational goals by letting employees know what is expected of them, and it gives information for making employment decisions, such as pay raises, promotions, and discharges.

(4) Performance incentives

Incentives are a type of reward system where somehow individuals receive some types of rewards for their performance. The incentive could be cash, a trip, a sports event ticket, paid holidays, or maybe even an award. Generally speaking, the incentives fall into three categories: monetary incentives, non-monetary incentives, and employee recognition.

Monetary incentive simply means giving the employees more money. The money can take the form of employee stock options, profit-sharing plans, paid time off, bonuses, and even cash. These rewards can be given over a period of time. They can be annual, semiannual, or any one of a number of options.

Non-monetary incentives do not use money but instead use perks or different types of rewards. For example, an organization might have flexible work hours, additional training opportunities, or the ability for an employee to take time off to go to school and learn a new trade. All of these are examples of non-monetary incentives.

Employee recognition is a means for employers to offer feedback and encouragement to their employees. This type of incentive can include verbal praise, some type of award, or maybe even a public announcement when an employee does an exceptional job. What this tells us is a job well done and recognition of that job by the organization is something that makes people feel motivated.

With all this focus on reward systems and incentives, we have to keep one point in our mind. For an incentive program to work, it must touch on the needs of the employees and it must match the goals of the organization.

7.5 Specific actions to increase employee motivation

After learning the theories of employee motivation, let's move on from theory to practice and study the specific actions managers can take to improve employee motivation. Actually, there are seven tips on how to increase employees' motivation quickly.

(1) To communicate responsibly and effectively any information employees need to perform their jobs most effectively

Employees want to be members of the well-informed people who know what is happening at work as soon as other employees know. They want the information necessary to do their jobs. They need enough information so that they make good decisions about their work. So, the managers are advised to meet with employees to update them about any company information that may impact their work. The managers may stop by the work area of employees who are particularly affected by a change to communicate more. Make sure the employee is clear about what the change means for his job, goals, time allocation, and decisions.

(2) To motivate employees by encouraging communication with senior managers

Studies indicate that the role of senior managers in attracting employee self-determined effort exceeded that of immediate supervisors. Therefore, the senior managers are advised to communicate openly, honestly and frequently with employees. They may implement an open-door policy for staff members to talk, share ideas, and discuss concerns. They may congratulate staff on life events such as new babies, inquire about vacation trips, and ask about how both personal and company events turned out.

(3) To provide the opportunity for employees to develop their skills and abilities

Employees often want to continue to develop their knowledge and skills. They do not want jobs that they perceive as no-brain drudge work. Therefore, the managers are advised to allow staff members to attend important meetings that are cross-functional, and that the supervisor normally attends. The managers may bring staff to interesting, unusual events, activities, and meetings. It's quite a learning experience for a staff person to attend an executive meeting with managers or represent the department. The managers may also provide the opportunity for the employees to cross-train in other roles and responsibilities.

(4) To motivate employees by giving them autonomy

Employees seek autonomy and independence in decision-making and in how they approach accomplishing their work and job. The managers are advised to provide more authority for the employees to self-manage and make decisions. Within the clear framework and ongoing effective communication, the managers can delegate decision-making after defining limits, boundaries, and critical points at which they want to receive feedback.

The managers may expand the job to include new, higher-level responsibilities. Assign responsibilities to the employees that will help them grow their skills and knowledge. They may also provide the employee with a voice in higher-level meetings, and more access to important and desirable meetings and projects.

(5) To address employees' concerns and complaints before they make an employee or workplace dysfunctional

The managers should listen to employees' complaints and keep the employees informed about how their complaints will be addressed. This is critical to producing a motivating work environment.

Even if the complaint cannot be resolved to the employees' satisfaction, the fact that the managers addressed the complaint and provided feedback about the consideration and resolution of the complaint to the employees is appreciated. The importance of the feedback loop in addressing employee concerns cannot be overemphasized.

The managers are advised to keep the door open and encourage employees to come to them with legitimate concerns and questions. The managers should provide feedback to the

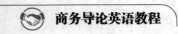

employees about the status of their expressed concerns. The concern or complaint cannot disappear into a dark hole forever. Nothing causes more anxiety or fear for an employee than the feeling that their legitimate concern went unaddressed.

(6) To recognize employees' performance

Many supervisors think reward and recognition are as important as monetary gifts in employee motivation. While employees appreciate money, they also appreciate praise, a verbal or written thank-you, out-of-the-ordinary job content opportunities, and attention from their supervisors. So the managers are advised to write a thank-you note that praises and thanks an employee for a specific contribution in as much detail as possible. This can let the employee know what behaviors they want to continue to see. The managers may also visit the employee in his workspace and verbally praise and recognize an employee for a contribution. The managers may give the employee a small token of gratitude. A small reward such as a card, their favorite candy bar, some fruits, and more, based on the traditions and interaction in the office, will make an employee feel greatly motivated.

(7) To establish a responsive and involved relationship between employees and their immediate supervisors

The managers are advised to avoid canceling regular meetings, and if it's a must, stop by the employees' work area to apologize, give them the reason, and immediately reschedule. Regularly missing employee meetings sends a powerful message of disrespect.

The managers are also suggested to talk daily with each employee who reports to them. The daily interaction builds the relationship and will stand for a lot when disappointments occur, or the managers need to address employee performance improvement.

The interaction of an employee with his immediate supervisor is the most significant factor in an employee's satisfaction with work. A supervisor should listen to his subordinates and encourage them to bring him an idea or improvement.

Remember that the supervisor's nonverbal communication is more expressive than the words in conveying their honest response to the employees' thoughts, concerns, and suggestions. Please keep in mind that the supervisor's relationship with reporting staff is the single most important factor in employee retention. The managers must know exactly what their staff need and want in order to provide a work environment for employee motivation.

Words and Phrases

time off		休假；请假
motivator	*n.*	动力；激励因素
intrinsic motivation		内在动机
extrinsic motivation		外在动机
stimulus	*n.*	刺激，激励
external reward		外在奖励
benefits package		福利待遇
bonus	*n.*	奖金
piece rate		计件工资，按件计酬
punch a card		打卡（上班）
Two-factor Theory		双因素激励理论
hygiene factor		保健因素
Maslow's Hierarchy of Needs		马斯洛需求层次理论
physiological needs		生理需求
safety needs		安全需求
social needs		社会需求
esteem needs		尊重需求
self-actualization needs		自我实现需求
vision	*n.*	愿景
commitment	*n.*	承诺；承担义务
job redesign		工作再设计
goal setting		目标设置
performance appraisal		绩效考核
performance incentive		绩效激励
job enrichment		工作丰富化
job enlargement		工作扩大化

job rotation		轮岗，岗位轮换
dysfunctional	*adj.*	机能失调的，功能障碍的
pay raise		加薪
promotion	*n.*	升职
discharge	*n.*	解雇
stock option		股票期权
perk	*n.*	额外收入；额外津贴
drudge	*n.*	苦力活
cross-train	*v.*	对……进行交叉训练（综合训练）

 **Exercises**

I. Answer the following questions according to the text.

1. What are the benefits of motivating employees?

2. Is money the only factor that can be used in motivating employees? Why or why not?

3. What's the difference between intrinsic motivation and extrinsic motivation?

4. In your opinion, which one of McGregor's Theory X and Theory Y is closer to the reality or more correct?

5. Try to differentiate "hygiene factors" and "motivators" by giving specific examples.

6. What are the main "motivators" according to Herzberg?

7. Why is Maslow's theory hierarchical rather than flat?

8. In what ways can interactions and communication between managers and employees be guaranteed?

9. How should managers handle employees' concerns and complaints?

10. What's the most important factor in employee retention? Why?

II. Decide whether the following statements are true (T) or false (F) according to the text.

1. Intrinsic motivation is based on taking pleasure in an activity rather than working towards an external reward. Extrinsic motivation refers to the performance of an activity in order to attain an outcome. (   )

2. Money is the only factor that can be used in motivating employees. (   )

3. At the very top of Maslow's hierarchy of five needs is our human need for safety. (   )

4. Employees often find interaction and communication with and attention from senior and executive managers motivational. (   )

5. Recognition of employees' performance is high on the list of employee needs for motivation. (   )

III. Read the following passage and fill in the blanks with the words given below. Change the form if necessary.

accuse	revolve	impact	assume	exhibit
foster	success	suppress	deliver	fulfill

Every employee is motivated about something in his life. Motivating employees about work is the activity of 1. _____ the employees' needs and expectations from work.

Too many workplaces still act as if the employee should be grateful to have a job. Managers are on power trips and employee policies and procedures are formulated based on the 2. _____ that you can't trust employees to do the right thing. Communication is never transparent and there is always a secret message or a hidden agenda. Motivating employees in this work environment is tough, if not impossible.

Fortunately, most work environments are not this extreme. They each have their own set of problems, but managers appreciate that motivating employees will bring positive results for the organization. The following ten tips about motivating employees provide a basic understanding of employee motivation. They also target key areas for 3. _____ in motivating employees.

(1) Every person is motivated. Whether that motivation 4. _____ around work, a hobby, the family, the spiritual side of life, or food, each person has some items or issues about which he feels motivated to take action in his life.

(2) Your actions in the workplace either encourage motivated behavior or discourage employee motivation. In some workplaces, company policies and management behavior actually 5. _____ motivation.

(3) Actions and activities in the workplace that provide an environment supportive of motivating employees don't have to be expensive. Activities and recognition that cost money are welcomed by employees as part of the motivation mix, but their 6. _____ on motivating employees is short-term and will not over-ride the consequences of how people feel treated every day in the workplace.

(4) Much of the workplace environment that encourages employee motivation involves management time and commitment: genuine interest and caring, employee-oriented policies and procedures, and attention from both senior managers and line managers are all appreciated and valued.

(5) Motivation is prevalent in workplaces where people are treated as valued human beings. Trust, respect, civil conversation, and listening prevail in a workplace that 7. _____ employee motivation.

(6) Clear direction plays a serious role in motivating employees. Employees want to know exactly what you expect from them. When they have the reassurance of clear direction, motivating employees becomes easier because you and they have created a framework for their expected performance.

(7) Supervisors can create an environment for motivating employees. You just do not consistently, in a disciplined manner, adhere to what you already know about motivating employees. To be perfectly honest, since I am often 8. _____ of viewing the world through rose-colored glasses, some supervisors just don't care. They work to collect a paycheck and all of this stuff about motivating employees is just gobbledegook.

(8) Employee motivation is a constant challenge. What motivates one employee is not motivating for another. After all, a workplace of happy employees is great, but it doesn't guarantee quality products 9. _____ on time, delighted customers, or profitability—all essential to providing those happy employees with jobs.

(9) Actively solicit information from employees about what motivates them. Responding to employee needs and complaints is key for motivating employees. People expect to see something changed as a result of their response. If it doesn't change, and you don't tell them why, you risk wasting all of your efforts in motivating employees.

(10) Motivation at work is a choice employees make. Employees choose to 10. _____ motivated behavior at work. You can know and do everything discussed here, but employees are ultimately in charge of motivating themselves.

IV. Translate the following sentences into Chinese.

1. If an employee's chosen course of action results in the anticipated outcome and reward, that person is likely to be motivated by the prospect of a similar reward to act the same way in the future. However, if the employee's action does not result in the expected reward, he is unlikely to repeat the behavior.

2. As a result of this, management believes that employees need to be closely supervised and comprehensive systems of controls need to be developed, and employees will show little ambition without an enticing incentive program and will avoid responsibility whenever they can. Theory X managers rely heavily on threat and coercion to gain their employees' compliance. Beliefs of this theory lead to mistrust, highly restrictive supervision, and a punitive atmosphere.

3. Maslow's higher levels of needs are less obvious and less easy to describe but of great importance. Social needs refer to love and belonging needs. We want to feel part of something we share in. A company can create the opportunity for its employees to share in its common goals and vision for the group. It does this by rewarding the people who contribute to its success through their commitment and hard work.

4. The managers are advised to provide more authority for the employees to self-manage and make decisions. Within the clear framework and ongoing effective communication, delegate decision-making after defining limits, boundaries, and critical points at which the managers want to receive feedback.

5. Even if the complaint cannot be resolved to the employees' satisfaction, the fact that the managers addressed the complaint and provided feedback about the consideration and resolution of the complaint to the employees is appreciated. The importance of the feedback loop in addressing employee concerns cannot be overemphasized.

Case Study

China's Greenland Offers Staff Bonuses to Hit Developer's Annual Sales Target

Greenland Holdings（绿地控股集团）has set aside CNY50 million (USD7 million) for bonuses to spur staff to achieve the property developer's CNY400 billion (USD56.5 billion) annual sales target. To that end, some employees have even been told to buy a home from the company. The inducement seeks to boost fourth-quarter sales. The Shanghai-based firm will grant the funds to each of its affiliated divisions to goad marketing teams into attaining the goal, which was set at the start of the year.

Chairman Zhang Yuliang is eager to counter a decline in the firm's sales and ranking in the sector. Real estate sales, its core business, began to fall each year after topping the nationwide list in 2014. Greenland came in sixth among rivals at the end of last year and slumped to seventh at the end of the third quarter of 2019, per data from the China Real Estate Information Circle Research Center (CREICRC) under Shanghai-based real estate services provider E-House China Holdings.

"Granting these bonuses is aimed mainly at achieving the annual sales target," a company insider said. "Each division will get incentives worth several million yuan, and the means by which the rewards are handed out will be independently determined per each division's situation."

Greenland had sales of CNY244 billion in the January to September period. It fell 32.6 percent to CNY20.2 billion last month from August, the CREICRC's data shows. September is generally peak season for the property sector, so a huge decline is seldom seen at that time. This means fourth-quarter sales need to reach CNY150 billion to reach the full-year target.

Each division will come up with their own ways to stimulate sales. The firm's Shanghai division 1 has opted to pay all employees in its marketing department 80 percent of their original salaries, with the portion withheld to be used as the marketing bonus.

The division in central Hunan Province requires all employees, even those still in their three-month probationary period, to buy a Greenland-developed home in the province by the end of this month, though they can enjoy preferential purchase conditions.

The firm's general operating performance has nonetheless still been quite good because of its efforts to diversify and deleverage in recent years. Its business revenue was RMB 201 billion in the first half, up 28 percent annually, with net profit of RMB 9 billion representing almost one-half rise of the year.

U.S. financial service company Standard & Poor's has also just raised its rating on Greenland based on the firm's faster-than-expected deleveraging, stable profit growth and cash flow, as well as low-cost land reserves.

 ## Questions for discussion

1. How does Greenland motivate its employees to attain the sales goal? Do you think this method is effective? Why?

2. What are the functions of Greenland's motivation plan?

3. Will you be attracted by Greenland's motivation? Why?

 # Assignments

1. Draw a diagram of Maslow's Hierarchy of Needs on a piece of paper. To each level of needs add the methods that are adopted by an organization of your choice to motivate its staff. A possible organization you could use is your school or college, as it should be easier to find out the relevant methods used.

2. Write a report of about 200 words in English to explain what you have learned from Maslow's Hierarchy of Needs.

Unit

8

Corporate Culture

Learning Objectives

After learning this unit, you should be able to:

- describe the factors affecting corporate culture;
- name the different types of organizational culture;
- explain the importance of corporate culture;
- know the differences between strong culture and weak culture;
- know the relation between national culture and corporate culture;
- understand the limitations of corporate culture.

1. What kind of colleague do you want to work with, an easy-going one or a competitive one?

2. How will you accomplish a task, all alone or with your workmates?

3. Talk about corporate culture in China and abroad.

 Reading

8.1 The concept of corporate culture

Every human being has certain personality traits that help them stand apart from the crowd. No two individuals behave in a similar way. In the same way, organizations have certain values, policies, rules and guidelines that help them create an image of their own.

Corporate culture is also known as organizational culture. It refers to the beliefs and principles of a particular organization. The culture followed by the organization has a deep impact on the employees and the relationships among themselves. Every organization has a unique culture, making it different from others and giving it a sense of direction. It is essential for employees to understand the culture of their workplace to adjust well.

In short, corporate culture is the total sum of the values, customs, traditions, and meanings that make a company unique. To be more specific, corporate culture is the collective behavior of people that are part of an organization. It is formed by the values, visions, norms, working language, systems, and symbols of the organization, and it includes beliefs and habits. It is also the pattern of such collective behaviors and assumptions that are taught to new organizational members as a way of perceiving, and even thinking and feeling.

8.2 Factors affecting corporate culture

Corporate culture represents the beliefs, ideologies, policies, and practices of an organization. It gives the employees a sense of direction and also controls the way they behave with each other. The work culture brings all the employees to a common platform and unites them at the workplace.

There are several factors that may affect the formation of corporate culture: the corporate vision, shared values, beliefs, history, leadership, and industry characteristics of an organization.

(1) Corporate vision

Corporate vision refers to the category of intentions that are broad, all-inclusive and forward-thinking. It is the image that a business must have of its goals before it sets out to reach them. It describes aspirations for the future, without specifying the means that will be used to achieve those goals.

Warren Bennis, a noted writer on leadership, says: "To choose a direction, an executive must have developed a mental image of the possible and desirable future state of the organization. This image, which we call a vision, may be as vague as a dream or as precise as a goal or a mission statement."

Corporate vision may contain commitment to:

- Creating an extraordinary customer value;

- Developing a great new product or service;

- Serving customers through the defined service portfolio;

- Ensuring quality and responsiveness of customer services;

- Providing an enjoyable work environment for employees;

- Ensuring financial strength and sustainable growth of the company for the benefit of its stakeholders.

A vision statement is a short, concise, and inspiring statement of what the organization intends to become and to achieve in the future. A carefully crafted vision statement is at the heart of every successful business. This statement clearly and concisely communicates a business' overall goals, and can serve as a tool for strategic decision-making across the company. A vision statement can be as simple as a single sentence or can be a short paragraph. All effective vision statements define the core ideas that give a business shape and direction. These statements also provide a powerful way to motivate and guide employees.

(2) Shared values

The values of a corporate culture influence the ethical standards within a corporation, as well as managerial behavior. Values are about how we have learned to think things ought to be or people ought to behave. Shared values are also the identity by which the organization is known throughout its business areas. These values must be stated as both corporate objectives and individual values. We shall notice that every organization and every leader will have a different set of values that are appropriate to its business situation.

Ensuring employees' understanding of an organization's values and vision requires the organization to have clearly defined values. Without this, the organization can get itself into real trouble. Defining shared values is more than putting words on paper. Most organizations have value statements or mission statements, yet many do not follow them. Winning organizations create successful cultures in a systematic way using various approaches that may include visual representations, training seminars, and/or socializing events.

(3) Beliefs

Beliefs are the assumptions we make about ourselves, about others in the world and about how we expect things to be. Beliefs are about how we think things really are, what we think is really true and what we therefore expect as likely consequences that will follow from our behavior. The clearer you are about what you value and believe in, the happier and more effective you will be.

Members of the same organization often share similar beliefs. For example, if a manager and his employee have similar beliefs, then the manager will be more comfortable to let the employee make the decision. In the same way, when performance depends on correct decisions, people in an organization prefer to work with others who have the same beliefs.

(4) History

A company's culture, particularly during its early years, is inevitably tied to the personality, background, and values of its founder or founders, as well as their vision for the future of the organization. This explains why culture is so hard to change: It is shaped in the early days of a company's history. When entrepreneurs establish their own businesses, the way they want to do business determines the organization's rules, the structure set-up in the company, and the people they hire to work with them.

(5) Leadership

Leadership is the process of directing the behavior of others toward the accomplishment of some common objectives. Leaders are important in creating and changing an organization's culture. There is a direct correspondence between a leader's style and an organization's culture. For example, when leaders motivate employees through inspiration, corporate culture tends to be more supportive and people-oriented. When leaders motivate employees by making rewards on performance, the corporate culture tends to be more performance-oriented and competitive. In these ways, what leaders do directly influences the cultures of their organizations.

Part of the leader's influence on corporate culture is through role modeling. Many studies have suggested that the leader's behavior, the consistency between organizational policy and the leader's actions, and the leader's role modeling determine the degree to which the organization's culture emphasizes ethics. The leader's own behaviors will show employees what is acceptable and what is unacceptable. In an organization in which high-level managers make the effort to involve others in decision-making and seek opinions from others, a team-oriented culture is more likely to evolve. By acting as role models, leaders send messages to the organization about the norms and values. And these messages can guide the actions of organizational members.

Leaders also shape culture by their reactions to the employees' actions. For example, do they praise a job well done, or do they praise a favored employee regardless of what was accomplished? How do they react when someone admits to making an honest mistake? What are their priorities? In meetings, what types of questions do they ask? Do they want to know what caused accidents so that they can be prevented, or do they seem more concerned about how much money was lost as a result of an accident? Do they seem outraged when an employee is disrespectful to a co-worker? Through their day-to-day actions, leaders shape and maintain an organization's culture.

(6) Industry characteristics

The industry characteristics also play a role in shaping the corporate culture. For example, despite some differences, many companies in the insurance and banking industries are stable and rule-oriented, many companies in the high-tech industry have innovative cultures, and companies in the non-profit industry tend to be people-oriented. If the industry has a large number of regulatory requirements, for example, banking, healthcare, and nuclear power plant industries, then we might see a large number of rules and regulations, a bureaucratic company structure, and a stable culture. Similarly, the high-tech industry requires agility, taking quick action, and low concern for rules and authority, which may create a relatively more innovative culture. It is also important to know the industry influence over culture, because this shows that it may not be possible to imitate the culture of a company in a different industry, even though it may seem admirable to outsiders.

8.3 Types of organizational culture

The practices, principles, policies, and values of an organization form its culture. The culture of an organization decides the way employees behave among themselves as well as the people outside the organization. There are different types of organizational culture that are prevalent throughout corporations and small businesses. Companies adopt a particular style based on their needs and expectations. Some of the major types of organizational culture will be discussed in this part.

(1) Normative culture

In such a culture, the norms and procedures of the organization are predefined and the rules and regulations are set according to the existing guidelines. The employees behave in an ideal way and strictly adhere to the policies of the organization. No employee dares to break the rules and everyone sticks to the already laid policies.

(2) Pragmatic culture

In a pragmatic culture, more emphasis is placed on the clients and the external parties. Customer satisfaction is the main motive of the employees in a pragmatic culture. Such organizations treat their clients as Gods and do not follow any set rules. Every employee strives hard to satisfy his clients to expect maximum business from their side.

(3) Academy culture

Organizations following academy culture hire skilled individuals. The roles and responsibilities are delegated according to the background, educational qualification and work experience of the employees. Organizations following academy culture are very particular about training the existing employees. They ensure that various training programs are being conducted at the workplace to improve the skills of the employees. The management makes great efforts to upgrade the knowledge of the employees to improve their professional competence. The employees in an academy culture stick to the organization for a longer duration and also grow within it. Educational institutions, universities, and hospitals practice such a culture.

(4) Baseball team culture

A baseball team culture considers the employees as the most treasured possession of the organization. The employees are the true assets of the organization because they have a major role in its successful functioning. In such a culture, the individuals always have an upper edge and they do not bother much about their organization. Advertising agencies, event management companies, and financial institutions follow such a culture.

(5) Club culture

Organizations following a club culture are very particular about their employees. The individuals are hired according to their specialization, educational qualification, and interests. Each one does what he is best at. The high potential employees are promoted suitably and appraisals are a regular feature of such a culture.

(6) Fortress culture

There are certain organizations where the employees are not very sure about their career and longevity. Such organizations follow a fortress culture. The employees are terminated if the organization is not performing well. Individuals suffer the most when the organization is at a loss. Stockbroking industries follow such a culture.

(7) Tough guy culture

In a tough guy culture, feedback is essential. The performance of the employees is reviewed from time to time and their work is thoroughly monitored. Team managers are appointed to discuss queries with the team members and guide them whenever required. The employees are under constant watch in such a culture.

(8) Bet your company culture

Organizations which follow such a culture take decisions with great potential risks and the consequences are also unforeseen. The principles and policies of such an organization are formulated to address sensitive issues and it takes time to get the results.

(9) Process culture

As the name suggests, the employees in such a culture stick to the processes and procedures of the organization. Feedback and performance reviews do not matter much in such organizations. The employees obey the rules and regulations and work according to the ideologies of the workplace. Many government organizations follow such a culture.

There's no correct corporate culture for all organizations. All types of culture promote some forms of behavior, and inhibit others. Some are well suited to rapid and repeated change, others to slow incremental development of the institution. The right culture will be one that closely fits the direction and strategy of a particular organization as it confronts its own issues and the challenges of a particular time.

8.4 The importance of corporate culture

Research suggests that numerous outcomes have been associated either directly or indirectly with corporate culture. A healthy and robust corporate culture may provide various benefits, including the following:

- Competitive edge derived from innovation and customer service;

- Consistent, efficient employee performance;

- Team cohesiveness;

- High employee morale;

- Strong company alignment towards goal achievement.

Although there is little empirical research to support the link between corporate culture and organizational performance, experts have no doubt that this relationship exists. Corporate culture can be a factor for an organization's survival or failure, although this is difficult to prove considering that the necessary longitudinal analyses are hardly feasible. The sustained superior performance of firms like IBM, HP, P&G, and McDonald's may be, at least partly, a reflection of their organizational cultures.

Corporate culture is reflected in the way people perform tasks, set objectives, and administer the necessary resources to achieve objectives. Culture affects the way individuals make decisions, feel, and respond to the opportunities and threats affecting the organization.

Experts find that job satisfaction is positively associated with the degree to which employees fit into both the overall culture and subculture in which they work. There is a misunderstanding of the organization's culture and what employees feel the culture should be. And this kind of misunderstanding is related to a number of negative consequences, including lower job satisfaction, higher job strain, general stress, and turnover intent.

It has been proposed that corporate culture may impact the level of employee creativity, the strength of employee motivation, and the reporting of unethical behavior, but more research is needed to support these conclusions.

Corporate culture also has an impact on recruitment and retention. Individuals tend to be attracted to and remain engaged in organizations that they perceive to be compatible. Additionally, high turnover may be a mediating factor in the relationship between culture and organizational performance. Deteriorating company performance and an unhealthy work environment are signs of an overdue cultural assessment.

The culture decides the way employees interact at their workplace. A healthy culture encourages the employees to stay motivated and loyal towards the management. The culture of the workplace also goes a long way in promoting healthy competition at the workplace. Employees try their best to perform better than their fellow workers and earn recognition and appreciation from their superiors. It is the culture of the workplace that actually motivates the employees to perform.

Every organization must have set guidelines for the employees to work accordingly. The culture of an organization represents certain predefined policies that guide the employees and give them a sense of direction at the workplace. Every individual is clear about his roles and responsibilities in the organization and knows how to accomplish the tasks ahead of the deadlines.

No two organizations can have the same work culture. It is the culture of an organization that makes it distinct from others. The work culture goes a long way in creating the brand image of the organization. The work culture gives an identity to the organization. In other words, an organization is known for its culture.

The organizational culture brings all the employees to a common platform. The employees must be treated equally and no one should feel neglected or left out at the workplace. It is essential for the employees to adjust well in the organizational culture to deliver their best.

The work culture unites the employees who are from different backgrounds, families and have varied attitudes and mentalities. The culture gives the employees a sense of unity at the workplace.

Certain organizations follow a culture where all the employees, irrespective of their ranks, have to step into the office on time. Such a culture encourages the employees to be punctual, which eventually benefits them in the long run. It is the culture of the organization that makes individuals successful professionals.

Every employee is clear about his roles and responsibilities and strives hard to accomplish the tasks within the desired time frame according to the set guidelines. Implementation of policies is never a problem in organizations where people follow a set culture. The new employees also try their best to understand the work culture and make the organization a better place to work.

The work culture promotes healthy relationships among the employees. No one treats work as a burden and molds himself according to the culture. It is the culture of the organization that extracts the best out of each team member. In a culture where management is very particular about the reporting system, the employees, however busy they are, would send their reports by the end of the day. No one has to force anyone to work. The culture develops a habit in individuals which makes them successful at the workplace.

So, all these factors are benefits that a healthy corporate culture may bring to a company.

8.5 Strong culture and weak culture

No two organizations can have the same culture. The values or policies of a non-profit organization would be different from those of a profit-making entity. Employees working in a restaurant would follow a different culture as compared with those working in the education industry or the manufacturing industry.

Broadly we can divide organizational culture into two types according to employees' alignment to the organizational culture. They are strong culture and weak culture. A strong corporate culture refers to a situation where the employees adjust well, respect the organization's policies and adhere to the guidelines. In such a culture people enjoy working and take every assignment as a new learning and try to gain as much as they can. They accept their roles and responsibilities willingly.

In a weak corporate culture, individuals accept their responsibilities out of fear of superiors and harsh policies. The employees in such a situation do things because of pressure. They just treat their organization as a mere source of earning money and never get attached to it.

A strong culture is said to exist where staff respond to stimulus because they are united by organizational values. In such environments, strong cultures help firms operate like well-oiled machines, running along with outstanding execution. Of course, sometimes there are also small adjustments to existing procedures here and there. On the contrary, in a weak culture staff are less united by organizational values and control must be exercised through extensive procedures and bureaucracy.

Now you may have a question in your mind: Which is more efficient and effective in management, a strong culture or a weak culture? Let's do a case analysis before we answer the question. There are two organizations: Organization A and Organization B. In Organization A, the employees are not at all disciplined and are least bothered about the rules and regulations. They reach their office at their own sweet time and spend their maximum time gossiping and loitering around. While Organization B follows employee-friendly policies and it is mandatory for all to adhere to them. It is important for the employees to reach their workplace on time and no one is allowed to unnecessarily roam around or spread rumors. Which organization do you feel would perform better? Obviously, it's Organization B. The employees follow a certain culture in Organization B, making it more successful than Organization A.

Research shows that organizations that foster strong cultures have clear values, and these values can give employees a reason to embrace the culture. A strong culture may be especially beneficial to firms operating in the service sector because members of these organizations are responsible for delivering the service. Research also indicates that organizations may get the following five benefits from developing strong and productive cultures:

- Being better united towards achieving its vision, mission, and goals;

- High employee motivation and loyalty can be obtained;

- Increased team cohesiveness among the company's various departments and divisions;

- Promoting consistency and encouraging coordination and control within the company;

- Shaping employee behavior at work, enabling the organization to be more efficient.

8.6 National culture and corporate culture

Sometimes, when it comes to the corporate culture, another kind of culture will also be mentioned at the same time. That is the national culture.

National culture is the values and attitudes shared by individuals from a specific country. It shapes behavior and beliefs. Getting information about cultural differences among countries is difficult. However, differences in national cultures may cause differences in the views on the management. Differences between national cultures are deep-rooted values of the respective cultures, and these cultural values can shape how people expect companies to be run, and how relationships between leaders and followers should be. This may lead to differences between the employer and the employee in expectations. So, the national culture determines the corporate culture, and influences the company's structure, its marketing behavior, and its views on the international business partners and contracts.

A question many people have asked is how national and organizational cultures are related and which of them is stronger. The answer is "It depends". There is no doubt that the two cultures both have powerful influences on people. It is anything but rare for employees to face conflicts between them, especially in foreign companies. A company's culture may be informal while a country's culture could be rather formal. A company may encourage and reward risk-taking in a country where people are generally risk-avoiding, or vice versa. Sometimes a national culture has more influence on employees than corporate culture, so it's important for multinational companies to hire applicants who can fit their organizational culture.

8.7 Limitations of corporate culture

It is essential for employees to adjust well in the organizational culture to deliver their best. However, it has been observed that in certain cases the employees might find themselves in trouble whenever there is a change in the work culture. The work culture might become a burden for the employees instead of giving them a sense of direction. The first and the foremost problem which arises out of a set work culture is adjustment.

The culture of an organization is not formed in a single day. A culture is the cumulative outcome of the interaction among the employees and their behavioral patterns at the workplace. A culture is formed when individuals follow certain values and adhere to guidelines over a considerable period of time. Problems arise when new employees step into the shoes of the existing ones and take charge. They bring new ideas, new plans of action and new concepts along with them and thus cause problems for the existing employees. They tend to hire their own people and eventually sideline the current employees.

Adjustment problems arise when new employees find it difficult to adjust to the prevailing work culture. They find it difficult to concentrate and tend to lose interest in work. For them, work becomes a burden and they simply attend the office to earn money. They never get attached to their workplace.

Culture in certain cases can also become a liability to an organization. Strict policies and harsh rules can sometimes create problems for the employees and they find it difficult to stick to the organization for a long time. Retaining the employee becomes a nightmare in cases of weak cultures. The policies must be employee-friendly and benefit one and all. An organization where male employees dominate the female counterparts follows a culture where late sitting is a regular feature. Male individuals might find this kind of culture extremely comfortable but a female employee would not be able to adjust well in such a culture. The youngsters would have a problem in organizations where the older generation decides the policies and forms the culture.

An individual working in any particular culture for quite some time would develop certain habits. It is not easy to get rid of a habit all of a sudden. Difficulties arise whenever employees wish to move on for better opportunities. The new organization might not promise them the same facilities and comforts that their previous organization offered. The incentive plan in this organization might not be as lucrative as it was in the previous organization.

An employee finds it difficult to implement new ideas and concepts in a culture which has been practiced for several years. For him, the culture becomes a limitation, where he has to work according to the set guidelines and predefined policies.

One should always remember that no culture is more important than employees. They are the true assets of an organization. The work culture should never bind the employees to do something innovative.

Words and Phrases

executive	n.	企业主管
customer value		顾客价值
service portfolio		服务组合
vision statement		愿景宣言；远景声明
role modeling		塑造典范
collective behavior		集体行为
stakeholder	n.	利益相关者
normative culture		规范型文化

pragmatic culture	实用主义型文化
academy culture	学院型文化
baseball team culture	棒球队型文化
club culture	俱乐部型文化
fortress culture	堡垒型文化
tough guy culture	硬汉型文化
bet your company culture	赌徒型文化
process culture	过程型文化
subculture	*n.* 亚文化

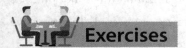 **Exercises**

I.　Answer the following questions according to the text.

1. What is corporate culture?

2. What are the commitments contained in corporate vision?

3. People in the same organization often share similar beliefs. Give an example.

4. How is a company's culture tied to its founder or founders?

5. How could the leaders of a company influence its corporate culture?

6. Can we find one correct corporate culture for all organizations? Why or why not?

7. What benefits can firms derive from developing strong and productive cultures?

8. How are national and organizational cultures related and which of them is stronger? Why?

9. Why is corporate culture important?

10. How does corporate culture influence recruitment and retention?

II.　Decide whether the following statements are true (T) or false (F) according to the text.

1. Corporate culture is the collective behavior of people that are part of an organization, it is also formed by the organization's values, visions, norms, working language,

systems, and symbols, and it includes beliefs and habits. (   )

2. The values of a corporate culture can only influence the top managers' behaviors. (   )

3. A strong corporate culture exists where staff respond to stimulus because of their respect to organizational values. Conversely, there is a weak culture where there is little respect to organizational values and strict control must be exercised. (   )

4. National culture is the values and attitudes shared by individuals from a specific country. It has no influence on the corporate culture. (   )

5. Corporate culture may impact the level of employee creativity and the strength of employee motivation. (   )

III. **Read the following passage and fill in the blanks with the words given below. Change the form if necessary.**

| loyalty | interest | speech | adaptive | cost |
| succession | colleague | sort | element | capacity |

We can learn a great deal from organizations whose strong and 1. _____ ownership cultures give them a powerful competitive edge. Here are our top eight lessons: (1) Leadership is critical in codifying and maintaining organizational purposes, values, and vision. Leaders must set an example by living the 2. _____ of culture: values, behaviors, measures, and actions. Values are meaningless without the other elements. (2) Like anything worthwhile, culture is something in which you invest. An organization's norms and values aren't formed through 3. _____ but through actions and team learning. Strong cultures are much more than slogans and empty promises. Some organizations choose to part ways with those who do not manage according to the values and behaviors that other employees embrace. Others accomplish the same objective more positively. (3) Employees at all levels in an organization notice and validate the elements of culture. As owners, they judge every management decision to hire, reward, promote, and fire 4. _____. Their reactions often come through in comments about subjects such as the "fairness of my boss". The underlying theme in such conversations, though, is the strength and appropriateness of the organization's culture. (4) Organizations with clearly codified cultures enjoy labor 5. _____ advantages. They often become better places to work. They become well known among prospective employees. The level of ownership—referral rates and ideas for improving the business of existing employees—is often high. The screening process is simplified because employees tend to refer acquaintances who behave like them. The pool of prospective employees grows. The cost of selecting among many applicants is offset by cost savings as prospective employees 6. _____ themselves into and out of consideration for jobs. This self-selection process reduces the number of mismatches among new hires. (5) Organizations with clearly codified and enforced cultures enjoy great employee and customer 7. _____ in large part because they are effective in either altering ineffective behaviors or disengaging from values-challenged employees in a timely manner. (6) An operating strategy based on a strong, effective culture is selective of prospective customers. It also requires the periodic "firing" of customers, as pointed out in our examples of companies like ING Direct, where thousands are fired every month. This strategy is especially important when customers "abuse" employees or make unreasonable demands on them. The result of all this is "the best serving the best," or as Ritz-Carlton's mission states, "Ladies and gentlemen serving ladies and gentlemen." This self-reinforcing source of operating leverage must be managed carefully to make sure that it does not result in the development of dogmatic cults with little 8. _____ for change. High-performing organizations periodically revisit and reaffirm their core values and associated behaviors. Further, they often subscribe to some kind of initiative that requires constant benchmarking and searching for best practices both inside and outside the organization. (7) Organizations with strong and adaptive cultures foster effective 9. _____ in the leadership ranks. In large part, the culture both prepares successors and eases the transition. (8) Cultures can sour. Among the reasons for this are success itself, the loss of curiosity and 10. _____ in change, the triumph of culture over performance, the failure of leaders to reinforce desired behaviors, the breakdown of consistent communication, and leaders who are overcome by their own sense of importance.

IV. Translate the following sentences into Chinese.

1. Beliefs are about how we think things really are, what we think is really true and what we therefore expect as likely consequences that will follow from our behavior. The clearer you are about what you value and believe in, the happier and more effective you will be.

2. Part of the leader's influence on corporate culture is through role modeling. Many studies have suggested that the leader's behavior, the consistency between organizational policy and the leader's actions, and the leader's role modeling determine the degree to which the organization's culture emphasizes ethics.

3. If the industry has a large number of regulatory requirements, for example, banking, healthcare, and nuclear power plant industries, then we might see a large number of rules and regulations, a bureaucratic company structure, and a stable culture. Similarly, the high-tech industry requires agility, taking quick action, and low concern for rules and authority, which may create a relatively more innovative culture.

4. Additionally, high turnover may be a mediating factor in the relationship between culture and organizational performance. Deteriorating company performance and an unhealthy work environment are signs of an overdue cultural assessment.

5. However, differences in national cultures may cause differences in the views on the management. Differences between national cultures are deep-rooted values of the respective cultures, and these cultural values can shape how people expect companies to be run, and how relationships between leaders and followers should be. This may lead to differences between the employer and the employee in expectations.

 **Case Study**

A True Global Culture

Across Europe, Huawei is sometimes perceived as a typical Chinese company. True, the Huawei headquarters are located in Shenzhen, a modern metropolis just next door to Hong Kong. But it's also true that Huawei operates in 170 countries across all continents, and that throughout its dynamic history it has embraced advice and guidance from all corners of the world. Through its participative corporate culture, input from employees of all nationalities shapes Huawei on a daily basis!

Huawei's culture is like an onion with many layers; one layer is the British culture, another layer is Chinese, and still another is American. For instance, the U.S.-based tech company IBM advised Huawei on its management system and has left a lasting imprint on Huawei's working

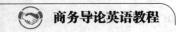

structure. Huawei could not have become a leading global ICT service provider without international expansion.

Arguably, the roots of its global outlook were already in place when Ren Zhengfei established Huawei in 1987—with a starting capital of just 21,000 yuan, less than 4,000 euros at that time. Back then, China was a very different country from what it is now: After 1978, the economy was only gradually opening up. Those who took the risk to set up their own companies were real pioneers—competition was fierce and success was all but guaranteed. After Huawei managed to survive the early years, this pioneer spirit naturally led Ren and his team to look beyond China. Already then, openness was the basis of Huawei's survival and growth.

Plunging into the sea of international expansion, Huawei had a chance to gain a foothold in markets as yet undeveloped by American and European telecom companies. As it happened, in the early 1990s, Africa was a continent offering numerous opportunities. Perseverance, one of Huawei's core values, was key in setting up networks in markets that competitors avoided entering. Had the Huawei executives thought about all that could go wrong when engaging in hardship locations, they would not have come very far. The spirit of openness, not the fear of unpredictable outcomes, drove investment decisions already back then.

At the end of 1997, Huawei founder Ren Zhengfei sold his second-hand Peugeot and bought a BMW. One day, when driving his BMW on Shennan Avenue in Shenzhen, Ren spotted then IBM chairman Louis Gerstner. "Do you know where the handbrake on this BMW is?" Ren asked Gerstner. One year later, IBM had successfully built up Huawei's modern business management system. By then, Ren knew where the handbrake was. Beforehand, he was so focused on expansion that he did not have enough time to think about the handbrake.

With an open mind, Huawei has developed a unique culture that combines both Western and Eastern characteristics. This, together with its core values, is the secret to its rapid growth and its perseverance in more challenging times such as in 2019 and 2020.

Invaluable experience comes from operating internationally in 170 countries. Everywhere Huawei operates, it abides by the local laws. Huawei also observes the conventions of the United Nations.

Questions for discussion

1. What are the key points of Huawei's corporate culture?

2. What role has corporate culture played in Huawei's growth into a global company?

3. Could you make some comments on the advantages and disadvantages of Huawei's corporate culture according to the text and your knowledge of this company?

Assignments

1. Suppose one of your friends has just been appointed as the manager of the American branch of a Chinese multinational company whose corporate culture is very different from the local culture. And most of his employees are local people. Write a note to give him some useful information and advice on how to deal with the conflicts between the corporate culture and local culture.

2. Interview several employees in different firms and ask about their corporate cultures, and then give a ten-minute presentation in English to the class.

Unit 9

Production and Product

Learning Objectives

After learning this unit, you should be able to:

- define production and product;
- know the factors of production;
- understand the classification of products;
- list the steps of developing new products;
- describe the product life cycle.

Warm-up Questions

1. What kinds of products do we use everyday? Give some examples.

2. What kinds of factors do you think are necessary in the production process?

3. Why do many products become less popular and at last withdraw from the market?

Reading

Production is the act of creating a good or service which has value and contributes to the utility of individuals. Any effort directed toward the realization of a desired product or service is a productive effort.

9.1 Factors of production

In economics, factors of production are used in the production process to produce output, including finished goods and services. Choices concerning what goods and services to produce are choices about an economy's use of its factors of production. The value, or satisfaction, that people can get from the goods and services they consume and the activities they pursue is called utility. An economy's factors of production create utility; they serve the interests of people.

Factors of production may refer specifically to items such as labor, capital, and natural resources. These are considered as primary factors. Materials and energy are considered secondary factors in classical economics because they are obtained from labor, capital, and natural resources. The primary factors facilitate production but neither become part of the product nor be transformed by the production process.

Labor is human effort that can be applied to the production of goods and services. People who are employed or would like to be are considered part of the labor available to the economy. Capital is a factor of production that has been produced for use in the production of other goods and services. Office buildings, machinery, and tools are examples of capital.

Natural resources are the resources of nature that can be used for the production of goods and services. These factors are also frequently labeled "industrial goods or services" to distinguish them from the goods or services purchased by consumers, which are frequently labeled "consumer goods or services". All the three factors are required in combination at a time to produce a commodity.

Recent usage has distinguished human capital from labor. Sometimes the technology and entrepreneurs are also considered as factors of production. The number and definition of factors of production varies, depending on theoretical purpose, empirical emphasis, or school of economics.

In this section, we will take a closer look at the factors of production we use to produce the goods and services we consume. The three basic building blocks of labor, capital, and natural resources may be used in different ways to produce different goods and services, but they still lie at the core of production. As economists began to grapple with the problems of scarcity, choice, and opportunity cost two centuries ago, they focused on these concepts, just as they are likely to do two centuries hence. We will also look at the roles played by technology and entrepreneurs in putting these factors of production to work.

(1) Labor

People who work to repair tires, pilot airplanes, teach children, or enforce laws are all part of the economy's labor. Some people would like to work but have not found a job. These unemployed people are also considered part of the labor available to the economy.

In some contexts, it is useful to distinguish two forms of labor. The first is the human equivalent of a natural resource. It is the natural ability an untrained, uneducated person brings to a particular production process. But most workers bring far more. The second is human capital. The skills a worker has as a result of education, training, or experience that can be used in production are called human capital. Students who are attending a college or university are acquiring human capital. Workers who are gaining skills through experience or training are acquiring human capital. Children who are learning to read are acquiring human capital.

The amount of labor available to an economy can be increased in two ways. One is to increase the total quantity of labor, either by increasing the number of people available to work or by increasing the average number of hours of work per week. The other is to increase the amount of human capital possessed by workers.

(2) Capital

Long ago, when the first human beings walked the earth, they produced food by picking leaves or fruit off a plant or by catching an animal and eating it. We know that very early on, however, they began shaping stones into tools, apparently for use in killing animals. Tools such as hammers, screwdrivers, and wrenches are also used as capital. Transportation equipment, such as cars and trucks, is capital. Facilities such as roads, bridges, ports, and airports are capital. Buildings are capital, too; they help us to produce goods and services.

Capital does not consist solely of physical objects. The score for a new symphony is capital because it will be used to produce concerts. Computer software used by business firms or government agencies to produce goods and services is capital. Capital may thus include physical goods and intellectual discoveries. Any resource is capital if it satisfies two criteria: Firstly, the resource must have been produced; secondly, the resource can be used to produce other goods and services.

What we should bear in mind is that money cannot be considered as capital. A firm cannot use money directly to produce other goods, so money does not satisfy the second criterion for capital. Firms can, however, use money to acquire capital. Money is a form of financial assets. Financial assets include money and other "paper" assets (such as stocks and bonds) that represent claims on future payments. These financial assets are not capital, but they can be used directly or indirectly to purchase factors of production or goods and services.

(3) Natural resources

There are two essential characteristics of natural resources. The first is that they are found in nature. No human effort has been used to make or alter them. The second is that they can be used for the production of goods and services. That requires knowledge; we must know how to use the things we find in nature before they become resources.

For example, oil in the ground is a natural resource because it is found (not manufactured) and can be used to produce goods and services. However, 250 years ago oil was a trouble, not a natural resource. In the 18th century, Pennsylvania farmers who found oil oozing up through their soil were anxious, not delighted. No one knew what could be done with the oil. It was not until the mid-19th century that a method was found for refining oil into fuel that could be used to generate energy, transforming oil into a natural resource. Oil is now used to make all kinds of things, including clothing, drugs, gasoline, and plastic. It became a natural resource because people discovered and implemented a way to use it.

Defining something as a natural resource only if it can be used to produce goods and services does not mean that a tree has value only for its wood or that a mountain has value only for its minerals. If people gain utility from the existence of a beautiful wilderness area, then that wilderness provides a service. The wilderness is thus a natural resource.

The natural resources available to us can be expanded in three ways. One is the discovery of new natural resources, such as the discovery of a deposit of ore. The second is the discovery of new uses for resources, as happened when new techniques allowed oil to be put to productive use or sand to be used in manufacturing computer chips. The third is the discovery of new ways to extract natural resources in order to use them. New methods of discovering and mapping oil deposits have increased the world's supply of this important natural resource.

(4) Technology and the entrepreneur

Goods and services are produced using the factors of production available to the economy. Two things play a crucial role in putting these factors of production to work. The first is technology, the knowledge that can be applied to the production of goods and services. The second is an individual who plays a key role in a market economy: the entrepreneur. An entrepreneur is a person who, operating within the context of a market economy, seeks to earn profits by finding new ways to organize factors of production. In non-market economies the role of the entrepreneur is played by government officials and other decision makers who respond to incentives other than profit to guide their choices about resource allocation decisions.

The interplay of entrepreneurs and technology affects all our lives. Entrepreneurs put new technologies to work every day, changing the way factors of production are used. Farmers, factory workers, engineers, electricians, technicians, and teachers all work differently than they did just a few years ago, using new technologies introduced by entrepreneurs. The music you enjoy, the books you read, the athletic equipment with which you play are produced differently than they were five years ago. The book you are reading was written and manufactured using technologies that did not exist ten years ago. We can dispute whether all the changes have made our lives better. What we cannot dispute is that they have made our lives different.

9.2 Classification of products

In general, the product is defined as a thing produced by labor or effort or the result of an act or a process. In economics and commerce, products belong to a broader category of goods.

In marketing, a product is anything that can be offered to a market that might satisfy a want or need. In retailing, products are called merchandise. In manufacturing, products are purchased as raw materials and sold as finished goods. Commodities are usually raw materials such as metals and agricultural products, but they can also be anything widely available in the open market. In insurance, the policies are considered as products offered for sale by the insurance company that created the contract.

Classifying products into meaningful categories can help managers decide which strategies and methods to take in the promotion of a product or service. Many types of classification exist. The key is to categorize the products in ways that make sense for a specific business. There are at least three different ways to classify different products.

(1) Consumer goods vs. industrial goods

Products generally fall into two categories based on their users: consumer goods and industrial goods.

Consumer goods are generally tangible personal properties for sale and they are used for other non-business purposes by individuals, families, or households.

Convenience goods are easily available to consumers, without any extra effort. At the end of the week when you go to the supermarket to complete the necessary shopping for the next week, you probably buy shampoo, soap, etc. This kind of product, which has become a habit and about which you don't think too much before buying is part of the convenience goods category. Another example would be when you enter into a shop, and when going to the cashier you see some umbrellas and take one just because it was raining outside and you went out unprepared. This is also an excellent example of impulse buying. Generally, for convenience goods, once customers make a choice for their preferred brand, then they stay loyal to that brand because it is convenient to keep repeating the choice over time. Other examples of such convenience purchases include bread, cold drinks, chewing gum, etc.

Shopping goods are another category of products. Compared with the convenience goods, the shopping goods are not so frequent. A relevant example can be clothing, electronics, etc. This category relies heavily on advertising and trained salespeople who can influence customers' choices. Companies usually set up their shops and show rooms in active shopping areas to attract customer attention to shopping goods. When buying shopping goods, consumers often do a lot of selection and comparison based on various information such as price, brand, style, textile, etc., before buying an item. Shopping goods are generally costlier than convenience goods.

Specialty goods refer to those goods that are very unique, unusual, and luxurious in nature. Specialty goods are mostly purchased by the upper-class of society as they are expensive in nature. The goods don't come under the category of necessity, and they are purchased on the basis of personal preference or desire. Brand name and unique and special features of an item are major attributes that attract customers to buy it.

For the unsought goods, consumers don't put much thought into purchasing them and generally don't have the compelling impulse to buy them. An example in this category would be life insurance.

Industrial goods are sometimes referred to as intermediate or intermediary goods. They are any types of products that are used in the production of other goods. This can include a wide range of raw materials, as well as various components that are eventually assembled to produce a finished product. Machinery used in the production process is also often classified as an industrial goods.

One of the more common types of industrial goods is the raw materials used in the creation of various products. These raw materials undergo some type of fashioning or transformation in preparation for use in the manufacturing of different kinds of goods and services. At times, these raw materials are leftovers from the creation of other products, as with the remnants of oil sludge that are used to create various types of artificial fibers. Those fibers are eventually used to manufacture upholstery for furnishings, car seats, and various other textile products.

In addition to raw materials, industrial goods also include the resources used in the actual production process. For example, hammers, drills, screwdrivers, and other types of tools would be considered industrial goods, since they are used in the process of assembling parts for the creation of different products. In like manner, machinery and equipment that is used in the manufacturing process would also be considered industrial goods. This would include heavy equipment such as molds for plastics and metals, heating and cooling chambers, and even machines used to automate the packing process for the finished goods.

(2) Durable goods vs. non-durable goods

Based on the variable of durability there are durable goods and non-durable goods. Consumers buy an enormous variety of products. Some are goods that will last for many years. Other items are consumed on the spot when we purchase them. These are known as durable and non-durable goods. Durable goods tend to have a long useful life. Goods consumed in a short time or that have useful lives of less than three years are classified as non-durable. The dividing line isn't always rigid. For example, people sometimes use a piece of clothing for more than three years. Durable goods include items like furniture, jewelry, and cars. Large appliances such as stoves and washing machines are durable goods. The category also includes defense and commercial procurement of heavy equipment and assets like aircraft, trucks and ships. Non-durable goods include food, medicines and other consumables, as well as products that last a limited lifetime, such as clothing, shoes, and small electronic devices.

(3) Tangible goods vs. intangible goods

Based on the variable of tangibility there are tangible goods and intangible goods. Tangible goods could be a road or a car, which has been built or manufactured over a period of time. When it is completed, you can see and touch it. On the contrary, the service is intangible, and you can't see it or touch it. You just know it's there to be provided if it's needed. It could be a service of law or accountancy.

9.3 Process of new product development

New product development is a crucial process for the survival of firms, especially small firms. The business environment today is very dynamic and competitive. In order to withstand competition, the firms have to continuously update their products to conform to current trends. The new product development process is the cycle that a new product has to undergo from conceptualization to the final introduction into the market. The following are the seven steps businesses often take in new product development.

(1) Idea generation

At this stage you are basically involved in the systematic search for new product ideas. A company has to generate many ideas in order to find one that is worth pursuing. The major sources of new product ideas include internal sources, customers, competitors, distributors and suppliers. Almost 55 percent of all new product ideas come from internal sources according to one study. Companies like 3M and Toyota have put in special incentive programs for their employees to come up with workable ideas. This stage is crucial as it lays the foundation for all the other stages. The ideas generated shall guide the overall process of product development.

(2) Idea screening

The generated ideas have to go through a screening process to filter out the viable ones. The purpose of idea generation is to create a large pool of ideas, while idea screening is to find out ideas that are genuinely worth pursuing. The business seeks opinions from workers, customers and other businesses to avoid the pursuit of costly unfeasible ideas.

Companies have different methods of doing the screening, from product review committees to formal market research. It is helpful at this stage to have a checklist that can be used to rate each idea, based on the factors required for successfully launching the product in the marketplace and their relative importance. Against these, management can assess how well the idea fits with the company's marketing skills and experience and other capabilities. Finally, the management can obtain an overall rating of the company's ability to launch the product successfully.

External industry factors can also influence the enterprise's decision criteria, such as competition, legislation, and changes in technology. At the end of the screening process, the firm remains with only a few feasible ideas from the large pool generated.

(3) Concept development and testing

An attractive idea has to be developed into a product concept. A product concept is a detailed version of the idea stated in meaningful consumer terms. This is different from a product image, which is the consumers' perception of an actual or potential product. Once the concepts are developed, they need to be tested within consumers either symbolically or physically. For some concept tests, a word or a picture may be sufficient, however, a physical presentation will increase the reliability of the concept test. After being exposed to the concept, consumers are asked to respond to it by answering a set of questions designed to help the company decide which concept has the strongest appeal. The company can then project these findings to the full market to estimate sales volume.

(4) Marketing strategy development

A marketing strategy statement consists of three parts. The first part describes the target market, the planned product positioning and the sales, market share and profit goals for the first few years. The second part outlines the product's planned price, distribution, and marketing budget for the first year. The third part of the marketing strategy statement describes the planned long-run sales, profit goals, and the marketing mix strategy. Once the management has decided on the marketing strategy, it can evaluate the attractiveness of the business proposal. Business analysis involves the review of projected sales, costs and profits to find out whether they satisfy a company's objectives. If they do, the product can move to the next stage.

(5) Product development

R&D or engineering develops the product concept into a physical product. This stage calls for a large investment. It will show whether the product idea can be developed into a full-fledged workable product. First, R&D will develop prototypes that will satisfy and attract customers and that can be produced quickly and at budgeted costs. When the prototypes are ready, they must be tested. Functional tests are then conducted under laboratory and field conditions to see whether the product performs safely and effectively.

(6) Test marketing

If the product passes the functional tests, the next stage is test marketing. At this stage the product and the marketing program are introduced to the real market. Test marketing gives the marketer an opportunity to adjust the marketing mix before the product launch. The amount of test marketing varies with the type of product. Costs of test marketing can be enormous and it can also allow competitors to launch a similar or even the same product. Hence, at times, the management may decide to do away with this stage and proceed straight to the next stage.

(7) Commercialization

Commercialization means to introduce the product to the market. It will face high costs for manufacturing and advertising and promotion. The company will have to decide on the timing and the location of the launch, whether regional, national or international. This depends a lot on the ability of the company to bear risk and the reach of its distribution network.

Because introducing new products on a consistent basis is important to the future success of many organizations, managers in charge of product decisions often follow these seven procedures for bringing products to market.

Today, in order to speed up to enter the market, many companies do not adopt this sequential approach to new product development. They are adopting a faster, more flexible, simultaneous development approach. Under the new approach, many company departments work closely together, overlapping the steps in the product development process to save time and increase effectiveness.

9.4 Product life cycle

Anything that satisfies a consumer's need can be called a "product". It may be tangible goods or intangible goods. All products introduced into the market undergo a common life cycle. To understand what this product life cycle theory is all about, let's have a quick look at its definition.

A product life cycle refers to the time period between the launch of a product into the market till it is finally withdrawn from the market. The product life cycle theory is used to comprehend and analyze various maturity stages of products. The term "product life cycle" was used for the first time in 1965, by Theodore Levitt in a *Harvard Business Review* article: "Exploit the Product Life Cycle".

Actually, this product life cycle is based on the biological life cycle, in which a seed is planted, germinates, sends out roots in the ground, and shoots with branches and leaves against gravity, thereby maturing into an adult. As the plant lives its life and nears old age, it shrivels up, shrinks and dies out.

Just like a plant, a product also has its own life cycle. A product's entry or launching phase into the market corresponds to the introduction stage. As the product gains popularity and wins the trust of consumers, it begins to grow. Further, with increasing sales, the product captures enough market share and gets stable in the market. This is called the maturity stage. However, after some time, the product gets overpowered by latest technological developments and entry of superior competitors in the market. Soon the product becomes obsolete and needs to be withdrawn from the market. This is the decline stage.

So, the product life cycle explains the product evolution stages. There are generally four stages in product life cycle: introduction, growth, maturity, and decline.

(1) Introduction

After conducting thorough market research, the company develops its product. Once the product is ready, a test market is carried out to check the viability of the product in the actual market, before it can set foot into the mass market. Results of the test market are used to make corrections. Then the product is launched into the market with various promotional strategies. The demand for the new product has to be created, and target customers are attracted to try the new product. Generally, during the market introduction stage, the revenues are very low and the investments are very high. Most businesses do not generate any profits during this stage. They use marketing and sales strategies and tactics to successfully position the new product or service in the marketplace. Identifying problems and solving them at this stage is crucial for the product's future. If solutions cannot be found or are impractical, the marketer withdraws the product from the market.

(2) Growth

Once the introductory stage goes as expected, the initial spark has been set, however, the fire has to be kindled carefully. The marketer has managed to gain the consumers' attention and works on attracting loyal customers. He also works on increasing his product's market share, by investing in aggressive advertising and marketing plans. He will also use different promotional strategies like offering discounts, etc. to increase sales. As output increases, economies of scale can be seen and better prices come about, which leads to profits in this stage. The marketer maintains the quality and features of the product and seeks brand building. The aim here is to let consumers prefer and choose this product over competitors' products. As sales increase, distribution channels are added and the product is marketed to a broader audience. Thus, rapid sales and profits are characteristics of this stage.

(3) Maturity

This stage views the most competition as different companies struggle to maintain their respective market shares. The "survival of the fittest" is applicable here. Companies are busy monitoring the product's value and its sales generation. Most of the profits are made at this stage and research costs are minimum. Any research conducted will be confined to product enhancement and improvement alone. The manufacturer is constantly on the lookout for new ideas, to improve his product and make it stand out among the competitors' products. His main aim is to attract new customers and increase the existing customer base. Since consumers are aware of the product, promotional and advertising costs will also be lower, as compared with the previous stages. In the fierce competition, companies may even reduce their prices in response to the tough times. The maturity stage is the stabilizing stage, in which sales are high, but the pace is slow, however, brand loyalty develops. Therefore, the company can make profits.

(4) Decline

After a period of stable growth, the revenue generated from sales of the product starts declining due to market saturation, stiff competition and latest technological developments. The consumer loses interest in the product and begins to seek other options. This stage is characterized by shrinking market share, decreasing product popularity and declining profits.

This is a very delicate stage and needs to be handled wisely. The type of response contributes to the future of the product. The company needs to take special efforts to raise the product's popularity in the market once again, either by reducing the cost of the product, tapping new markets or withdrawing the product from the market. The manufacturer will cut down all non-profit distribution channels and continue to focus on improving the product design and features, so as to gain back the lost customer base. However, if this strategy fails, the manufacturer will have no option but to withdraw the product from the market.

It is important to note that not all products go through the entire life cycle. Not all products launched into the market succeed. Some fail at the introductory stage, while some fail to capture market shares. Moreover, some marketers quickly change strategies when the product reaches the decline phase and by various promotional strategies regain the lost glory, thereby achieving cyclic maturity phases. Also, there are no time frames for the stages. The growth stage for a product may take a very long time, while the maturity stage may be extremely short. Time frame for each stage differs from one product to another.

The application of product life cycle is especially important to marketers because through this analysis they can decide when it is appropriate to advertise, reduce prices, explore new markets or create new packaging. A well-managed product life cycle leads to a rise in profits and does not necessarily end. Product innovations and new marketing strategies can keep the product attractive to customers for a very long period of time.

Words and Phrases

factor of production		生产要素
output	*n.*	工业产出
utility	*n.*	功用，效用
finished goods		（工业）制成品
labor capital		劳动力资本
scarcity	*n.*	稀缺性
opportunity cost		机会成本
incentive	*n.*	（物质）刺激
non-market economy		非市场经济

allocation	n.	分配
consumer goods		消费品
convenience goods		便利品；日用品
shopping goods		选购品
specialty goods		特殊品
unsought goods		非需品
industrial goods		工业品
intermediate/intermediary goods		中间产品；半成品
assemble	v.	组装，装配
retailing	n.	零售业
durable goods		耐用品
non-durable goods		易耗品
tangible goods		有形产品
intangible goods		无形产品
screening	n.	筛选
launch	v.	发布（产品）
commercialization		商品化，商业化
product life cycle		产品生命周期
cashier	n.	出纳员；收银员
introduction stage		导入期
growth stage		成长期
maturity stage		成熟期
decline stage		衰退期
automate	v.	自动化
procurement	n.	采购
accountancy	n.	会计工作；会计职位
conceptualization	n.	概念化
unfeasible	adj.	不能实行的

 **Exercises**

I. Answer the following questions according to the text.

1. What is production and product?

2. What are the two forms of labor?

3. Is money considered capital? Why?

4. What are the essential characteristics of natural resources?

5. Who will play the role of the entrepreneur in non-market economies?

6. What are the main subcategories of consumer goods?

7. What are industrial goods?

8. How many steps should be taken in the new product process? What are they?

9. Could a business generate a lot of profits during the introduction stage of the product life cycle? Why?

10. What do most companies do when both revenues and profits decline?

II. Decide whether the following statements are true (T) or false (F) according to the text.

1. In economics production just means the manufacturing of physical goods with exchange value. It doesn't include the provision of services. (   )

2. The basic factors of production in an economy include labor, capital, and natural resources. (   )

3. Goods generally fall into two categories: consumer goods and industrial goods. (   )

4. The first stage in the new product development process is idea generation. At this stage a company is basically involved in the systematic search for new product ideas within the company. (   )

5. A product life cycle refers to the time period of producing a product from the beginning to the end. (   )

III. Read the following passage and fill in the blanks with the words given below. Change the form if necessary.

share	abandon	design	respond	maturity
specific	release	saturate	fluctuation	distinct

Product life cycle is the theory that recognizes four separate developmental stages in the life span of a product, with each stage characterized by its own 1. _____ marketing opportunities and restraints. The theory of a product life cycle was first introduced in the 1950s to explain the expected life cycle of a typical product from 2. _____ to obsolescence. The advantage of the product life cycle concept is that it provides a basic structure that allows you to see where you are, and what lies ahead. There are four components to the cycle: introduction, growth, 3. _____ and decline.

The first component is fairly self-explanatory; when a new product is introduced, market gain tends to be very slight, and it is almost impossible to spot any kind of emerging patterns in demand. Depending on how you launch the product, marketing costs may be high, and it is unlikely that there will be any profits as such. After the creation and subsequent 4. _____ of your product, this often boils down to gritting your teeth and waiting. If this stage doesn't lead into the next, then it may be time to jump ship.

The growth stage exhibits a rapid increase in both sales and profits, and this is the time to try and increase your product's market 5. _____. By now you should be seeing where your demand is coming from, and which of your efforts is worth spending time and energy on. With a little bit of luck, you might even have knocked some of the competition out of the way too!

As more and more competitors come into the market, the product enters into the third stage in which the product becomes "mature" and the market gets 6. _____. Price wars often break out. The total sales volume begins to fall, and the profits start to shrink.

The final stage in the life cycle is the decline. This doesn't necessarily mean that it's time to 7. _____ your product altogether, but rather that the introduction of new strategies might be in order. These could include new versions, new distribution methods, price reductions, in short, anything that will inject a little life into the cycle.

Each of the four stages has its own characteristics, and each is open to different strategies being implemented. Theoretically, the product life cycle is a smooth and elegant curve; in reality, there are constant short-term 8. _____ due to external factors.

The advantages of the product life cycle concept speak for themselves. Once you've applied this model to your product, there are numerous options and strategies that may be implemented, according to the 9. _____ of your product and its current stage in the life cycle. For example, you may wish to consider product life cycle acceleration strategies, or at the very least recognize where you are, and what lies ahead. Before 10. _____ to any of the stage characteristics, don't forget to consider the external factors, particularly in response to the decline phase.

IV. **Translate the following sentences into Chinese.**

1. The skills a worker has as a result of education, training, or experience that can be used in production are called human capital. Students who are attending a college or university are acquiring human capital. Workers who are gaining skills through experience or training are acquiring human capital. Children who are learning to read are acquiring human capital.

2. In the 18th century, Pennsylvania farmers who found oil oozing up through their soil were anxious, not delighted. No one knew what could be done with the oil. It was not until the mid-19th century that a method was found for refining oil into fuel that could be used to generate energy, transforming oil into a natural resource.

3. Specialty goods are mostly purchased by the upper-class of society as they are expensive in nature. The goods don't come under the category of necessity, and they are purchased on the basis of personal preference or desire. Brand name and unique and special features of an item are major attributes that attract customers to buy it.

4. In like manner, machinery and equipment that is used in the manufacturing process would also be considered industrial goods. This would include heavy equipment such as molds for plastics and metals, heating and cooling chambers, and even machines used to automate the packing process for the finished goods.

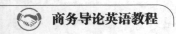

5. The application of product life cycle is especially important to marketers because through this analysis they can decide when it is appropriate to advertise, reduce prices, explore new markets, or create new packaging. A well-managed product life cycle leads to a rise in profits and does not necessarily end. Product innovations and new marketing strategies can keep the product attractive to customers for a very long period of time.

 **Case Study**

A Look Inside Alibaba's Smart Factory That Gives Micro Merchants Fast-Fashion Speed

Xunxi (迅犀) factory, or Rhino Smart Manufacturing (犀牛智造), was officially unveiled in September after three years of trial runs. Imagine this: you are an entrepreneur leading a small garment store or boutique. For your next production order, you can simply access an online portal, input the design elements of your new collection, along with the colors, sizes, and quantities, and hve personalized items like coats and jackets will be delivered to you in just ten days. This is what Alibaba offers to merchants with its new smart production manufacturing platform Xunxi, or Rhino.

The e-commerce juggernaut opened its first Xunxi factory as early as 2017 to test its capabilities in new manufacturing, a concept included in Jack Ma's "Five New" strategy, presented in 2016. However, Xunxi was only unveiled officially in September 2020 after three years of trial runs. Rhino Smart Manufacturing's factory is a fully digitized facility leveraging intelligent manufacturing and automation. Raw materials are all coded and assigned with a unique ID, along with a QR code. Cutting, sewing, and printing machines are all connected to Xunxi's digital systems, on which the entire production process is planned, managed, and tracked. For example, a fabric-cutting machine can determine how to fully utilize an entire sheet of cloth, enabled by the system's artificial intelligence. Automated guided vehicles, pick-and-place robotic arms, and conveyor belts are used to transport materials to workers around the plant.

Targeting the fast-paced clothing industry

Xunxi has served about 200 merchants in China's clothing sector so far, and plans to work with over 10,000 retailers all over the world, said Gao Xiang, chief technology officer of Xunxi.

However, he did not offer a specific timeline for this goal. According to Gao, China's apparel market is currently worth RMB 3 trillion (USD 457.5 billion), but clothing's short product life cycle leads to hundreds of billions in sunk costs due to unsold inventory. He explained that data-driven, on-demand manufacturing can reduce waste in the garment industry, adding that one out of every four pieces of clothing bought in China is purchased from Alibaba's platforms, such as Taobao and Tmall. This means the company has sufficient data to predict sales trends and guide production.

While Alibaba's marketplaces cover business-to-business (B2B), business-to-customer (B2C), and customer-to-customer (C2C) channels, some might question whether Xunxi might give Alibaba the capability of developing its own clothing brand and put the firm in direct competition with its garment clients.

However, Xunxi's CEO Alain Wu explained that Alibaba will not develop Xunxi as a B2C brand. "We just want to build Xunxi as a smart supply chain provider for small and medium-sized companies, which allows them to decide how much to produce based on market demands," he said during a visit to the factory.

Xunxi has already opened two plants in Hangzhou and another in Suzhou, Anhui province, with different digital systems. The first Hangzhou plant was set up with the aim to develop a digital system to optimize production processes for different types of apparel, such as jeans and coats, while the second facility streamlines logistics operations between different factories in the city. The plant in Suzhou is testing a controlling system for production involving raw materials located in different provinces. "We cannot empower a complicated traditional sector, with a history of over 100 years, without actually being in it," Wu said.

Giving small merchants access to fast-fashion speed

Alibaba has reduced the need for apparel merchants to hold inventory by 30%, shortened the delivery time by 75%, and even cut water consumption by 50%, according to the World Economic Forum, which recognized Xunxi as a "lighthouse" factory, or a globally advanced production facility that may redefine the standards for apparel manufacturing.

The plant allows merchants to order as few as 100 pieces of one item, while it is able to fulfill production orders in seven days and deliver finalized products within an additional three days—that's a mere ten-day lead time from when a merchant confirms their order. In comparison, existing clothing manufacturers ask for a minimum of 5,000 units on average and sometimes take months to fulfill an order. Xunxi's speed puts the smart retailing arm in line with fast fashion companies such as Japanese casual wear retailer Uniqlo, which compressed its design-to-deliver supply chain down to just 13 days by 2017, and Spanish company Zara, which has managed to produce and ship garments within three weeks.

However, the business model of Uniqlo is different from Xunxi's, according to Wu, who served the Japanese company for 16 years in senior positions. Uniqlo produces a large number of standardized products, while Xunxi serves retailers on Taobao, Tmall, and cross-border e-commerce platform Kaola to produce a wide variety of personalized goods, he explained. Wu added that production efficiency at a large scale is normally high, while at a small scale it is generally low, which is why Xunxi has a comparative advantage. "Xunxi has actually beaten our expectations in terms of efficiency improvement for small-batch production," he said.

While Alibaba's smart manufacturing division currently focuses on the garment industry due to its large addressable market, Wu revealed that the model could be expanded to items such as footwear, bags, and suitcases, addressing a market with a current combined value of RMB 2–3 trillion (USD 304–457.5 billion).

Questions for discussion

1. How did technology improve the production process in Xunxi factory?

2. What's the difference between Xunxi factory and other fast fashion companies?

3. What do you think of Xunxi's prospects?

Assignments

1. Suppose you are a product manager in a firm that manufactures toys. The branded toy line is five years old and the profit is less and less. Propose some strategies based on the brand's current product life cycle position.

2. Form small groups and generate ideas for a new consumer product that satisfies an existing need but does not currently exist. Give a ten-minute presentation to introduce the idea of your group to the class.

Unit

10

Marketing

Learning Objectives

After learning this unit, you should be able to:

- define marketing correctly;
- understand the functions of marketing;
- list the 7 Ps of the marketing mix;
- know the three key elements to marketing environment;
- describe the three key marketing strategy decisions.

Warm-up Questions

1. What do you know about marketing? Can you give some examples of successful marketing?

2. In your opinion, how can a product become famous in the fierce competition?

3. If you are a manager of a small company, what strategies would you take to expand your market share?

Reading

10.1 The definition of marketing

Marketing is a term so widely accepted that we might take its meaning for granted. Although few people could define it, most people would know it when they saw it. In some ways marketing is as old as civilization itself. You may have seen films based in ancient Greece or Rome with images of busy market stalls and traders actively engaged in persuasive communications. Of course, these traders would not have called their activities marketing and their activities may seem far removed from someone ordering airline tickets via a website. Marketing involves selling products and services, but that doesn't mean marketing is limited to sales activities.

We might accept that marketing is so broad in its scope that no one explanation can cover all its meanings. Here are three frequently cited definitions:

The Chartered Institute of Marketing (CIM) defines marketing as "the management process which identifies, anticipates, and supplies customer requirements efficiently and profitably".

The American Marketing Association (AMA) defines marketing as "the process of planning and executing the conception, pricing, promotion and distribution of ideas, goods and services to create exchange and satisfy individual and organizational objectives".

Philip Kotler, distinguished professor of International Marketing at Northwestern

University, defines marketing as "a social and managerial process by which individuals and groups obtain what they need and want through creating and exchanging products and value with each other".

There are many other definitions, but from these three we can see consistency in the scope of marketing. Marketing is a management process; it is about the exchange of goods and services; it anticipates and meets consumers' needs; it creates profits.

Definitions of marketing describe it as a business function rather like accounting, or human resource management. Marketing is therefore to manage a complex business process.

Marketing is about exchanges. Normally this is expressed as the exchange of goods or services for payment. But more recent applications of marketing techniques have complicated this definition. For example, "political marketing" might be seen as the exchange of a preferred set of policies in return for a vote and ongoing support.

Central to the idea of marketing is that individuals have needs and wants that can be met through the purchase of goods and services. These needs are most obviously physical, but may also be social, and psychological.

Now obviously in modern Western society most people have enough to eat and drink and have reasonably safe and secure accommodation, so the focus of much modern marketing is actually on meeting the social and psychological needs. Any particular need may also be met by a number of different products or services. Although absent from the definitions, "providing choices" becomes a central aspect of modern marketing.

Psychological and social needs can be met through a wide variety of services and products, so marketing also ensures competition. For example, the "need" to be respected by others could be met by an expensive luxury car, a designer suit, an adventure holiday, or a higher degree. Each organization attempts to produce goods or services that are more effective at meeting needs. Organizations also attempt to find new ways to meet new needs.

In return for satisfying consumers' needs, organizations expect to make a profit. In other words, marketers do not manage solely with the aim of meeting consumer needs, they select those needs which their organization can meet most profitably. This also suggests that choice is a key aspect of marketing management. Organizations select what they judge to be the most profitable markets from all the possible markets they can enter.

However, we can note that some definitions suggest "organizational objectives" or "value" rather than profit. These definitions accept that in the short term at least, organizations might want to grow their volume of customers at the expense of profit. They also allow the marketing concept to be applied to a wider range of organizations such as charities and political parties, where profit is not an objective.

10.2 The concept of marketing

The concept of marketing that we now see has more to do with developments during the Industrial Revolution in the 18th and 19th centuries. This was a period of rapid social change driven by technological and scientific innovation. For example, the invention of the steam engine, camera, and telephone all happened at that time. One result was that for the first time the production of goods was separated from their consumption. Mass production, developing transport infrastructure and growing mass media meant that producers needed to, and could develop more sophisticated ways of managing the distribution of goods. Since then, we went through different eras that emphasized the different aspects of a business.

What philosophy should guide a company's marketing and selling efforts? What relative weights should be given to the interests of the organization, the customers, and society? These interests often clash; however, an organization's marketing and selling activities should be carried out under a well-thought-out philosophy of efficiency, effectiveness, and social responsibility, which is just the concept of marketing.

There are five different concepts of marketing: production concept, product concept, selling concept, marketing concept, and societal marketing concept.

These concepts vary in the function that they deal with. For example, production concept deals with production and selling concept deals with selling. Each of the concept is developed according to the need of the market. As the market changes, so do the concepts of marketing. In this part we are going to look at all five concepts of marketing and what they represent respectively.

(1) The production concept

This is the oldest concept in business. It holds that consumers will prefer products that are widely available and inexpensive. For most time of the Industrial Revolution, goods were generally scarce, and producers could sell all that they could produce as long as people could afford to buy them. Managers focusing on this concept concentrate on achieving high productivity, low costs, and mass distribution. They assume that consumers are primarily interested in product availability and low prices. This orientation makes sense in developing countries, where consumers are more interested in obtaining the product than in its features.

(2) The product concept

This concept holds that consumers will favor those products that offer the highest quality, performance, or innovative features. Managers focusing on this concept concentrate on making superior products and improving them over time. They assume that buyers admire well-made products and can appraise quality and performance. However, these managers are sometimes obsessed with their products and do not realize what the market needs.

(3) The selling concept

This is another common business orientation. It holds that consumers and businesses, if left alone, will ordinarily not buy enough of the selling company's products. The organization must, therefore, undertake an aggressive selling and promotion effort. This concept assumes that consumers typically show buying resistance and must be persuaded into buying. It also assumes that the company has all kinds of effective selling and promotional tools to stimulate more buying. Most firms practice the selling concept when they have overcapacity. Their aim is to sell what they make rather than make what the market wants.

From the start of the 20th century to the period following the World War II, competition grew and the focus of marketing turned to selling. Communications, advertising and branding started to become more important as companies needed to sell an increasing number of products in an increasingly crowded market. Marketing was therefore still a "slave" to production, but focused on distribution, communication and persuading customers that one manufacturer's goods were better than another's.

(4) The marketing concept

This is a business philosophy that challenges the above three business concepts. It holds that the key to achieving its organizational goals is that the company should be more effective than its competitors in creating, delivering, and communicating its value to the selected target customers.

From the 1960s onwards most markets have become saturated but the size of the market remains the same. This means that there is now intense competition for manufacturers. The sophistication of marketing management has therefore developed into what we see now in a modern marketing department.

Marketers are involved at a strategic level within the organization and therefore inform an organization about what should be produced, where it should be sold, how much should be charged for it and how it should be communicated to consumers. Modern marketers research markets and consumers. They attempt to understand consumer needs and potential needs and allocate organizational resources appropriately to meet these needs. Modern marketers are particularly interested in brands. They are also increasingly interested in ensuring that employees understand marketing; everyone within the organization involves himself/herself with marketing activities.

(5) The societal marketing concept

Nowadays the marketing concept has evolved into a fifth and more refined company orientation: the societal marketing concept. This concept is more theoretical and will undoubtedly influence future forms of marketing and selling approaches.

This concept holds that the organization's task is to determine the needs, wants, and interests of target markets and to deliver the desired satisfaction more effectively and efficiently than its competitors. This is the same as marketing concept. Additionally, it holds that these must be done in a way that preserves or enhances the consumer's and the society's well-being.

This orientation came out as some people questioned whether the marketing concept is an appropriate philosophy in an age of environmental deterioration, resource shortages, explosive population growth, world hunger and poverty, and neglected social services. Are companies that do an excellent job of satisfying consumer wants necessarily acting in the best long-run interests of consumers and society?

The marketing concept possibly sidesteps the potential conflicts among consumer wants, consumer interests, and long-run societal welfare. For example, the fast-food hamburger industry offers tasty but unhealthy food. Hamburgers have a high fat content, and restaurants promote fries and pies, two products high in fat. These products are wrapped in convenient packaging, which leads to much waste. In satisfying consumer wants, these restaurants may hurt consumers' health and cause environmental problems.

So, all the above-mentioned five concepts are the most important ones in the history of marketing. To better understand the marketing concepts, it is worthwhile to put them in perspective by reviewing other philosophies that once were predominant. While these alternative concepts prevailed during different historical time frames, they are not restricted to those periods and are still practiced by some firms today.

10.3 The functions of marketing

The functions of marketing are embodied in economic activities related to the transfer of property rights, selling and buying, the transport and storage of goods, distribution, packaging, financing and procurement. All these areas involve numerous marketing actions. There are actually twelve functions of marketing that span everything from distribution to pricing.

(1) Gathering and analyzing market information

It is an important function of marketing. Under it, an effort is made to understand the consumer thoroughly in the following ways: What do the consumers want? In what quantity? At what price? When do they want it? What kind of advertisement do they like? Where do they want it? What kind of distribution system do they like? All the relevant information about the consumer is collected and analyzed. On the basis of this analysis, an effort is made to find out which product has the best opportunity in the market.

(2) Marketing planning

In order to achieve the marketing objectives of an organization, a marketer should work out his marketing plan. For example, a company has a 25 percent market share of a particular product. The company wants to raise it to 40 percent. In order to achieve this objective, the marketer has to prepare a plan in respect of the level of production and promotion efforts. It will also be decided as to who will do what, when and how. To do this is known as marketing planning.

(3) Product designing and development

Product designing plays an important role in product selling. The company whose product is better and attractively designed sells more than a company whose product design happens to be weak and unattractive.

In this way, it can be said that the possession of a special design gives a company a competitive advantage. It is important to remember that it is not sufficient to prepare a design for a product, but it is more important to develop it continuously.

(4) Standardization and grading

Standardization refers to determining the standards regarding size, quality, design, weight, color, raw material to be used, etc., in respect of a particular product. By doing so, it is ascertained that the given product will have some peculiarities.

Products having the same characteristics or standard are placed in a given category or grade. This placing is called grading. For example, a company produces commodity X, having three grades, namely "A" "B" and "C", representing three levels of quality—best, medium, and ordinary respectively. Customers who want the best quality will be shown a grade "A" product. In this way, the customer will not doubt that a high grade product has been given to him. Grading, therefore, makes sales and purchases easy. Grading process is mostly used in the case of agricultural products like food grains, cotton, tobacco, apples, mangoes, etc.

(5) Packaging and labelling

Packaging aims at avoiding breakage, damage, and destruction of the goods during transit and storage. Packaging facilitates handling, lifting, and conveying of the goods. Many a time, customers demand goods in different quantities. It makes special packaging necessary. Packing material includes bottles, cans, bags, boxes, etc.

A label is a slip which is found on the product itself or on the package. It provides all the information regarding the product and its producer. This can either be in the form of a cover or a seal. For example, the name of the medicine is printed on the slip on its bottle along with the manufacturer's name, the formula used for making the medicine, date of manufacturing, expiry date, batch number, and price. It gives all the information about the medicine to the consumer. The slip carrying all these details is called a label, and the process of preparing it is labelling.

(6) Branding

Every producer or seller hopes that his product should have a special identity in the market. In order to realize his wish, he has to give a name to his product which has to be distinct from other competitors.

Giving a distinct name to one's product is called branding. Thus, the purpose of branding is to show that the product of a given company is different from that of its competitors, so that the product has its own identity.

(7) Customer support service

The customer is the king of the market. Therefore, it is one of the chief functions of a marketer to offer all possible help to the customers. A marketer offers primarily the following services to the customers: after-sales services, customers' complaints handling, technical services, credit facilities, and maintenance services.

Helping the customer in this way offers him satisfaction and in today's competitive age, customer's satisfaction happens to be the most important thing. This encourages a customer's attachment to a particular product and he starts buying that product time and again.

(8) Pricing of products

It is the most important function of a marketing manager to fix the price of a product. The price of a product is affected by its cost, profit margin, price of its competing product, policy of the government, etc. The price of a product should be fixed in a manner that it should not appear to be too high and at the same time it should make enough profit for the organization.

(9) Promotion

Promotion means informing the consumers about the products of the company and encouraging them to buy these products. There are four methods of promotion: advertising, personal selling, sales promotion, and publicity. Every decision taken by the marketer in this respect affects the sales. These decisions are taken according to the budget of the company.

(10) Physical distribution

This function of marketing is about carrying goods from the place of production to the place of consumption. To accomplish this task, four factors need to be considered, namely transportation, inventory, warehousing, and order processing. By taking things to the right place and at the right time, physical distribution creates time and place utility.

(11) Transportation

Production, sale, and consumption of products often happen at different places. Transport facility is needed for the produced goods to reach the hands of consumers. So the enterprises must have an easy access to means of transportation.

We can often see private vehicles belonging to Pepsi, Coca-Cola, or other companies on the road. These are the living examples of transportation function of marketing. Place utility is thus created by transportation activity.

(12) Storage or warehousing

There is a time gap between the producing and selling of goods, so it is very essential to store the goods at a safe place during this time interval. Warehouses are used for this purpose. Keeping goods in warehouses until they are sold is called storage.

For the marketing manager, storage is an important function. Any negligence on his part may damage the entire stock. Time utility is thus created by storage activity.

All these twelve functions happen in the process of marketing. Marketing is about the exchange of goods and services. Through performing all these functions, the marketers bring the goods and services to the place of consumption, and satisfy the needs of the customers.

10.4 Marketing mix

The marketing mix is a basic concept in marketing. It has been defined as the "set of marketing tools that the firm uses to pursue its marketing objectives in the target market". Marketing mix is often crucial when determining a product or brand's unique selling point, which is the unique quality that differentiates a product from its competitors, and is often explained with the 4 Ps: product, price, promotion, and place. This is the famous 4 Ps model, and it was introduced around 1960. And in 1981, some scholars proposed a marketing mix model of 7 Ps, comprising the original 4 Ps plus people, process, and physical evidence. This model is said to be more applicable for services marketing. Since then, there have been a number of different proposals for a services marketing mix.

(1) Product

Product refers to what the business offers for sale and may include products or services. Product decisions include the quality, features, benefits, style, design, branding, packaging, services, warranties, guarantees, life cycles, investments and returns. No matter what products you are selling, it's important to have a clear grasp of exactly what your product is and what makes it unique before you can successfully market it.

(2) Price

Price refers to decisions surrounding list pricing, discount pricing, special offer pricing, credit payment or credit terms. It also refers to the total costs for the customer to acquire the product, and may involve both monetary and psychological costs, such as the time and effort expended in acquisition.

The price of an item is clearly an important determinant of the value of sales made. In theory, price is really determined by the discovery of what customers perceive is the value of the item on sale. Researching consumers' opinions about pricing is important because it shows how they value what they are looking for as well as what they want to pay. An organization's pricing policy will vary according to time and circumstances. Generally speaking, the value of water in the Lake District will be considerably different from the value of water in the desert.

(3) Promotion

Promotion refers to the marketing communication used to make the offer known to potential customers and persuade them to investigate it further. Promotion elements include advertising, public relations, direct selling and sales promotions.

Promotion is the business of communicating with customers. It will provide information that will assist them in making a decision to buy a product or service.

The cost of promoting or advertising goods and services often represents a sizeable proportion of the overall cost of producing an item. However, successful promotion increases sales so that advertising and other costs are spread over a larger output. Though increased promotional activity is often a sign of a response to a problem such as fierce competition in the market, it can help an organization send messages to the consumers and can be extremely cost-effective.

(4) Place

Place is defined as the direct or indirect channels to market, geographical distribution, territorial coverage, retail outlet, market location, catalog, inventory, logistics and order fulfilment. Place refers either to the physical location where an organization carries out business or the distribution channels used to reach markets. Place may also refer to a retail outlet, including virtual stores such as a mail order catalog, a telephone call center, or a website.

Although figures vary widely from product to product, roughly one fifth of the cost of a product is spent on getting it to the customer. Simple speaking, "place" is concerned with various methods of transporting and storing goods, and then making them available to the customer. Getting the right product to the right place at the right time involves the distribution system. The choice of distribution method will depend on a variety of circumstances. It will be more convenient for some manufacturers to sell to wholesalers who then sell to retailers, while others will prefer to sell directly to retailers or customers.

(5) People

An essential ingredient to any service provision is the use of appropriate staff. Recruiting the right staff and training them appropriately in the delivery of their service is essential if the organization wants to obtain a form of competitive advantage. Consumers make judgments and deliver perceptions of the service based on the employees they interact with. Staff should have the appropriate interpersonal skills, attitude, and service knowledge to provide the service that consumers pay for.

(6) Process

Process refers to the systems used to assist the organization in delivering the service. The systems and processes of the organization affect the execution of the service. So, you have to make sure that you have a well-tailored process in place to minimize costs. It could be your entire sales system, a pay system, distribution system and other systematic procedures and steps to ensure everything is running effectively. Some measures can be taken to "tighten up" a business to minimize costs and maximize profits.

(7) Physical evidence

In the service industries, there should be physical evidence that the service was delivered. Additionally, physical evidence influences how a business and its products are perceived in the marketplace. If you walk into a restaurant, you expect a clean and friendly environment. On an aircraft if you travel first class you expect enough room to be able to lie down. Physical evidence is an essential ingredient of the service mix; consumers will make perceptions based on their sight of the service provision.

Besides the 4 Ps and 7 Ps marketing mix models, there is a 4 Cs model. It is a modification of the 4 Ps model. Now that you know what is included in the 4 Ps, you should have noticed that the 4 Ps take the point of view of the seller and not the one of the buyer. From the buyer's point of view, the 4 Ps are transformed into the 4 Cs. Here are the components of this marketing mix model: Product is transformed into customer solution, price is transformed into cost, promotion is transformed into communication, and place is transformed into convenience.

According to this theory, buyers don't see the product as a selling item but rather as a possible solution to their problems. They see how much they would have to spend to benefit from the product. Sellers try to choose the right places to sell their products in order to make it convenient for buyers. And finally, buyers don't think about how sellers promote their products, they think about the way sellers communicate with them.

Whether you are using the 4 Ps, the 7 Ps, or the 4 Cs model, your marketing mix plan plays a vital role. It is important to devise a plan that balances profit, customer satisfaction, brand recognition, and product availability. By understanding the basic concept of the marketing mix and its extensions, you can stand a larger chance to achieve financial success.

10.5 Marketing environment

A company's marketing environment consists of the internal factors and forces, which affect the company's ability to develop and maintain successful transactions and relationships with the company's target customers. The marketing environment surrounds and impacts upon the organization. The marketing environment can be divided into two parts: internal environment and external environment. The external environment can be subdivided into microenvironment and the macroenvironment. Therefore, the internal environment, the microenvironment and the macroenvironment are three key elements of the marketing environment.

Why are they important? Well, marketers build both internal and external relationships. Marketers aim to deliver value to satisfied customers, so we need to assess and evaluate our internal business/corporate environment and external environment. The detailed and continuous process by which an organization monitors its internal and external environment is termed as "environmental scanning". This process is aimed at identifying the risks and opportunities that can affect an organization's prospect or direction.

10.6 Three key marketing strategy decisions

(1) Market segmentation

Market segmentation is the process of dividing a broad consumer or business market into sub-groups of consumers. These sub-groups are known as segments. Market segmentation is based on some shared characteristics. In dividing or segmenting markets, researchers typically look for shared characteristics such as common needs, common interests, similar lifestyles, or even similar demographic profiles. The overall aim of segmentation is to identify high yield segments—that is, those segments that are likely to be the most profitable or that have growth potential—so that these can be selected for special attention and become target markets. There are many different ways to segment a market.

Market segmentation assumes that different market segments require different marketing programs—that is, different offers, prices, promotion, distribution, or some combination of marketing variables. Market segmentation is not only designed to identify the most profitable segments, but also to develop profiles of key segments in order to better understand their needs and purchase habits. Findings from segmentation analysis are subsequently used to support marketing strategy development and planning.

(2) Market targeting

Market targeting is a broad term. It is used to describe the process of identifying groups of consumers who are highly likely to purchase a specific product or service. There are several different approaches to this process. Some of them allow for a broad cultivation of a market, while others are focused more on identifying markets. These markets are small but somewhat lucrative. Businesses of all sizes adopt some forms of market targeting in order to secure and maintain customers.

There are three approaches to market targeting. One is known as broad or undifferentiated marketing. It does not attempt to tailor marketing and sales strategies to cultivate sales within one or two groups of consumers. It is a marketing campaign aimed at covering customers from all walks of life. Market targeting may also take on a form that is known as selective or differentiated marketing. With this approach, the business will identify two or more specific consumer groups. These groups are highly likely to become loyal customers. A third approach to market targeting is known as focused or concentrated marketing. With this strategy, the business will identify a specific group of consumers that is highly likely to generate enough revenue to allow the company to enjoy a profit.

(3) Market positioning

Market positioning is the manipulation of a brand or family of brands to create a positive perception in the eyes of the public. If a product is well positioned, it will have strong sales, and it may become the particular brand for people who need that particular product. Poor positioning, on the other hand, can lead to bad sales and a dubious reputation.

Market positioning is a tricky process. Companies need to see how consumers perceive their product, and how differences in presentation can impact perception. Periodically, companies may reposition, trying to adjust their perception among the public.

Companies also engage in depositioning, in which they attempt to alter the perception of other brands. While outright attacks on rival brands are frowned upon and may be illegal unless they are framed very carefully, companies can use language like "compared with the leading brand" or "we're not like those other brands".

Developing a market positioning strategy is an important part of the research and development process. The marketing department may provide notes during product development which are designed to enhance the product's position, and they also determine the price, where the product should be sold, and how it should be advertised. Every aspect of the product's presentation will be carefully calculated to maximize its position, with the goal of market positioning being domination.

Words and Phrases

trader	*n.*	交易员；贸易商
stall	*n.*	货摊
concept of marketing		营销理念
production concept		生产观
product concept		产品观
selling concept		销售观
marketing concept		营销观
societal marketing concept		社会营销观
marketing planning		营销策划
branding	*n.*	品牌推广
consumption	*n.*	消费
infrastructure	*n.*	基础设施
overcapacity	*n.*	产能过剩
deliver	*v.*	递送；发表
after-sales service		售后服务
marketing mix		营销组合
credit payment		赊账
retail outlet		零售商店
distribution channel		分销渠道
market segmentation		市场细分
market targeting		目标市场选择
market positioning		寻找市场定位
market segment		细分市场

 **Exercises**

I. Answer the following questions according to the text.

1. Can you give a definition of marketing?

2. How did marketing develop in history?

3. What are the functions of marketing?

4. Can you list the 7 Ps of marketing mix?

5. What is the major difference between the 4 Ps and the 4 Cs?

6. What's the importance of recruiting the right staff and training them appropriately when delivering a service?

7. What are the three key elements to the marketing environment?

8. What is a market segment?

9. What are the approaches to market targeting?

10. Can you describe the process of marketing positioning?

II. Decide whether the following statements are true (T) or false (F) according to the text.

1. Marketing involves selling products and services, but that doesn't mean marketing is limited to sales activities. (   )

2. An organization's marketing and selling activities should be carried out under a well-thought-out philosophy of efficiency, effectiveness, and social responsibility, which is just the concept of marketing. (   )

3. The marketing mix is the set of ideas that the firms have in doing its marketing. (   )

4. The function of marketing is only about selling and buying of products or services. (   )

5. Market segmentation is the process of dividing a broad consumer or business market into sub-groups of consumers. (   )

III. Read the following passage and fill in the blanks with the words given below. Change the form if necessary.

| inferior | benefit | promotion | increase | establish |
| purchase | live | reduction | target | market |

While all marketers do not agree on a common definition of marketing strategy, the term generally refers to a company plan that allocates resources in ways to generate profits by positioning products or services and 1. _____ specific consumer groups. Marketing strategy focuses on long-term company objectives and involves planning marketing programs so that they help a company realize its goals. Companies rely on marketing strategies for 2. _____ product lines or services as well as for new products and services.

While marketing practices no doubt have existed as long as commerce has, marketing did not become a formal discipline until the 1950s. At this point, businesses began to investigate how to better serve and satisfy their customers and deal with competition. Consequently, marketing became the process of focusing business on the customer in order to continue providing goods or services valued by consumers. Marketing includes a plethora of decisions that affect consumer interest in a company: advertising, pricing, location, product line, promotions, and so forth. The major concerns of marketing are usually referred to as the 4 Ps, or the " 3. _____ mix": product, price, place, and promotion.

Hence, marketing involves establishing a company vision and implementing policies that will enable a company to 4. _____ up to its vision or maintain its vision. Marketing strategy is the process of planning and implementing company policies towards realizing company goals in accordance with the company vision. Marketing strategies include general ones such as price 5. _____ for market share growth, product differentiation, and market segmentation, as well as numerous specific strategies for specific areas of marketing.

Competition is the primary motivation for adopting a marketing strategy. In industries monopolized by one company, marketing need only be minimal to spur on increased consumption. Utilities long enjoyed monopolized markets, allowing them to rely on general mass marketing programs to maintain and 6. _____ their sales levels. Utility companies had rather fixed market positions and steady demand, which rendered advanced concern for marketing unnecessary. Now, however, most companies face some form of competition, no matter what the industry is, because of deregulation and the globalization of many industries. Consequently, marketing strategy has become all the more important for companies to continue being profitable.

Contemporary approaches to marketing often fall into two general but not mutually exclusive categories: customer-oriented marketing strategies and competitor-oriented marketing strategies. Since many marketers believe that striving to satisfy customers can 7. _____ both consumers and businesses, they contend that marketing strategy should focus on customers. This strategy assumes that customers tend to make more 8. _____ and remain loyal to specific brands when they are satisfied, rather than dissatisfied, with a company. Hence, customer-oriented marketing strategies try to help establish long-term relationships between customers and businesses.

Competitor-oriented marketing strategy, on the other hand, focuses on outdoing competitors by strategically manipulating the marketing mix. Competitor-oriented strategies will lead companies to imitate competitor products, match prices, and offer similar 9. _____. This kind of marketing strategy parallels military strategy. For example, this approach to marketing strategy leads to price wars among competitors. Successful marketing strategies, however, usually incorporate elements from both of these orientations, because focusing on customer satisfaction alone will not help a company if its competitors already have high levels of customer satisfaction and because trying to outdo a competitor will not help a company if it provides 10. _____ products and customer service.

IV. Translate the following sentences into Chinese.

1. This was a period of rapid social change driven by technological and scientific innovation. One result was that for the first time the production of goods was separated from their consumption. Mass production, developing transport infrastructure and growing mass media meant that producers needed to, and could develop more sophisticated ways of managing the distribution of goods.

2. The price of an item is clearly an important determinant of the value of sales made. In theory, price is really determined by the discovery of what customers perceive is the value of the item on sale. Researching consumers' opinions about pricing is important

because it shows how they value what they are looking for as well as what they want to pay. An organization's pricing policy will vary according to time and circumstances.

3. The cost of promoting or advertising goods and services often represents a sizeable proportion of the overall cost of producing an item. However, successful promotion increases sales so that advertising and other costs are spread over a larger output. Though increased promotional activity is often a sign of a response to a problem such as fierce competition in the market, it can help an organization send messages to the consumers and can be extremely cost-effective.

4. In dividing or segmenting markets, researchers typically look for shared characteristics such as common needs, common interests, similar lifestyles, or even similar demographic profiles. The overall aim of segmentation is to identify high yield segments—that is, those segments that are likely to be the most profitable or that have growth potential—so that these can be selected for special attention and become target markets.

5. Companies also engage in depositioning, in which they attempt to alter the perception of other brands. While outright attacks on rival brands are frowned upon and may be illegal unless they are framed very carefully, companies can use language like "compared with the leading brand" or "we're not like those other brands".

 Case Study

Nostalgia Marketing: Case Studies of Brands Sparking Cherished Memories

Nostalgia marketing（怀旧营销）aims to capture or recapture the customer's attention through appealing to cherished memories. Some brands have taken full advantage of nostalgia marketing in China and have resulted in high sales and brand awareness. Whether it is a cartoon, a candy, or even characters from a textbook, items from childhood and teenage years tend to leave a strong impression on the emotions. A common practice of nostalgia marketing is to partner with a brand that is was dear to the target market during these formative ages.

Wahaha（哇哈哈）& Zhongxuegao（钟薛高）: You are young today

The Wahaha Group Co., Ltd. is the largest beverage producer in China. AD calcium milk is one of its products carrying many memories of the post-80s and 90s generation. "Zhong Xuegao" was the three surnames from Hundred Family Surnames, which is an authentic Chinese ice-cream brand. The brand uses an unique Chinese tile design, supplemented by the top " 回 " pattern in Chinese, meaning "back" to the original taste.

In March 2020, Wahaha and Zhongxuegao jointly launched AD calcium milk flavor ice cream "pre-adulthood ice cream". The main target customers of the new ice cream are adults who have grown up but "don't want to grow up", mainly millennials and Gen Z. Wahaha and Zhongxuegao made the flavor of 'Pre-adulthood ice cream' in layers; the first taste is rich, delicate with milk flavor. After that, Brazilian orange juice and French lemon puree bring fresh fruit flavor and restore the flavor of AD milk drink.

As Generation Z has become an emerging consumer force, domestic brand Wahaha has been trying to communicate with young people. AD calcium milk, as one of the largest IP of Wahaha, has a highly recognizable taste. As a famous product in the 1990s, AD calcium milk still reaches many generations. Wahaha uses the marketing theme of "don't want to grow up" to label young people as "babies" and arouses the resonance of more young people.

The cases of nostalgic marketing in China of these two F&B brands have attracted many consumers. Apart from this, the co-branding nostalgia marketing campaigns in China between brands from different industries also worked.

White Rabbit（大白兔）& Scent Library（氣味圖書館）: Be a little bit childish

White Rabbit is a brand of milk-flavored candies. Originally from Shanghai, the brand has a history of more than 70 years. It cooperated with Scent Library, a domestic fragrance brand which is regarded as 'National fragrance cleaning and care brand' in 2019. They launched a variety of skincare and beauty products including perfume, fragrance, lotion and shower gel. All the products from the collaboration incorporate the White Rabbit's signature milk candy flavor.

Moreover, the co-branded products were strategically launched during Children's Day, which triggered the feeling of nostalgia among millennial consumers. More than 14,000 collaborated products were sold out in the first 10 seconds after the collaboration was launched on T-mall on May 23rd, 2019. In addition, in the two months after rabbit launched its online store, the campaign generated 15 times increase in visit and 1.6 times increase in sales revenue.

Scent Library is not White Rabbit's only partner in Chinese nostalgia marketing. The candy brand also launched a limited-edition lip balm with Maxam and milk-candy gift box with Agnesb which did the test for its future brand co-operations. Through the nostalgia marketing campaigns in China, White Rabbit has capitalized on taste, smell, and appearance that has already left an impression on Chinese millennials during childhood. Now that their target market is all grown up, White Rabbit successfully morphed its brand image from an old brand to a classic, and fashionable brand.

Even though the products used in nostalgia marketing are usually domestic brands or domestic cartoons, this doesn't mean this kind of marketing strategy is limited to domestic brands. Foreign brands also take Chinese consumers for a stroll down memory lane through co-branding.

McDonald's (麦当劳) & Li Lei and Han Meimei (李雷和韩梅梅): The classic characters from English textbook in China

Li Lei and Han Meimei were the two main characters in the English textbooks of junior high school published by People's Education Publishing House from 1990 to 2000. These two characters accompanied a total of 100 million people in their English learning journey. As a result, the classic lines including "How are you?", "Fine, thank you and you" have become Chinese millennials' first impression of English.

McDonald's used this memory for reference and leveraged Li Lei and Han Meimei in the mini comic where they taught students how to order food in English. In the advertisement, Li Lei and Han Meimei went abroad with their classmates. Li Lei struggled to order food at McDonald's because of his poor English while Han Meimei as a top student, teaches Li Lei how to order food.

The two familiar characters combine Chinese and McDonald's elements, refining the original memories by blending the old with the new. In the collaboration with Li Lei and Han Meimei, McDonald's chose the topic of ordering food in English, which is very consistent with its own brand tone and also a practical and interesting topic. Indeed, as one of the largest fast-food chains in the world, McDonald's has about 30,000 sub branches around the world and the context of ordering in English in the ads fits the reality of many Chinese consumers traveling overseas.

✔ Questions for discussion

1. What are the similarities and differences in the marketing strategies of these three cases?

2. What are the benefits of adopting nostalgic and co-branding marketing strategy for businesses?

3. In your opinion, why consumers are attracted to nostalgia and co-branded marketing?

Assignments

1. Find some information about Chinese national brands which become internationally famous. Discuss how they succeed and what other home brands can learn from them.

2. Form small groups and suppose that each group will start their own business. Try to describe the process of entering the market and developing some major marketing strategies.

Unit

11

Financial Management

Learning Objectives

After learning this unit, you should be able to:

- know the meaning of financial management;
- understand the functions of financial management;
- understand the objectives of financial management;
- know the contents of financial management;
- understand accounting and financial management systems.

商务导论英语教程

Warm-up Questions

1. In your opinion, what activities in a company can be considered as financial management?

2. How can companies raise money for production? Discuss with your classmates.

3. What measures can be taken to improve the financial management?

Reading

11.1 The importance of financial management

The business owners and managers must have some basic skills in financial management. Totally depending on others in the organization to manage finances can be dangerous sometimes. Basic skills in financial management start in the critical areas of cash management and bookkeeping. The financial management should be done according to certain financial controls to ensure integrity in the bookkeeping process. The business leaders and managers should learn how to generate financial statements from bookkeeping journals, and analyze those statements to understand the financial condition of the business. Financial analysis shows the "reality" of the situation of a business. Thus, financial management is one of the most important practices in management. This unit will help you understand basic practices in financial management, and build the basic systems and practices needed in a healthy business. In this text, we will study the functions, objectives and contents of financial management.

Briefly speaking, financial management is the management of monetary resources. It involves planning accurately, directing the monetary resources at the correct time, and controlling the financial activities of a firm. Financial management is very important for a business to ensure it can run smoothly. Finance is an aspect which, if neglected, can lead to severe losses and closure of a firm.

If you are inexperienced in financial management, then you should get an accountant to help you set up your financial system, generate financial statements, and do some basic financial analysis. But don't count on an accountant to completely take over your responsibility for financial management. The accountant can help you with the financial management, but you have to understand financial data. You should understand the effects of your management decisions, the current condition of your business, and how the decisions will affect the financial condition of your business in the future.

11.2 The functions of financial management

Financial management is a business process that allows a company to record operating transactions and then prepare financial statements. These financial statements should be accurate, complete and in compliance with generally accepted accounting principles (GAAP) and industry practices. Financial management is very useful in financial planning and decision-making processes.

A financial management specialist prepares fair and complete financial statements. He must ensure that internal controls, policies and procedures around financial reporting mechanisms are adequate and functional. A financial management specialist may also analyze operating data and business performance to recommend investment ideas to a firm's senior management.

Generally speaking, the functions of financial management fall into three categories: financial planning, financial control, and financial decision-making.

(1) Financial planning

Financial planning is the task of determining how a business will afford to achieve its strategic goals and objectives. Usually, a company creates a financial plan immediately after the vision and objectives have been set. The financial plan describes the activities, resources, equipment and materials that are needed to achieve these objectives, as well as the timeframes involved.

It is the duty of management to ensure that adequate funds are available to meet the needs of the business. In the short term, funds are required to pay the employees or to make investments. In the middle and long term, funds are required to increase the productive capacity of the business.

(2) Financial control

Financial control ensures that financial transactions are recorded and maintained accurately, and that personnel don't unintentionally or intentionally corrupt the financial management system. Financial control can be very basic sometimes, but it can also be very complex, like yearly financial audits.

Financial control helps the business to ensure that it is meeting its goals. Through financial control the firm decides how much to invest in short-term assets and how to raise the required funds.

(3) Financial decision-making

The three primary aspects of financial decision-making are investment, financing, and dividends. Investment must be financed in some way for which various alternatives are available. A financing decision is to retain the profits earned by the business or to make sure that the profits are distributed among the shareholders via dividends.

11.3 Financial management objectives

Financial management objectives give an overview of how an organization will allocate and monitor its income, expenditures, and assets. Typically, financial management objectives are used to create practical policies and procedures. They include the following types:

(1) Budget creation and management

One of the main objectives of financial management is to create, and stick to, a budget. A budget depicts what you expect to spend and earn over a time period. Amounts are categorized according to the type of business activities, or accounts, for example, telephone bills, sales of catalogs, etc. Budgets are useful for planning your finances and then tracking if you're operating according to your plan. They are also useful for projecting how much money you'll need for a major initiative, for example, buying a facility, hiring some new employees, etc. There are yearly operating budgets, project budgets, cash budgets, etc. The overall format of a budget is a record of planned income and planned expenses for a fixed period of time.

A budget deviation analysis regularly compares what you planned to spend with what you actually spent. It can be used to detect how well you're tracking your plans, how to accurately budget in the future, where there may be upcoming problems with spending, etc.

Budget creation and management is important if you are going to make a profit in business. Budget projections should be made to fit in with the organization's financial year and should be regularly reviewed. Financial resources should only be used for the purposes that have been set out in the budget. And expenditures should be monitored to ensure that every department is keeping to its allocated funds.

(2) Income management

Financial management objectives should include aims for your organization's income. For example, all income (both cash and bank credits) should be properly recorded and banked and invoices should be raised in a timely manner.

For a new business, the biggest challenge is likely to be managing the cash flow. Probably the most important financial statement for a new business is the cash flow statement. The overall purpose of managing your cash flow is to make sure that you have enough cash to pay current bills. Businesses can manage cash flow by examining a cash flow statement and cash flow projection. Basically, the cash flow statement includes total cash received minus total cash spent. One of your biggest challenges in managing cash flow may be decisions about granting credit to customers or clients, and how to collect payment from them.

And clear recovery action policies are in place for overdue accounts or payment failure. Once your income objectives have been created, you need to develop policies and procedures to allow the objectives to be met.

(3) Establishment of accountability systems for finances

Financial management objectives should include establishing systems of accountability for finances. The best way to achieve this is to appoint authorized personnel who have to approve all transactions (typically by signing a document) before the funds can be released. This makes it easier to trace financial irregularities in the accounts to a specific individual or department. They may have mistakenly entered figures or, in more extreme cases, might be embezzling funds. For larger organizations, accountability-related objectives include having an annual audit of accounts. Audits are typically undertaken by an external organization. And audits are a legal requirement for some businesses.

(4) Assets management

To be comprehensive, financial management should not just focus on the tangible annual income and expenditure, but also include the organization's assets. Consequently, one financial management objective should be to keep accurate and up-to-date records of all items of value, such as furniture and vehicles. It should also be made clear who has ownership

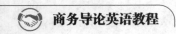

and responsibility for these assets; for example, an organization might not have ownership of its office building, but it might be responsible for its upkeep for the duration of the lease. Allowances for the maintenance of assets should be included in the budget.

11.4 Contents of financial management

In general, financial management consists of four kinds of management: investment management, capital raising management, working capital management, and profit distribution.

(1) Investment management

Investment management is the professional management of various securities and assets, such as shares, bonds and other securities, and real estate. Its purpose is to meet specified investment goals for the benefit of the investors. Investors may be institutions like insurance companies, pension funds, corporations, charities, educational establishments, etc. They may also be private or individual investors. For a business, investment management is the activities to increase fund and to enlarge operation scale for short-term and long-term development.

(2) Capital raising management

Large corporations could not have grown to their present size if they couldn't find innovative ways to raise capital to finance expansion. Corporations have five primary methods for obtaining that money.

Issuing bonds

A bond is a written promise to pay back a specific amount of money at a certain date or dates in the future. In the interval, bondholders receive interest payments at fixed rates on specified dates. Holders can sell bonds to someone else before they are due.

Corporations benefit by issuing bonds because the interest rates they must pay investors are generally lower than rates for most other types of borrowing and because interest paid on bonds is considered to be a tax-deductible business expense. However, corporations must make interest payments even when they are not showing profits. If investors doubt a company's ability to meet its interest obligations, they either will refuse to buy its bonds or will demand a higher rate of interest to compensate them for their increased risk. For this reason, smaller corporations can seldom raise much capital by issuing bonds.

Issuing preferred stock

A company may choose to issue new preferred stock to raise capital. Buyers of these shares have special status in the event that the underlying company encounters financial trouble. If profits are limited, preferred-stock owners will be paid their dividends after bondholders receive their guaranteed interest payments but before any common stock dividends are paid.

Selling common stock

If a company is in good financial health, it can raise capital by issuing common stock. Typically, investment banks can help companies issue stock. They will agree to buy any new shares issued at a set price if the public refuses to buy the stock at a certain minimum price. Although common shareholders have the exclusive right to elect a corporation's board of directors, they rank behind holders of bonds and preferred stock when sharing profits.

Investors are attracted to stocks in two ways. Some companies pay large dividends, offering investors a steady income. But others pay little or no dividends, instead they attract shareholders by improving corporate profitability. And hence, the value of the shares increases. In general, the value of shares increases when investors expect corporate earnings will rise.

Borrowing

Companies can also raise short-term or long-term capital by getting loans from banks or other lenders. In finance, a loan is the lending of money from one individual or organization to another individual or organization. A loan is a debt provided by an entity to another entity at an interest rate, and evidenced by a promissory note which specifies the principal amount of money borrowed, the interest rate the lender is charging, and date of repayment. In a loan, the borrower initially receives an amount of money, called the principal, from the lender, and is obligated to pay back an equal amount of money to the lender at a later time. The loan is generally provided at a cost, referred to as interest on the debt, which provides an incentive for the lender to engage in the loan. In a legal loan, each of these obligations and restrictions is enforced by contract.

Using profits

As noted, companies can also finance their operations by retaining their earnings. Strategies concerning retained earnings vary. Some corporations, especially electric, gas, and other utilities, pay out most of their profits as dividends to their stockholders. Others distribute about 50 percent of earnings to shareholders in dividends, keeping the rest to pay for operations and expansion. Still, other corporations, often the smaller ones, prefer to reinvest

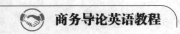

most or all of their net income in research and expansion. They hope to reward investors by rapidly increasing the value of their shares.

(3) Working capital management

Decisions relating to working capital and short-term financing are referred to as working capital management. It is related to the management of current assets and current liabilities. The goal of working capital management is to ensure that the firm is able to operate, and that it has sufficient cash flow to service long-term debt, and to satisfy both maturing short-term debt and upcoming operational expenses.

The policy is another element that cannot be ignored in working capital management. Policies are the guidelines. They are helpful to direct business. Finance managers can also make working capital policies. Here are the two main capital policies of business.

Liquidity policy

Under this policy, a finance manager will increase the amount of liquidity to reduce the risk of business. If a business has a high volume of cash and bank balance, then the business can easily pay its debts. But a finance manager should not forget that the excess cash will not produce, and earning and return on investment will decrease.

Profitability policy

Under this policy, a finance manager will keep a low amount of cash in business and try to invest the maximum amount of cash and bank balance. It will ensure that the profit of business will grow due to increasing investment in a proper way. But at the same time, the risk of business will also increase because the liquidity of business will decrease. And it can lead to bankruptcy of the business. So, a finance manager should keep a balance between the two policies. And after this, both two policies will be helpful for proper management of working capital.

(4) Profit distribution

The specific way that a company distributes profits varies from company to company. Some companies distribute a greater share of profits to investors, while others retain earnings within the company. In a general sense, corporate profits are used to satisfy both the operations necessary within the company and the demands of investors who own shares in the company.

Operating needs

The most immediate use of profits in most corporations is for maintenance and expansion of corporate properties. When a company is profitable, it is likely to build additional plants, expand its sales force, or undertake other actions that expand its ability to generate additional profits. Depending on the structure of the company, the decision on where to allocate these profits can lie with the CEO, the board of directors, or other company officers.

Dividends

Dividends are a physical distribution of the cash profits of a company to its shareholders. In times of rising profits, a corporation may declare an increased dividend to allow shareholders to share the company's growing profit. A high dividend may also attract additional investors to a company's stock, which in turn could drive the stock price higher. Companies that pay high dividends are generally not in a high-growth phase. Therefore, they do not need all the cash generated from operations to fuel additional growth.

Bonuses

Some corporations tie the compensation of certain employees to the profitability of the company. When the company generates a higher profit, these employees get higher pay in the form of a bonus. This compensation system allows the corporation to avoid paying high salaries to employees.

Profit-sharing plans

Profit-sharing plans are a type of retirement benefit that some companies offer as a perk for employees. Company contributions to profit-sharing plans are not mandatory but are based on the amount of profit that a company earns in any given year. Employees benefit by having funds available for distribution at retirement, without having to contribute their own money along the way.

11.5 Accounting and financial management systems

Accounting and financial management systems help businesses, small and large, with reports and queries. These systems provide managers with information to make good decisions based on facts, not gut feelings. Accounting and financial management systems serve the various needs of a firm, such as manufacturing cost information and the development and control of budgets.

A business without an accounting or financial system in place is functioning without a compass, with decisions based on gossip, memory and biased data. The main advantage of a financial and accounting system is that the data is objective and unbiased. Managers can rely on the system to get data based on actual business events, not hear-say. Another advantage of an accounting system is that it organizes your data, making it easy to find information without going through many files. For example, if you want to know how much a client owes you, you can look it up in the accounting system, which often stores many kinds of data.

(1) Financial statements and ratios

To really understand the current and future conditions of your business, you have to look at certain financial statements. These statements are generated by organizing and analyzing numbers from your accounting activities. You should understand the two primary financial statements: One is the profit and loss statement or income statement, and the other is the balance sheet. There are other primary statements, such as the cash flow statement. However, the income statement and balance sheet are the two standard statements for any business.

The income statement depicts the status of the overall profits. This statement includes how much money you've earned and how much you've spent, resulting in how much money you've made or lost. Basically, this statement includes total sales minus total expenses. It presents the nature of your overall profit and loss over a period of time. Therefore, the income statement gives you a sense for how well the business is operating.

Whereas the income statement depicts the overall status of your profits or deficits by looking at income and expenses over a period of time, the balance sheet depicts the overall status of your finance at a fixed point of time. It totals all your assets and subtracts all your liabilities to calculate your overall net worth. This statement is referenced particularly when buying or selling a business, or applying for funding.

There are also a variety of ratios that can be used to help determine the current and future condition of a business. These ratios are produced from numbers on the financial statements. The finance managers often compare ratios from different time periods in the same business, for example, manufacturing, wholesale, service, etc.

After you have got all kinds of financial statements and ratios, you need to do a financial analysis. A financial analysis can tell you a lot about how your business is doing. Without this analysis, you may end up staring at a bunch of numbers on budgets, cash flow projections and profit and loss statements. You should spend at least a few hours every month doing financial analysis. Analysis includes cash flow analysis and budget deviation analysis. It also includes balance sheet analysis and income statement analysis. There are some techniques and tools to help in financial analysis, for example, profit analysis, break-even analysis and ratios analysis.

They can substantially help to simplify and streamline financial analysis. How you carry out the analysis depends on the nature and needs of the business.

(2) Manual and computerized financial management systems

Accounting and management accounting systems can be divided into two main kinds: manual or computerized. Basically, these systems help businesses in many processes, such as paying bills, controlling expenses and recording revenues. Financial management programs can give managers required reports and analysis with the focus on timeliness and reliability of information.

The business owners are strongly suggested to get a software package to manage their accounting books. There are a number of useful software packages that will help you automate bookkeeping, generate financial statements and analyze them. An accounting software package can greatly reduce the time to record and manage accounting transactions, and generate financial statements. However, you still should have at least a basic understanding of the accounting process for your organization, including what journals are used and what general accounts exist. You must have a good understanding of financial statements and how to analyze them. An accounting package cannot do this for you.

(3) Internal controls

A financial and accounting management system is not perfect—it may contain errors. The internal controls can prevent or identify mistakes, making the financial system more accurate and reliable. One common feature of internal controls is to separate the duties of accounting personnel if more than one employee is involved in conducting accounting tasks from the beginning to the end of a process. For example, internal controls in paying bills include a person approving the bill and another one processing payment. This setup makes it harder for errors to go undetected.

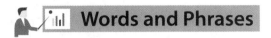 **Words and Phrases**

financial management		财务管理
bookkeeping	*n.*	记账
financial statement		财务报表
financial condition		财务状况

generally accepted accounting principles (GAAP)		一般公认会计原则
decision-making process		决策过程
internal control		内部控制
timeframe	*n.*	时间表
financial transaction		金融交易
audit	*n.*	审计
investment financing		投资融资
working capital		周转资金
preferred stock		优先股
common stock		普通股
dividend	*n.*	股息；分红
operating budget		营业预算
project budget		项目预算
current bill		活期票据
current asset		流动资产
overdue account		逾期账款
accountability system		问责制
embezzle	*v.*	贪污；挪用
external organization		外部组织
duration of the lease		租赁期限
budget creation		预算制定
budget deviation analysis		预算差异分析
income management		收入管理
balance sheet		资产负债表
income statement		损益表
net worth		净值；资产净值
ratio	*n.*	比率
break-even analysis		盈亏平衡分析

 **Exercises**

I. Answer the following questions according to the text.

1. What is financial management?

2. What are the functions of financial management?

3. What are the objectives of financial management?

4. What are the four kinds of financial management?

5. How do corporations raise money?

6. What is the goal of working capital management?

7. How do corporations distribute their profits?

8. What are the types of accounting and financial management systems?

9. What are the advantages of accounting and financial management systems?

10. How can mistakes be prevented or identified in the financial system?

II. Decide whether the following statements are true (T) or false (F) according to the text.

1. Financial management is the management of monetary resources. It involves planning accurately, directing the monetary resources at correct time and controlling the financial activities of a firm. (   )

2. Financial management should just focus on the tangible annual income and profit. (   )

3. In general, financial management consists of four kinds of management: investment management, capital raising management, working capital management, and profit distribution. (   )

4. The only function of accounting and financial management system is to prevent financial risks. (   )

5. Internal controls can prevent or identify mistakes, making the financial system more accurate and reliable. (   )

III. Read the following passage and fill in the blanks with the words given below. Change the form if necessary.

address	cash	operation	alternative	pay
acquire	track	accurate	management	subset

The financial 1. _____ system for a small business includes both how you are financing it as well as how you manage the money in the business.

In setting up a financial management system, your first decision is whether you will manage your financial records yourself or whether you will have someone else do it for you. There are a number of 2. _____ ways you can handle this. You can manage everything yourself; hire an employee who manages it for you; keep your records in-house, but have an accountant prepare specialized reporting such as tax returns; or have an external bookkeeping service that manages financial transactions and an accountant that handles formal reporting functions. Some accounting firms also handle bookkeeping functions. Software packages are also available for handling bookkeeping and accounting.

Bookkeeping refers to the daily 3. _____ of an accounting system, recording routine transactions within the appropriate accounts. An accounting system defines the process of identifying, measuring, recording, and communicating financial information about the business. So, in a sense, the bookkeeping function is a(n) 4. _____ of the accounting system. A bookkeeper compiles the information that goes into the system. An accountant takes the data and analyzes it in ways that give you useful information about your business. They can advise you on the systems needed for your particular business and prepare 5. _____ reports certified by their credentials. While software packages are readily available to meet almost any accounting need, having an accountant at least review your records can lend credibility to your business, especially when dealing with lending institutions and government agencies.

Setting up an accounting system, collecting bills, and 6. _____ employees, suppliers, and taxes correctly and on time are all part of running a small business. And, unless accounting is your small business, it is often the bane of the small business owner. Setting up a system that does what you need with the minimum of maintenance can not only make running a small business more pleasant, but also save you from problems down the road.

The basis for every accounting system is a good bookkeeping system. What is the difference between that and an accounting system? Think of accounting as the big picture of how your business runs—income, expenses, assets, liabilities—an organized system for keeping 7. _____ of how the money flows through your business to see that it goes where it is supposed to go. A good bookkeeping system keeps track of the nuts and bolts—the actual transactions that take place. The bookkeeping system provides the numbers for the accounting system. Both accounting and bookkeeping can be contracted out to external firms if you are not comfortable with managing them yourself.

Even if you outsource the accounting functions, however, you will need some type of recordkeeping system to manage the day-to-day operations of your business, in addition to a financial plan and a budget to make certain you have thought through where you are headed in your business finances. And your accounting system should be producing financial statements. Learning to read them is an important skill to 8. _____.

Another area that your financial management system needs to 9. _____ is risk. Any good system should minimize the risks in your business. Consider implementing some risk management strategies in your business. Certainly, insurance needs to be considered not only for your property, office, equipment, and employees, but also for loss of critical employees. Even in businesses that have a well set up system, 10. _____ flow can be a problem.

Clearly, financial management encompasses a number of crucial areas of your business. Take time to set them up right. It will make a significant difference in your stress level and in the bottom line for your business.

IV. Translate the following sentences into Chinese.

1. A financial management specialist prepares fair and complete financial statements. He must ensure that internal controls, policies and procedures around financial reporting mechanisms are adequate and functional. A financial management specialist may also analyze operating data and business performance to recommend investment ideas to a firm's senior management.

2. Corporations benefit by issuing bonds because the interest rates they must pay investors are generally lower than rates for most other types of borrowing and

because interest paid on bonds is considered to be a tax-deductible business expense. However, corporations must make interest payments even when they are not showing profits.

3. Profit-sharing plans are a type of retirement benefit that some companies offer as a perk for employees. Company contributions to profit-sharing plans are not mandatory but are based on the amount of profit that a company earns in any given year. Employees benefit by having funds available for distribution at retirement, without having to contribute their own money along the way.

4. Accounting and financial management systems help businesses, small and large, with reports and queries. These systems provide managers with information to make good decisions based on facts, not gut feelings. Accounting and financial management systems serve the various needs of a firm, such as manufacturing cost information and the development and control of budgets.

5. One common feature of internal controls is to segregate the duties of accounting personnel if more than one employee is involved in conducting accounting tasks from the beginning to the end of a process. For example, internal controls in paying bills include a person approving the bill and another one processing payment. This setup makes it harder for errors to go undetected.

 **Case Study**

What's Behind Luckin Coffee's Massive Stock Plunge?

Starbucks' Chinese competitor Luckin Coffee (瑞幸咖啡) went through its darkest day as its shares dropped as much as 81 percent on Thursday after an internal investigation unveiled fabricated transactions. Luckin disclosed that "the aggregate sales amount associated with the fabricated transactions from the second quarter of 2019 to the fourth quarter of 2019 amount to around 2.2 billion yuan (10.02 million U.S. dollars)." "As a result, investors should no longer rely upon the company's previous financial statements and earning releases..." the company told investors.

The huge scandal has caught officials' eyes. The China Securities Regulatory Commission on Friday denounced Luckin for financial misconduct, saying listed companies should strictly obey related market law and rules, and fulfill the information disclosure obligations truthfully and completely, no matter where they are.

Just two months ago, on the last day of January, short-seller Muddy Waters Research shorted the stock, citing an anonymous report revealing that Luckin "played tricks" in financial and operating numbers from the third quarter of 2019. The 89-page report, consisting of tons of photos, videos, receipts, and even transaction and WeChat records, claimed to find credible evidence to prove the number of items per store was inflated by at least 69 percent in Q3 and 88 percent in Q4 2019.

The stock dropped more than 10 percent after the report came out. But three days later, Luckin said the methodology was flawed and the allegations were "unsupported speculation and malicious interpretation of events." The stock price went back to where it was at before the report. However, Luckin did not give substantiated financial data and evidence to support its rebuttal at the time.

17 months from trial to debut on Nasdaq: Who's the captain?

The fast-growing chain has been a superstar for investors. After starting a trial operation on the first day of 2018, Luckin spent just 17 months before being listed on the Nasdaq Stock Market, becoming the fastest Chinese company to issue an initial public offering in the U.S. The chairman of the coffee chain, Lu Zhengyao, is also the boss of the Hong Kong-listed car rental company CAR Inc. Beyond the chairman, Luckin's founder and CEO Qian Zhiya used to be the COO of CAR and its parent company UCAR Technology Inc. Her colleague Yang Fei, chief marketing officer, played the same role when he was in UCAR. And the troubled COO Liu Jian has served as the deputy general manager of the vehicle management center in CAR and was the person in charge of benefits management from 2008 to 2015. After that, he was the director of the benefits management of UCAR for three years.

So now it is clear that this UCAR crew is driving the coffee boat. According to Wind, Lu holds 23.94 percent of Luckin's shares and he and his wife Guo Lichun hold 29.76 percent of CAR's shares. His current position indirectly dragged CAR's share down by as much as 70 percent on Friday.

Why it's up, why it's down

So, what makes this coffee brand so different? Targeted at the young generation of white-collar workers, Luckin aims to challenge Starbucks' dominance in China. Most of the domestic coffee company locations are "pick-up stores" that offer limited seating and are in office buildings and other areas where the demand is high. Within just several months from its founding in October 2017, Luckin quickly grew to thousands of stores across the country.

According to Luckin Coffee's official website, it operated 4,507 stores by the end of 2019 in China and vows to open 10,000 stores by the end of 2021. However, the unit performance is far weaker than expected and the fast expansion has burdened Luckin's financial pressure. The firm's operating expenses were 1.6 billion yuan for the second quarter last year, a 244 percent increase year-on-year, according to its financial report. "The average Starbucks store does about 1 million dollars in annual sales. At the start of 2019, Luckin's coffee houses were averaging about 150,000 dollars in revenue per store," said Luke Lango, a market analyst at InvestorPlace. To gain more market share, the coffee provider launched hand-brewed tea drinks to attract tea enthusiasts in the middle of last year, and added smart vending machines called Luckin Pop earlier this year to sell coffee more conveniently.

Luckin started with coffee, but not just coffee. From coffee to tea, from stores to vending machines, Luckin has been constantly breaking boundaries. However, judging from the actual situation, Luckin's various businesses are not as financially healthy as portrayed. The business is maintaining consumers by offering dramatic discounts and vouchers, not by the taste of its offerings. It always uses a cheap price to keep customers loyal. Many Chinese netizens have complained online, saying the lower price is the only reason that they choose Luckin rather than Starbucks. Some even said that Luckin is "burning cash" to occupy the market.

In fact, though it was worth more than 8 billion U.S. dollars in 2019, China's coffee industry is still far from being saturated, said Daxue Consulting. The second-largest economy has the largest population on earth but one of the world's lowest coffee consumption rates. Data from Euromonitor shows that the per capita coffee consumption on the Chinese mainland is only at 4.7 cups in 2018, which is far less than Japan, South Korea and the United States. For coffee fans, taste is always the priority. According to a survey conducted by Aurora Market Research, almost 70 percent of coffee consumers will consider the taste and 28.1 percent will consider the price. But only 6 percent will consider the brand. So, there are market chances for newcomers. But quality will always win out.

Questions for discussion

1. According to the text, what negative impact did the financial mismanagement (financial fraud) of Luckin coffee have on the company?

2. What do you think are the reasons for the massive losses and financial mismanagement of Luckin coffee?

3. In what ways do you think financial management is important to a company?

Assignments

1. Interview some shopkeepers of small businesses on your campus. Ask them about their methods of financial management. Write a report of about 200 words in English.

2. Collect information of three companies who have been troubled by poor financial management. Analyze the reasons of their problems and how they get out of the trouble. Give a ten-minute presentation to the class.

Unit

12

Financing

Learning Objectives

After learning this unit, you should be able to:

- describe the time frame of financing sources;
- describe the advantages and disadvantages of debt financing;
- describe the advantages and disadvantages of equity financing;
- know how to choose the appropriate financing sources.

Warm-up Questions

1. How do you get money when you need it in an emergency?

2. What are the financing options available to start-up businesses?

3. What is the cost of borrowing money from banks or other investors?

Reading

Financing, generally speaking, is a means of currency transaction. When a company's income exceeds its expenditure, it can lend or invest the excess income. On the other hand, when a company's income is less than its expenditure, it can raise capital by borrowing, selling stocks, decreasing its expenses, or increasing its income. The lender can find a borrower, a financial intermediary such as a bank, or buy notes or bonds in the bond market. The lender receives interest, the borrower pays a higher interest than the lender receives, and the financial intermediary earns the difference for arranging the loan.

Every business owner has a vision for his company, and that vision is frequently manipulated by managing the use of financial resources. The ability to raise capital is important for businesses because they need funds for business growth, market competition, and to keep their business operational and maintain their customer base. So financing is critical for the survival and success of a business. Therefore, it's necessary for us to understand the different types of financing options, and know how to select the best financing source.

12.1 The time frame of financing sources

Businesses need finance for daily operations and to meet essential expenses and payments. Expenses are either short term, such as payroll payments, or long term, such as purchasing buildings. The time frame can dictate which type of finance source works best for funding. Bank is an obvious choice and works well for covering many short-term, medium-term, and long-term financial requests. However, venture capital, private funding, and trade credit are also sources of business financing. On the basis of different time frames, there are short-term, medium-term, and long-term financing.

(1) Short-term financing sources

Short-term finance solutions are needed on a daily, weekly, and monthly basis to pay for office supplies, rent, utilities, equipment, and payroll. A business may establish credit with local trades and businesses, which is known as trade credit. Credit cards and trade credit can help a business with managing cash flow. The use of itemized statements allows for a clear visual representation of where the cash is being spent and a single payment can be made instead of multiple payments. Many businesses arrange for short-term lines of credit with their bank, referred to as working capital, used to manage everyday business operations. Lines of credit are typically 90-day loans obtained through a commercial bank to assure that payrolls and suppliers are paid on time, every time.

(2) Medium-term financing sources

Medium-term financing is used to fund a special business project or expansion that will increase production and revenue. Banks are a first stop when searching for this type of financing. Through letters of credit and equipment leases, banks can help with some financial risks involved with medium-term funding. Venture capital is also a financing source for expansion and special projects. Businesses offer venture capitalists a level of ownership in the business when they contribute funding. Another medium-term finance source is capital contributed by the existing owners. This is an additional investment that the business owners make directly to the business and it is called owners' equity. Owners' equity is considered as a debt owed by the business to the owners of the business.

(3) Long-term financing sources

Any financial need requiring very large amounts of cash receives long-term funding. These sources of financing are generally designed to be paid off in one or more years and not in a few months. Businesses use this type of financing to purchase other businesses or buildings, or to invest in long-term product development. Bank loans, venture capital, and private financing are sources for long-term funding. Long-term financing can be a combination of funding sources that covers overall costs together. For example, a private financing source (such as a car manufacturer like Ford or Honda) could cover the cost of the initial purchase of vehicles needed for a business expansion. In addition, a local commercial bank loan could cover the purchase of the buildings to house the vehicles, and a line of credit could be used to cover payroll during the training of all the employees needed to run the expanded business. So, in this case three financing sources are involved—the company itself, a local commercial bank, and a line of credit.

Apart from the above-mentioned three types, there are some other ways to classify financing sources: debt financing and equity financing.

12.2 Debt financing

Debt financing deals with borrowing money and repaying it with interest. It includes both secured and unsecured loans. Security involves a form of collateral as an assurance that the loan will be repaid. If the debtor fails to pay back the loan, that collateral is forfeited to satisfy payment of the debt. Most lenders will ask for some sort of security on a loan. Few, if any, will lend you money based on your name or idea alone.

You can also try to acquire debt financing through an unsecured loan. In this type of loan, your credit reputation is the only security the lender will accept. You may receive a personal loan for several thousand dollars—or more—if you have a good relationship with the bank. But these are usually short-term loans with very high rates of interest.

Briefly speaking, the debt financing can be a secured loan which requires guarantees by your property, or an unsecured loan which only requires your reputation.

Most outside lenders are very conservative and are unlikely to provide an unsecured loan unless you've done a tremendous amount of business with them in the past and have performed above expectations. Even if you do have this type of relationship with a lender, you may still be asked to post collateral on a loan due to the general economic conditions or your present financial condition.

The most common source of debt financing for start-ups often isn't a commercial lending institution, but family and friends. When borrowing money from your relatives or friends, have your attorney draw up legal papers dictating the terms of the loan. Why? Because too many entrepreneurs borrow money from family and friends on an informal basis. The terms of the loan have been discussed but not written down in a contract.

Lending money can be tricky for people who can't view the transaction at arm's length; if they don't feel you're running your business correctly, they might step in and interfere with your operations. In some cases, you can't prevent this, even with a written contract, because many state laws guarantee voting rights to an individual who has invested money in a business. This can, and has, created a lot of hard feelings. You'd better check with your attorney before accepting any loans from family or friends.

Besides borrowing money from family or from an agency formally, one of the most popular ways of obtaining start-up capital is using credit cards. Although most credit cards charge high interest rates, they provide a way to get a sum of money quickly without the trouble of paperwork. Of course, you need to pay back the money in a timely fashion, because interest payments on credit-card debt add up quickly.

For example, if you have three credit cards with a credit line of 5,000 yuan on each card and you want to start a small business that you think will require about 8,000 yuan, you could take a cash advance on each card and start that business. Within six months, if you build up a profitable business and approach your local bank for a 10,000 yuan loan at about 10 percent interest, you could use this money to pay off your credit-card balances. After another six months, you could pay off the bank loan of 10,000 yuan.

A small-business loan usually costs a little more than a loan at the regular prime rate. The prime rate is the interest rate that banks charge their most favored customers. Small businesses usually pay one to three percentage points above that prime rate. Most small-business owners are more concerned with finding the right loan at the right terms than with the current interest rate. So, they will just look around for it.

At the same time, banks tend to shy away from small companies experiencing a temporary decline or a seasonal slump. In addition, firms that are already highly leveraged (a high debt-to-equity ratio) will usually have a hard time getting more bank funding.

The advantages and disadvantages of raising capital through debt financing are as follows.

(1) Advantages

Maintain ownership

A primary advantage of issuing bonds and borrowing money from lenders is that a company maintains complete ownership. This is not the case with equity financing because stockholders have ownership rights in a company. The benefit of maintaining ownership is that management has complete control over the decisions made on behalf of the company. Management also has the ability to choose its own board members. The only obligation a debtor has to a lender is to pay back the principal and interest.

Tax benefits

Another advantage of debt financing is that companies receive tax deductions for the interest paid on debt. In most cases, the government considers the interest paid to be a business expense and allows businesses to deduct the payments from their corporate income taxes. This is beneficial for businesses because it allows them to use the money saved to grow the business.

Greater freedom

Businesses using debt financing to raise capital have more flexibility than those using equity financing because they are only obligated to the investor or lender for the repayment period. After all the money is paid back, the business is completely free from its obligation. Companies also have greater flexibility because the paperwork to obtain debt financing is less complicated and less expensive than equity financing.

(2) Disadvantages

Repayment

A disadvantage of debt financing is that businesses are obligated to pay back the principal borrowed along with interest. Businesses suffering from cash flow problems may have a difficult time repaying the money. Penalties are given to companies who fail to pay their debts on time.

Credit rating

Another disadvantage is that debt financing affects the credit rating of a business. A company that has a significantly greater amount of debt financing than equity is considered as a risky business. A company with a lower credit rating that issues bonds typically will have to pay a higher interest rate to attract investors. Companies who have to pay more in interest may experience a cash flow problem in the future.

Cash qualifications

Companies seeking debt financing must meet the lender's cash requirement, which means companies must have sufficient cash on hand. This is difficult for businesses depending on debt financing for a cash infusion. Some companies may have to put up collateral to qualify for financing. This may put assets at risk if they fail to repay the debt.

12.3 Equity financing

Debt is the loans taken by the business from banks or other sources which must be repaid along with interest, while equity is the form of capital raised from investors in exchange for a share in ownership of the business. Briefly speaking, equity refers to stocks or other securities representing ownership in the business.

Equity financing is a method of financing in which a company issues shares of its stock and receives money in return. This method is quite different from debt financing, and most small or growth-stage businesses use limited equity financing. As with debt financing, additional equity often comes from non-professional investors such as friends, relatives, employees, customers, or industry colleagues. However, the most common source of professional equity funding comes from venture capitalists. These are institutional risk takers and may be groups of wealthy individuals, government-assisted sources, or major financial institutions. Most specialize in one or a few closely related industries. The high-tech industry of California's Silicon Valley is a well-known example of capitalist investing.

Venture capital is one of the more popular forms of equity financing used to finance high-risk, high-return businesses. The amount of investment by a venture capitalist depends on the company's stage of development when the investment occurs, the perceived risk, the amount invested, and the relationship between the entrepreneur and the venture capitalist.

Venture capitalists usually invest in businesses of every kind. Many individual venture capitalists are known as angels. They prefer to invest in industries that are familiar to them. The reason is that, while angels don't actively participate in the daily management of the company, they do want to have a say in strategic planning in order to reduce risks and maximize profits.

On the other hand, private venture capital partnerships and industrial venture capitalists like to invest primarily in technology-related industries, especially applications of existing technology such as computer-related communications, electronics, genetic engineering, and medical or health-related fields. There are also a number of investments in service and distribution businesses and even a few in consumer-related companies that attract venture capitalists.

In addition to the type of business they invest in, venture capitalists often define their investments by the business' life cycle. For example, it could be seed financing, start-up financing, second-stage financing, bridge financing, and leveraged buyout. Some venture capitalists prefer to invest in firms only during start-up, where the risk is highest but so is the potential for return. Other venture capital firms deal only with second-stage financing for expansion purposes or bridge financing where they supply capital for growth until the company goes public. Finally, there are venture capital companies that concentrate solely on supplying funds for management-led buyouts. A management buyout, or MBO, is a form of acquisition where a company's existing managers acquire a large part or all of the company from either the parent company or from the private owners.

Generally, venture capitalists like to finance firms during the early and second stages when growth is rapid and cash out of the venture once it's established. At that time, the business owner either takes the company public, repurchases the investor's stock, merges with another firm; or in some circumstances, liquidates the business.

Before approaching any investor or venture capital firm, you must do your homework and find out if your interests match their investment preferences. The best way to contact venture capitalists is through an introduction from another business owner, banker, attorney, or other professional who knows you and the venture capitalist well enough, then you approach them with the proposition.

The advantages and disadvantages of raising capital through equity financing are as follows.

(1) Advantages

Less burden

With equity financing, there is no loan to repay. This offers relief in several ways. First, the business doesn't have to make a monthly loan payment. This can be particularly important if the business doesn't initially generate a profit. This also frees you to channel more money into growing the business.

Better credit

If a business lacks creditworthiness because it has no credit history, or it lacks a financial track record, equity financing can be preferable or more suitable than debt financing.

With equity financing, you might form a partnership with more knowledgeable or experienced individuals. Some might be well-connected. You may learn and gain from partners. If so, your business could benefit from their knowledge and their business network.

(2) Disadvantages

Loss of control

The major disadvantage of equity financing is the dilution of your ownership interests and the possible loss of control that may accompany a sharing of ownership with additional investors.

Shared profit

Your investors will take a piece of your profits. However, it could be a worthwhile trade-off if you are benefiting from the value they bring as financial backers and their business expertise and experience.

Potential conflict

Sharing ownership and having to work with others could lead to some tension and even conflicts if there are differences in vision, management style and ways of running the business. It can be an issue to consider carefully.

In summary, debt financing is somewhat about borrowing money either from an individual like a family member or from an institution like a local bank. And equity financing is attracting investment by giving away part of the rights or shares of the company to the investors. They both have some advantages and disadvantages. Either of them can be a good approach as long as you use them carefully.

12.4 How to choose the appropriate financing sources

While poor management is cited most frequently as the reason businesses fail, inadequate or ill-timed financing is a close second. Whether you're starting a business or expanding one, sufficient ready capital is essential. It is not, however, enough to simply have sufficient financing; knowledge and planning are required to manage it well. These qualities ensure that entrepreneurs avoid common mistakes like securing the wrong type of financing, miscalculating the amount required, or underestimating the cost of borrowing money.

Choosing between equity and debt financing is one of the most common decisions made by business managers while raising capital. However, deciding between the two options is a challenge for virtually all entrepreneurs that need seed capital to start a new business or expand an existing one. Why? Because choosing a source of capital is a decision that will have a long-term influence on the business.

We have learned the advantages and disadvantages of debt financing and equity financing, and next we will talk about how to determine which funding option is best for your business.

Before deciding the financing options for your business, you need to spend some time thinking about the following questions:

- Do you need more capital or can you manage existing cash flow more effectively?

- How do you define your need? Do you need money to expand or as a cushion against risk?

- How urgent is your need? You can obtain the best terms when you anticipate your needs rather than looking for money under pressure.

- How great are your risks? All businesses carry risks, and the degree of risk will affect cost and available financing alternatives.

- In what state of development is the business? Needs are most critical during transitional stages.

- For what purposes will the capital be used? Any lender will require that capital be requested for very specific needs.

- What is the state of your industry? Depressed, stable, or growth conditions require different approaches to money needs and sources. Businesses that prosper while others are in decline will often receive better funding terms.

- Is your business seasonal or cyclical? Seasonal needs for financing generally are short term. Loans advanced for cyclical industries such as construction are designed to support a business through depressed periods.

- How strong is your management team? Management is the most important element assessed by money sources.

- Perhaps most importantly, how does your need for financing mesh with your business plan? If you don't have a business plan, make writing one your first priority. All capital sources will want to see your business plan for the start-up and growth of your business.

If you would be going in the way of debt financing, you should try to start with family and friends because they would most likely loan you the necessary funds at lower interest rates and better repayment terms. If the funds still don't add up, then you can approach a commercial lender who gives loans to small business owners. In fact, these may be the only debt financing options you have if you are just starting a new business, because most banks and other credit-issuing institutions don't give loans to finance new businesses. However, if you are trying to expand an already existing business, then you have brighter chances of getting loans from banks and other finance institutions.

Equity financing involves bringing in investors or partners who provide capital in exchange for a share of the ownership of your business. So, if you have friends, family, or other people who want to invest in your business and become part owners instead of simply lending you money, you can raise money for your small business this way, too. These investors or partners generally invest because they expect to make a profit when the business becomes successful. However, it is important to keep in mind that allowing people to own part of your business comes with its own set of disadvantages.

Which is the best for your business, debt financing or equity financing? There isn't a definite answer to this question, because the financing source you choose depends on your needs and your business' capacity. If you are trying to finance a start-up venture, it is better to seek equity investments, because you generally only have to repay investors if the business turns a profit. And if the business tanks, you don't have to repay.

For ongoing needs like working capital funds, loans are better for businesses with an established reputation and predictable cash flow that allows for realistic repayment schedules.

Because each type of financing has its own appeal, some entrepreneurs opt for a blend of both equity and debt financing to meet their needs when expanding a business. The two forms of financing together can work well to reduce the downsides of each. The right ratio will vary according to your type of business, cash flow, profits and the amount of money you need to expand your business.

Lastly, it is important that you look at the benefits of each to see which may most help your business, and compare the typical debt-to-equity ratios of other businesses in your industry when deciding what type of financing to seek.

Words and Phrases

payroll payment		工薪支付
equity	*n.*	股本；股权；所有者权益
debt financing		债务融资
equity financing		股权融资
secured loan		有担保贷款
unsecured loan		无担保贷款
commercial lending institution		商业贷款机构
attorney	*n.*	律师
pay off		偿清（欠款等）

regular prime rate		定期利率
seasonal slump		季节性下滑
leverage	n.	杠杆作用
principal	n.	本金
paperwork	n.	文书工作
credit rating		信贷评级
infusion	n.	投入
securities	n.	证券
growth-stage business		成长期的企业
government-assisted		政府扶助的
high-tech industry		高科技产业
venture capital		风险投资
business life cycle		企业生命周期
seed financing		种子资金
leveraged buyout		杠杆收购
bridge financing		过渡性融资
management-led buyout		管理层收购
liquidate	v.	清偿；结算
creditworthiness	n.	信誉
track record		业绩记录
dilution	n.	稀释
trade-off	n.	交换；权衡
business expertise		业务专长
tension	n.	张力，拉力
cushion against risk		风险对冲
financing alternative		融资方案
construction	n.	建造，建设
mesh	v.	与……相适应

credit-issuing institution		授信机构
business capacity		业务能力
tank	*v.*	财务状况很差（美式英语口语表达）
debt-to-equity ratio		资产负债率

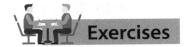 **Exercises**

I. Answer the following questions according to the text.

1. What is financing?

2. How many sources of financing are there? What are they?

3. What do businesses use long-term financing to do?

4. What is only accepted by the lender in unsecured loans?

5. Why does the author ask people to draw up legal papers when borrowing money from relatives and friends?

6. What kinds of companies will banks probably refuse to fund?

7. Why do most individual venture capitalists prefer to invest in industries that are familiar to them?

8. What is business life cycle?

9. Why do venture capitalists like to finance firms during the early and second stages of the life cycle?

10. What risks does equity financing bring to businesses?

II. Decide whether the following statements are true (T) or false (F) according to the text.

1. Financing is the commercial activity of providing funds for business activities, making purchases or investing. (   )

2. Equity financing deals with borrowing money and repaying it with interest. (   )

3. The debt financing can be a secured loan which requires guarantees by your property, or an unsecured loan which only requires your reputation. (   )

4. Venture capital is one of the popular forms of debt financing used to finance high-risk, high-return businesses. (   )

5. Debt financing and equity financing provide different opportunities for raising funds, and a commercially acceptable ratio between debt and equity financing should be maintained. (   )

III. Read the following passage and fill in the blanks with the words given below. Charge the form if necessary.

appealing	trust	generate	mainstream	belly-up
promissory	covert	liquidity	accountable	frequent

When it comes to the financing popularity contest, equity funding is currently in vogue. Articles in the 1. _____ media about venture capital have glamorized the concept of selling stock in your start-up, and entrepreneurs across the board would much prefer to raise money in the form of equity rather than debt.

Why is equity so 2. _____? Because it feels like you're getting "free" money during the start-up stage. There are usually no repayment obligations and no interest payments due to equity investors. You'll also have some say in negotiating the price of your stock, any dividend payments, and the position the investor will have in your company. If your business goes 3. _____, it's their loss (unless, of course, your investors can prove in court that you didn't disclose critical information that would have influenced their decision to invest).

Besides providing funding, equity investors can be helpful in other ways as well. They bring their business experience and lessons learned to bear on your company, and they can become a(n) 4. _____ advisor, mentor, or board member. The best equity investors are those with expertise in your industry, experience in launching a business, a cool temperament, and deep pockets. Some say choosing an equity investor is like getting married—you're making yourself 5. _____ to this person through thick and thin, so choose carefully.

Before you go investor shopping, though, you should carefully think about just what you're selling and what having equity investors really means to you and your business. Very few businesses will ever be able to deliver a decent return on investment (ROI) for equity investors. The typical restaurant or retail store, for example, is unlikely to have any 6. _____ for its shares. And even if you plan to have a high-growth tech business, the chance of reaching liquidity for your early investors is low. You must be honest with yourself about whether your investors expect to be paid back.

Assuming you won't have a glamorous initial public offering, you'll need to find a way to allow your investors a graceful exit. One option is to find a new wave of investors willing to buy out the old ones at a share price that feels like a win-win for all. Another option for investors—especially friends and family who want to stay involved—is to 7. _____ equity positions into loans. In my role as president of Circle Lending, I've encountered these loan conversions quite 8. _____, even though equity investors typically have no legal recourse in the event the business fails. This is one of the hidden secrets of start-up financing that equity investments from relatives, friends, and other start-up investors often morph into loans if the businesses fail.

But what about good, old-fashioned loans? If the sheen of equity capital is tarnished by the reality of having to 9. _____ a respectable ROI, you can fall back on the old familiar friend: a loan. The good news about debt financing is that you're still completely in charge of your business—your only duty to your lender is to make your payments on time, as spelled out in your 10. _____ note. As long as you do that, your lender has no right to meddle in your business. Interest payments are typically a deductible business expense, and if your lender is someone you know well, you may be able to get favorable repayment terms that can make the loan walk and talk much like an equity investment.

IV. Translate the following sentences into Chinese.

1. Credit cards and trade credit can help a business in managing cash flow. The use of itemized statements allows for a clear visual representation of where the cash is being spent and a single payment can be made instead of multiple payments.

2. In addition, a local commercial bank loan could cover the purchase of the buildings to house the vehicles, and a line of credit could be used to cover payroll during the training of all the employees needed to run the expanded business.

3. Lending money can be tricky for people who can't view the transaction at arm's length; if they don't feel you're running your business correctly, they might step in and interfere with your operations. In some cases, you can't prevent this, even with a written contract, because many state laws guarantee voting rights to an individual

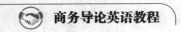商务导论英语教程

who has invested money in a business.

4. However, the most common source of professional equity funding comes from venture capitalists. These are institutional risk takers and may be groups of wealthy individuals, government-assisted sources, or major financial institutions. Most specialize in one or a few closely related industries.

5. Some venture capitalists prefer to invest in firms only during start-up, where the risk is highest but so is the potential for return. Other venture capital firms deal only with second-stage financing for expansion purposes or bridge financing where they supply capital for growth until the company goes public. Finally, there are venture capital companies that concentrate solely on supplying funds for management-led buyouts.

 Case Study

Chinese Uber-like Manbang Group Plans Overseas IPO

Richard Zhang, Manbang Group's chief executive officer, revealed to Bloomberg on September 13 that the company was considering an overseas IPO plan due to better financial performance—but the schedule was not clear yet. Besides, the company may seek one more funding round before the IPO.

The largest Chinese truck logistics unicorn Manbang Group（满帮集团）is a merged company between Yunmanman（运满满）and Huochebang（货车帮）that provides truck-hailing services in China. Like Uber, it acts as a middleman, connecting service providers to customers throughout the vast, freight-hungry country.

Nearly five months after its founding in November 2017, the merged company completed its first corporate funding after the merger on April 24 last year, raising USD 1.9 billion from 18 global institutional investors such as SoftBank Vision Fund, China Reform Fund, Google Capital, Baillie Gifford, Farallon Capital, Sequoia China Capital, Tencent, ABC International, Hillhouse Capital, GGV Capital and so on. Among the investors, SoftBank Vision Fund and China Reform Fund led the fundraising.

The valuation of Manbang surged to USD 6.5 billion after the funding, making the company a super unicorn (worth more than USD 1 billion) in truck-hailing logistics industry.

It is also worth mentioning that Manbang was reported to be pursuing a USD 1 billion financing in August last year, which would further boost its valuation to between USD 9 billion and USD 10 billion. However, the deal could not finally be completed, according to Richard Zhang.

Before the merger, Yunmanman and Huochebang were two leading providers of online truck logistics platforms, offering integrated services to truckers and shippers in China. Founded in 2013, Yunmanman closed an extended Series D funding on October 31, 2017, one month prior to the merger. The valuation of Yunmanman was propelled to more than USD 13 billion after that funding. Huochebang , meanwhile, was established in 2008 and completed an extended Series B on August 18, 2017. Though the latest valuation after funding was not released, valuation after cash of the company also exceeded USD 1 billion, considering how the fundraising size compared closely with Yunmanman. As of November 27, the two companies completed the merger and formed a new company Manbang Group whose main business also lay in truck-hailing services. Yunmanman and Huochebang would still operate independently but complement each other with advantages in business.

The merger created the most dominant truck freight service provider on the market, possessing almost monopoly market power. According to public data, 5.2 million of the 7 million freight trucks and 1.25 million of the 1.5 million logistics enterprises are members of Manbang. By the end of August, 7 million truck drivers and 2.25 million goods shippers have been registered with Manbang. The total user number is expected to exceed 10 million this year. The company's delivery network covers 339 cities and 110 thousand routes in China, with an annual GMV of CNY 800 billion.

China has the largest logistics market in the world with annual delivering fees reaching USD 1.6 trillion, almost double the American market. Notably, Manbang accounts for three-quarters of the Chinese market share. Hong Kong's Financial Secretary Paul Chan Mo-po said in May last year that a Guizhou-based unicorn company had shown their interests in IPO at HKEX. However, Manbang is the only unicorn company headquartered in Guizhou. "Manbang is in talks with Hong Kong's Financial Secretary regarding going public in Hong Kong, but we have no explicit schedule for it yet," said Yunmanman's co-founder and president Miao Tianye in response to the IPO issue.

Questions for discussion

1. How does financing (before IPO) benefit Manbang?

2. In your opinion, how was Manbang able to attract so many well-known institutions and investors?

3. Many companies, including Manbang, have gone public to raise capital, while tech giant Huawei has not. Could you make some comments on this issue?

Assignments

1. Read reports of some businessmen who ran into the problem of finance before and came through it by financing via banks or other investors. Ask them about the brief steps and specific situation of the financing process. And write a report of about 200 words in English.

2. Prepare a ten-minute presentation to introduce the procedures of applying for a loan from a commercial bank.

Corporate Social Responsibility

Learning Objectives

After learning this unit, you should be able to:

- know the basic ideas and the development course of corporate social responsibility;
- tell the importance of socially responsible actions for a business;
- know how a business can shoulder its social responsibility;
- discuss the relation between socially responsible actions and economic performance;
- understand the development of corporate social responsibility.

Warm-up Questions

1. How much do you know about corporate social responsibility?

2. What do you think is the most important factor for a business? Profits or reputation?

3. Can you list any companies which are both socially responsible and committed to profits?

Reading

13.1 The definition of corporate social responsibility

Social responsibility is defined as a theory that obligates individuals and groups to act in a way that benefits the whole society. Applied to businesses, if a company's main objectives and practices not only respect laws and regulations, but also contribute to the growth and well-being of the community, then it can be defined as a socially responsible business.

Corporate social responsibility (CSR) was first used in the late 1960s by multinationals. And it is defined as a form of self-regulated social responsibility within a business model. The objective of CSR is to encourage actions that have a positive impact on employees, stakeholders, clients, and the environment. There are various CSR actions.

(1) Community-based development

This approach to CSR encourages businesses to work with local communities to better themselves. A good example of this is Tyson Food, one of the biggest producers and marketers of chicken, beef, and pork products in the world. This company practices community-based development through its Know Hunger program. By collaborating with the Food Research and Action Center, the Tyson initiative helps raise awareness of hunger in America.

(2) Philanthropy

Another common approach to social responsibility in business is through philanthropy. This can include financial aid and donations of time, gifts or expertise. When companies decide to make donations to a community that is faced with a natural disaster such as a flood or an earthquake, they are exercising philanthropic social responsibility.

(3) Creating shared value

The shared value model is based on the belief that a company and its community's well-being are interdependent. This approach encourages businesses to focus on social problems it can help resolve through its own specialization, so as to create economic and social values toward the community. For example, car manufacturers have been introducing hybrid and electric cars for the benefit of a healthier environment.

(4) Making laws and regulations

A particular feature of CSR is that it's a self-governing principle. Although this means no law or regulation makes CSR obligatory, ISO 26000 was put in place in November 2010. ISO 26000 is a recognized international standard put in place to provide guidelines and encourage voluntary commitment to social responsibility. It targets a wide range of organizations in both the public and private sectors.

13.2 The history of corporate social responsibility

While most people demand ethical conduct for their idols and political leaders, few do so for businessmen. Ever since they came into being, businessmen have been regarded as cold-blooded creatures, and they are by nature profit-thirsty, unscrupulous, and unethical. As an old Chinese saying goes, "No businessman is not unscrupulous." But nowadays businessmen have been exerting ever-growing influence, more and more people demand businessmen to behave more ethically and become more responsible toward the society.

As early as 1969, corporations had been paying attention to their impact on the local community and the world. Arising from the social justice movement of the 1960s, companies have found that it is good for their bottom line to be involved, to invest in their local community, to pay living wages and offer health benefits to their employees, to provide safe and sanitary work environments, to take care to avoid child or slave labor when purchasing parts and materials from overseas suppliers, to reduce pollutants produced by their product and to promote responsible business practices worldwide. Rather than bending laws or asking for exceptions, these companies strive to go beyond the law to ensure that what they do to make a profit is not at the expense of quality of life, sustainability or fairness to community members, suppliers, employees, investors or customers.

The earliest example of a corporate social and environmental responsibility report, according to professors Alice and John Tepper Marlin, was made in 1972 by Abt and Associates. There were no standards set at this time. The professors helped develop standards of accountability for future reports in 1973, including the recommendation that the auditors for those reports would be certified by a third party. Shell Oil followed with its own report in 1991. The Body Shop also followed soon after. An organization named Social Accountability International was founded in 1997 to certify corporate responsibility auditors. Avon Corporation was certified under its standards in 1998.

Corporate social responsibility includes making certain that suppliers are treating their workers well, paying a living wage, providing opportunities for education and advancement, investing in their communities and protecting the environment. This is not always an easy standard to meet. Efforts to change practices overseas do not always have these results. Poverty relief efforts, such as securing a clean water supply for the community, providing access to public health clinics and ensuring that children get needed food and vaccines must take place before pressure can be put on local governments to enforce worker health, safety and wage laws. The benefit to the company is a new group of loyal customers for its products, resulting in dollars spent being at least partially returned to company coffers.

13.3 The importance of corporate social responsibility in business

The main reason why social responsibility is so important to current and long-term business success is that corporate social responsibility has become a widely recognized business process in the early 21st century. Many entrepreneurs consider CSR as an evolution of corporate ethics because it involves balancing the social expectations of all stakeholders, including shareholders, citizens, providers and customers, along with environmental responsibility. The importance of CSR in business can be reflected in the following three points.

(1) Basic integrity

Today, most experts and CSR analysts agree that this broad business concept is an evolution of basic business ethics and integrity. Treating stakeholders with respect and earning the trust of customers through ethical business operations is the foundation of CSR. The importance of internal business controls requires ethics from corporate leaders and employees.

(2) Community relations

The word "social" is the key to understanding how CSR goes beyond basic integrity. As a CSR adherent, a company must remain involved in community-related issues and activities thereby demonstrating that it is a responsible community contributor. This community involvement and participation shows the marketplace that the company is interested in something more than just taking money from their pockets. In the long run, this strategy leads to a stronger public reputation and more profitable business relationships.

(3) The environment

The reason CSR is much broader than conventional business ethics is its necessary inclusion of environmental responsibility. Environment-friendly practice was once an opportunity for companies to add value and enhance their brand image, but now it is a societal requirement with CSR. Preserving the environment, optimizing efficient use of natural resources, such as renewing, reuse and recycle, and reduction of waste are all important environmental components of CSR. Companies that do not consider these points could make the government, public and consumer groups angry.

13.4 How can a business be socially responsible?

For a business to be socially responsible, it means that the business is aware of the environment in which it operates. The environmental conditions that influence the activities of a business define the society that the business is indebted to. Therefore, social responsibility is a way of giving back and in doing so businesses aim at improving the welfare of the society in general.

The major purpose of businesses is making profits and creating wealth for the owners. But they must provide goods and services. The provision of goods and services is itself a form of responsibility. Once they make profits, business must pay taxes. Then the government uses the tax to provide essential services to the society at large. This setup does not free businesses from voluntary corporate social responsibility. They should go further and serve the society because it allows them to use scarce resources. Social responsibility is all about being ethical. Businesses should view the society as the host of the factors of production, the source of profits and as shareholders to the scarce resources.

There are mainly five reasons why businesses own to the society. The first one is that they are part of the society's problems. Secondly, they have a moral duty to help. As an entity, a business should mind the welfare of everyone in society. Thirdly, businesses expect that they will continue operating in the society in future. This calls on them to protect the host society. Fourthly, businesses have caused many social ills, so they must correct them where possible. Finally, social responsibility improves the image of businesses and makes them more popular in the society.

The stakeholders in the society include the consumers, the workers, shareholders, local authorities and the general public. Actually, there are two major ways that a business can give back to these groups of stakeholders.

One is giving preference to the immediate public when it comes to hiring. This makes the public feel attached. The businesses should give fair wages and never be seen to be exploiting workers. They should set fair prices for the goods and services provided. Again, exploiting the consumers is irresponsible. They should aim at quality production and customer satisfaction, because they are the pillars of establishing good relationships and gaining respect. They may also set up social welfare facilities. For example, businesses can use part of their profits to build schools and healthcare facilities.

The other way is participating in social activities. The businesses may sponsor sporting events and tournaments that involve the host society. Organizing community forums to share ideas and intelligence is also one way of enhancing interactions with the society. It can help people come up with plans and strategies on how to solve common problems. The businesses should communicate their actions to the public and give periodic assessment reports, so that their activities and achievements are known by the public. They can use part of the business resources to fund research and development that is aimed at creating solutions to problems of the entire society. For example, a business can fund research on how to find a cure for a common disease. This mainly works in developing countries where governments cannot take care of such needs on their own. This can make the society happy and one aim of being socially responsible is just to keep the society happy. The businesses can also pay attention to minorities such as the disabled. It is good to come up with a program that encourages and promotes equity among all members of the society. It is the contemporary way of being responsible. In some places such as Africa, people are increasingly becoming aware of the role of multinational corporations in environmental degradation. So, businesses in these areas have a duty to show respect to the environment by leading the way in its conservation.

The examples above do not exhaust ways that businesses can participate in corporate social responsibility. They can introduce many ways of being helpful by seeking to protect all the stakeholders' interests. In one word, the key to social responsibility is giving back.

13.5 The relation between socially responsible actions and economic performance

Over the past decade, more companies have embraced CSR and now disclose their activities to investors on an annual basis. The growth of CSR is partly due to the expectation that companies can profit by serving the greater social good. For example, one of the justifications for CSR is that it builds pride and cohesion among employees, which results in better operational performance. Many corporations have sought to use social impact as a core element of business strategy, identifying benefits and making informed choices. Others have proceeded in a more casual way, assuming that markets and customers would reward them for their corporate citizenship and virtue.

Proponents of CSR tend to justify their position by arguing that these expenditures improve a company's economic performance. So, the company can earn higher profits through enhanced brand reputation, more-productive employees, and insulation from regulatory penalties. In other words, executives promote the company's own interests by pursuing a strategy of "doing well by doing good".

In contrast, economist Milton Friedman proclaimed in 1970 that in a free society, "there is one and only one social responsibility of business—to use its resources and engage in activities designed to increase its profits, so long as it stays within the rules of the game." Obviously, there is a contradiction between Friedman and CSR proponents.

Actually, not all companies agree on the value of corporate social responsibility efforts as they apply to the bottom line. Philanthropy that does not produce a return of some kind becomes a mistake if it drives the company out of business. If consumers are unaware of the efforts the company has made and how those efforts affect costs of production, they may buy a competing product at a lower price.

About this point, the underlying question seems to be whether CSR operations improve a company's economic performance. David Vogel argued in his 2008 Forbes article that "CSR Doesn't Pay." He said that, operating under CSR guidelines is not likely to produce higher tangible profits for a company throughout time. Now that socially responsible behavior is expected, it goes largely unnoticed. However, he does agree that companies that ignore CSR may experience public resistance and negative business consequences. Still, many advocates of CSR believe that companies can still profit in the long run through stronger business and customer relationships.

Therefore, there are some considerations for both companies and consumers.

On the one hand, companies must make sure that consumers know about their socially responsible efforts. But this can be tricky. Striking the right note between informing the consumer and corporate bragging can be difficult. Sometimes the companies could even be accused of deception. The tobacco companies serve as a good example, because their products may cause health problems, even death. No amount of fair-trade practices can make up for that.

On the other hand, consumers must take responsibility. They should know about the practices of the companies whose products they buy most often. They can switch brands when they find a company whose ethics match their own, choose products from companies practicing fair and sustainable trade, and do their best to limit pollution and other environmental damage.

The consumers can also let responsible companies know why they are buying from these companies. This increases the likelihood that the companies will continue the efforts to create safer products free of chemicals, genetically altered materials, antibiotics or hormones. Workers at fair-trade companies will have more money available, much of which will return to the local economy. This helps raise the standard of living in an area, and puts pressure on irresponsible companies to raise wages and offer better benefits to prevent workers from leaving to join other companies.

Actually, the corporate social responsibility truly brings some potential on many aspects. If every consumer buys from responsible companies, other companies would have to become more socially responsible in order to compete. Lower pollution levels would result in fewer visits to the doctor or hospital. Workers would have fewer absences due to injury and illness. Families could afford to buy homes, cars and other items needed. With companies' donations, the schools would have more money to spend on improvements. Forests would be planted rather than mowed down and chewed into paper and siding.

13.6 The development of corporate social responsibility in China

CSR has increasingly been seen as important in China, yet the evolution of CSR in China has its own features. It is widely accepted that the evolution of CSR in modern China is linked to economic reform and opening up policy.

There are two driving forces for the development of CSR in China: external change of institutional framework and internal motivation. Externally, the change of institutional framework and policy in relevant areas, such as environmental protection, labor practice, and the demand from the public for high social responsibility have pushed the business to contribute to society. Internally, encouraging managers to follow the Confucian view and be ethical is important too. So, a combination of the two aspects has promoted CSR greatly in China.

The Chinese government is strongly encouraging companies to adhere to high standards of behavior. Responsible business conduct (RBC) is written into the Company Law, which requires companies to comply with laws and regulations, social morality and business morality. A code of conduct has been established for the companies in all sectors, and the government has prepared RBC guidelines for all industries. The proponents of RBC are making a business case for it based on the notion of "soft competitiveness".

At the same time, the Chinese government is developing framework conditions to enable RBC in China. It has put in place a series of measures to ensure disclosure by enterprises of both financial and non-financial information. It has enacted laws to protect the rights of workers, including women workers and children, and it is also taking measures to protect the environment. Responding to the concerns of domestic and international consumers, the Chinese government is taking measures to improve product safety.

The Chinese government is striving to ensure corporate compliance with laws relating to RBC. Further development of the legal system that better ensures judicial competence and independence would facilitate these efforts. Stakeholder and public consultation on the development of legislation is improving. Consultation and arbitration procedures are available. The Chinese government is using RBC as an instrument to ensure legal compliance.

The Chinese authorities are also promoting RBC in overseas operations of Chinese enterprises. The main Chinese banks providing loans for investment overseas have started to implement environmental lending criteria. China has signed and ratified international agreements relevant to promoting RBC. Chinese companies are seeking to learn about RBC standards. The Shenzhen Stock Exchange has published an instruction on social and environmental standards for listed companies.

Improved conduct by businesses operating in China can help address domestic challenges, including environmental pollution and occupational health and safety. It can also support

China's export industries by helping to relieve the concerns of international consumers, such as those concerns about product safety. CSR can facilitate sustainable overseas investment by Chinese enterprises. Policies to encourage CSR can produce both tangible and intangible net benefits for Chinese enterprises, including order retention, reduced staff turnover, increased productivity and improved product quality.

However, for a developing country like China, high profit is still the most important goal of many companies. If it can be proven that high CSR leads to improved economic performance and this, in turn, leads to increased CSR, then this virtuous circle may stimulate low CSR companies to invest in CSR. However, where exactly is the point that the right balance between CSR investment and economic performance can be found? How much exactly do firms have to invest in CSR so as to generate the highest profit? There is clearly a need for much more research in this area.

Words and Phrases

corporate social responsibility		企业社会责任
multinational	*n.*	跨国公司
philanthropy	*n.*	慈善事业
financial aid		财政补助
donation	*n.*	捐赠
philanthropic	*adj.*	博爱的，慈善的
well-being	*n.*	福利
corporate ethics		企业道德
ethical conduct		道德行为
bottom line		底线
sustainability	*n.*	可持续性
standard of accountability		责任标准
coffer	*n.*	保险柜，金库
business process		业务流程
business concept		经营理念

indebted	*adj.*	负债的
sponsor	*v.*	赞助，主办
periodic assessment report		定期评估报告
degradation	*n.*	下降，降级
staff turnover		员工离职率；人员流动率

 **Exercises**

I. Answer the following questions according to the text.

1. What is corporate social responsibility?

2. How can companies shoulder the corporate social responsibility?

3. What is the first example of corporate social responsibility?

4. What is the relation between corporate social responsibility and corporate ethics?

5. Why should a company make its consumers know its efforts in CSR?

6. How is the importance of CSR reflected in business?

7. How will consumers respond to a company's social responsible actions?

8. What was Vogel's argument on CSR?

9. What other social responsibilities does a company have apart from paying taxes?

10. What should a company do to pay back the society?

II. Decide whether the following statements are true (T) or false (F) according to the text.

1. As the economy develops and businessmen have been exerting ever-growing influence, more and more people demand businesses to behave more ethically and become more responsible toward the society. (   )

2. The objective of corporate social responsibility is to encourage actions that promote activities that have a positive impact on employees, stakeholders, clients and the environment. (   )

3. Social responsibility is very important to the short-term business success. (   )

4. A socially responsible business means that the business is conscious of the environment in which it operates. (   )

5. A company can shoulder its social responsibility in different ways, such as giving fair wages to workers, sponsoring sporting events, or helping the public solve common problems. (   )

III. Read the following passage and fill in the blanks with the words given below. Change the form if necessary.

result	principle	dynamic	precede	performance
mutual	expectation	distinct	conflict	imply

Although economic and legal responsibilities embody ethical norms about fairness and justice, ethical responsibilities embrace those activities and practices that are expected or prohibited by societal members even though they are not codified into law. Ethical responsibilities embody those standards, norms, or 1. _____ that reflect a concern for what consumers, employees, shareholders, and the community regard as fair, just, or in keeping with the respect or protection of stakeholders' moral rights.

In one sense, changing ethics or values 2. _____ the establishment of law because they become the driving force behind the very creation of laws or regulations. For example, the environmental, civil rights, and consumer movements reflect basic alterations in societal values and thus may be seen as ethical bellwethers foreshadowing and 3. _____ in later legislation. In another sense, ethical responsibilities may be seen as embracing newly emerging values and norms society expects business to meet, even though such values and norms may reflect a higher standard of 4. _____ than that currently required by law. Ethical responsibilities in this sense are often ill-defined or continually under public debate as to their legitimacy, and thus are frequently difficult for businesses to deal with.

Superimposed on these ethical expectations emanating from societal groups are the 5. _____ levels of ethical performance suggested by a consideration of the great ethical principles of moral philosophy. This would include such 6. _____ as justice, rights, and utilitarianism.

No metaphor is perfect, and the CSR pyramid is no exception. It is intended to portray that the total CSR of business comprises 7. _____ components that, taken together, constitute the whole. Though the components have been treated as separate concepts for discussion purposes, they are not 8. _____ exclusive and are not intended to juxtapose a firm's economic responsibilities with its other responsibilities. At the same time, a consideration of the separate components helps the manager see that the different types of obligations are in constant but 9. _____ tension with one another. The most critical tensions, of course, would be between economic and legal, economic and ethical, and economic and philanthropic. The traditionalist might see this as a(n) 10. _____ between a firm's "concern for profits" versus its "concern for society", but it is suggested here that this is an oversimplification. A CSR or stakeholder perspective would recognize these tensions as organizational realities, but focus on the total pyramid as a unified whole and how the firm might engage in decisions, actions, and programs that simultaneously fulfill all its component parts.

In summary, the total corporate social responsibility of business entails the simultaneous fulfillment of the firm's economic, legal, ethical, and philanthropic responsibilities. Stated in more pragmatic and managerial terms, the CSR firm should strive to make a profit, obey the law, be ethical, and be a good corporate citizen.

IV. Translate the following sentences into Chinese.

1. This approach encourages businesses to focus on social problems it can help resolve through its own specialization, so as to create economic and social values toward the community. For example, car manufacturers have been introducing hybrid and electric cars to the benefit of a healthier environment.

2. Poverty relief efforts, such as securing a clean water supply for the community, providing access to public health clinics and ensuring that children get needed food and vaccines must take place before pressure can be put on local governments to enforce worker health, safety and wage laws.

3. The reason CSR is much broader than conventional business ethics is its necessary inclusion of environmental responsibility. Environment-friendly practice was once an opportunity for companies to add value and enhance their brand image, but now it is a societal requirement with CSR.

4. They should go further and serve the society because it allows them to use scarce resources. Social responsibility is all about being ethical. Businesses should view

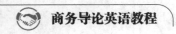

the society as the host of the factors of production, the source of profits and as shareholders to the scarce resources.

5. Workers at fair-trade companies will have more money available, much of which will return to the local economy. This helps raise the standard of living in an area, and puts pressure on irresponsible companies to raise wages and offer better benefits to prevent workers from leaving to join other companies.

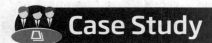 **Case Study**

JD.com'S Popular Free-Range Chicken Program Helps Farmers, Delights Customers

Sales double as JD.com's（京东商城）Farm-To-Table "Running Chicken"（京东走地鸡）Program provides jobs to people in impoverished areas and high-quality, blockchain-traced poultry to urban consumers.

Back in 2016, JD.comturned its hand to revolutionizing a whole new industry: raising chickens. With the launch of its "Running Chicken" initiative, JD established a free-range chicken farm in China's economically disadvantaged Wuyi County, in Hebei province. The program has gone on to reduce poverty in one of the country's historically poorest regions while providing top-quality chicken to discerning shoppers on the JD platform. It has been a resounding success, with sales of the free-range chicken products doubling on JD in its first two years.

The 27-hectare "Running Chicken" farm exemplifies JD's commitment to both giving back to society and providing goods of unmatched quality. By offering interest-free loans to farmers, the program has helped nearly 500 families in the area earn thousands of RMB per year, improving their quality of life and helping to remove Wuyi County from China's national poverty list. Professional breeders hired by JD take the lead in tending to the chickens, while local farmers are offered part-time jobs maintaining farms and growing vegetables, fruit and grain for chicken feed.

Chickens raised on the JD farm also provide a more ethical and healthier choice for consumers in an industry dominated by "battery farms," where animals spend their lives caged in windowless sheds. Free-roaming chickens spend at least 50 percent of their time outdoors, so they can exercise in fresh air and sunshine and interact with other chickens. Studies have shown that free-range chicken meat can have lower levels of harmful cholesterol and saturated fat and higher levels of beneficial omega -3 acids, beta-carotene and vitamins A, B and E.

JD fits each chicken with a specially designed pedometer, with the aim of having each bird take one million steps during the rearing process. The company uses blockchain technology for maximum quality assurance and full traceability. Since early 2018, JD customers have been able to review details about the rearing process for every chicken they buy. A scan of the QR code on the poultry's packaging allows buyers to view detailed information on sourcing, feeding intervals and more. The chickens are delivered via JD's self-operated logistics network, which covers 99% of China's population and offers same and next-day delivery to most customers.

"We are thrilled to see the 'Running Chicken' initiative find so much success with consumers just two years after its launch," said Xiaowen Liu, key projects lead, fresh food sourcing, JD.com. *"The project showcases how e-commerce can benefit society as a whole by alleviating poverty while bringing high-quality, safer, and better tasting produce to consumers."*

Following the chicken project's initial success, JD has expanded its philanthropic reach and range of premium produce by launching two similar farm-to-table initiatives: "Swimming Duck" in Jiangsu Province and "Flying Pigeon" in Hebei Province. Since 2012 JD has also opened more than 200 Poverty Alleviation Local Specialty Malls on JD.com covering 25 provinces. The malls help promote and market local agricultural products on a national scale, both benefitting disadvantaged farmers and providing access to more locally-sourced products for consumers.

 ## Questions for discussion

1. How did JD's "Running Chicken" program "help farmers" and "delight customers"?

2. Why did JD launch such a program?

3. Do you know of any other cases of JD's corporate social responsibility?

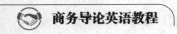

Assignments

1. Interview the managers of some companies which are doing well in CSR. Ask them about the advantages and benefits from CSR, and the disadvantages and problems they met. Write a report of about 200 words in English.

2. Prepare a ten-minute presentation to introduce how the governments of different countries encourage businesses to comply with CSR and why it is so important for both the businesses and the society.

Going to the International Market

Learning Objectives

After learning this unit, you should be able to:

- understand the meaning of globalization;
- know the key factors to be considered when entering the international market;
- understand the reasons of going international;
- describe some challenges and opportunities of going to the international market;
- know the principal modes of going international.

Warm-up Questions

1. What foreign products or services have you used?

2. Which countries are China's major trade partners?

3. What do you think of economic globalization?

Reading

14.1 The background of globalization

The international business is developing rapidly under the background of globalization. Globalization refers to the increasingly global relationships of culture, people, and economic activity. It is generally used to refer to economic globalization: the global distribution of the production of goods and services, through reduction of barriers to international trade such as tariffs, export fees, and import quotas and the reduction of restrictions on the movement of capital and on investment. Globalization may contribute to economic growth in developed and developing countries through increased specialization and the principle of comparative advantage. The term can also refer to the transnational circulation of ideas, languages, and popular culture. Economic globalization includes at least two aspects: the globalization of markets and the globalization of production.

(1) The globalization of markets

A powerful force drives the world toward a converging commonality, and that force is technology. It has facilitated international communication, transport, and travel. It has made isolated places and impoverished peoples eager for modernity. Almost everyone everywhere wants all the things they have heard about, seen, or experienced via the new technologies.

The result is a new commercial reality—the emergence of global markets for standardized consumer goods on a previously unimagined scale of magnitude. Corporations geared to this new reality benefit from enormous economies of scale in production, distribution, marketing, and management. By translating these benefits into reduced world prices, they can beat competitors that still live in the disabling grip of old assumptions about how the world works.

(2) The globalization of production

The globalization of markets forced everyone in the business to be involved in this new trend, otherwise they could fail. At the same time, besides the market, the production methods around the world also experienced the globalization.

The globalization of production means that the world has become the global village and now the producers can get cheap labors all around the world. Now many companies move from their home countries to other parts of the world where they can produce the products at the lowest cost. For example, a large number of famous brands like Nike and Adidas all located their plants in Asia, so that they can lower their labor cost. And it is a truth universally acknowledged that the labor cost in Asia is much lower than that in America. There is another reason for this. Besides the labor cost, this movement of production happened due to the natural resources the Asian countries have and the favorable policies they made to facilitate foreign investors to come to their countries. By entering these Asian countries, Nike and Adidas can reduce the cost of production, produce innovative products, and compete in the market in a better way.

Now the whole scenario has changed the manufacturing companies who are producing things in different countries. We can take Honda as an example, who is making the spare parts in China, assembling the products in Pakistan and designing the engine in Japan. So, the production is distributed into three places. This can be described as the globalization of production. The production which needs high technological knowledge is given to those countries where the people are highly skilled.

14.2 Key factors to be considered when entering the international market

Although the same basic business principles used in the domestic market will still work in the international market, there are some differences. The international market presents some added uncertainties. Many factors, like culture and legal restrictions, are typically cited as major barriers in international business. These factors must be accurately interpreted. When entering new markets, these factors might require the companies to change their pricing structure, promotional strategies, distribution policies, and the product itself.

Indeed, there are a host of factors that need to be researched and evaluated when preparing an international marketing strategy. Key aspects of entering any potential foreign market include demographic and physical environment, economic environment, social and cultural environment, legal environment, and political environment.

(1) Demographic and physical environment

Elements that fit under this category include population size, growth, and distribution; climate factors that could impact on business; shipping distances; time zones; and natural resources.

(2) Economic environment

Factors in this area include disposable income and expenditure patterns, per capita income and distribution, currency stability, inflation, level of acceptance of foreign businesses in economy, Gross Domestic Product (GDP), industrial and technological development, available channels of distribution, and general economic growth. Obviously, the greater a nation's wealth, the more likely it will be that a new product or service can be introduced successfully. Conversely, a market in which economic circumstances provide only a tiny minority of citizens with the resources to buy televisions may not be an ideal one for a television-based marketing campaign.

(3) Social and cultural environment

This category includes a wide range of considerations, many of which can significantly affect a business' marketing efforts. These include literacy rates, general education levels, language, religion, ethics, social values, and social organization. Attitudes based on religious beliefs or cultural norms often shape marketing choices in fundamental ways as well. Cultures differ in their values and attitudes toward work, success, clothing, food, music, sex, social status, honesty, the rights of others, and much else. For example, if a company tries to sell short pants or mini skirts in some Middle East countries where women are supposed to wear scarfs, this business is doomed to fail. Bargain is never done by the Dutch, often by Brazilians, and always by the Chinese. The company that does not take the time to understand these differences may have the risk of failing in international marketing.

(4) Legal environment

This includes limitations on trade through tariffs or quotas; documentation and import regulations; various investment, tax, and employment laws; patent and trademark protection; and preferential treaties. These factors range from huge treaties that profoundly shape the international transactions of many nations to trade barriers erected by a single country.

(5) **Political environment**

Factors here include the system of government in a targeted market, political stability, dominant ideology, and national economic priorities. This aspect of an international market is often the single most important one, for it can be so influential in shaping other factors. For example, a government that is distrustful of foreigners or intent on maintaining domestic control of an industry or industries might erect legal barriers. These legal barriers are designed to restrict the business opportunities of foreign firms.

To sum up, we should be cautious when we choose to go to the international market, and minimize the risk by seriously analyzing all kinds of environments that may influence us, so that we can succeed in the international business world.

The list of factors that affect the success or failure of a business venture is almost unending. A country's level of economic development, trade barriers, geography, competition, the political and legal environment, and culture are a few important factors. It is impossible to expand successfully into a new market without taking these factors into consideration and adapting to them. The willingness to change is therefore, a prerequisite to going international.

14.3 Reasons for going to the international market

Most companies take their business overseas for different reasons. These companies adopt the reactive or defensive approach to stay ahead of the competition. A few of them take the proactive or aggressive approach to accomplish the same purpose. Most of them choose to adopt both approaches to avoid a decrease in their competition. In order to remain competitive, companies move as quickly as possible to secure a strong position in some of the key world or emerging markets. They often make the products customized for the needs of the people in these markets they plan to enter. Most of these world markets are using very good incentives to attract companies with new capital investments.

(1) **The reactive or defensive reasons**

The reactive or defensive reasons for going global are as follows:

- Trade barriers;

- Customer demands;

- Globalization of competitors;

- Regulations and restrictions.

In the case of trade barriers, companies move from exporting their products to manufacturing them overseas. The purpose is to avoid the burden of tariffs, quotas, the policy of buy-local, and other restrictions that make export too expensive to foreign markets. For example, if Adidas manufactured a pair of shoes in America, it would cost much more for us to buy them because some tariffs will be imposed on the imported shoes.

Companies respond to customer demands for effective operations and product assurance and reliability, and/or logistical problem solutions. Most foreign customers who seek accessibility to suppliers may request that supply stay local in order to enhance the flow of production. Companies usually follow that request to avoid losing the business.

The companies realize that if they leave opponent companies overseas too long without challenge or competition, these opponent companies' investments or foreign operations in the world market may be so solid that competing with them will be difficult. Therefore, they try to act quickly.

Some companies' home government may have regulations and restrictions that are so inconvenient and expensive, thus limiting the expansion, taking away the companies' profits, and making their costs uncontrollable. This is the reason for the companies to move to a different market environment with few foreign restrictive operations.

(2) The proactive or aggressive reasons

The proactive or aggressive reasons for going global are as follows:

- Growth opportunities;

- Economies of scale;

- Incentives;

- Resource access and cost saving.

Many companies prefer to invest their excess profits in order to expand, but sometimes they are limited because of the maturity of the markets in their area. Therefore, they seek the overseas new markets to provide such growth opportunities. So, these companies, in addition to investing their excess profits, also try to maximize efficiency by employing their underutilized resources in human and capital assets such as management, machinery, and technology. Companies seek economies of scale in order to achieve a higher level of output spread over large fixed costs to lower the per-unit cost. They also want to maximize the use of their manufacturing equipment and spread the high cost of research and development over the product life cycle. Some developing countries that need improvement and development through capital infusion, skills, and technology voluntarily provide incentives such as fixed assets, tax exemptions, subsidies, tax holidays, human capital, and low wages. These incentives seem attractive to these companies due to their increase in profits and reduction of risks.

The company must have some reasons to go to the international market, either being reactive or proactive. As a business, their primary reason is to gain benefit and sustain long-term development, and going globally will help them achieve the goal.

14.4 The challenges and opportunities of going to the international market

Once a company decides to go to the global market, they will enter a new world, which is filled with all kinds of opportunities and challenges.

(1) Opportunities

On the one hand, international markets can offer companies significant opportunities to expand and diversify their product and service offerings, increase brand awareness and drive revenues.

One benefit for companies to go international is that they can diversify their consumer base and revenue sources. A company that markets only to local consumers is especially vulnerable to domestic economic trends. With consumers in other countries buying products and services from the international division, the company can maintain revenue streams in foreign markets and stay afloat even when the local economy fails to provide enough consumers.

When a company is going global, it increases the ability of the business to attract large companies as clients. These companies already have their own global operations, and they need to give their business to globalized companies diversified and structured to accommodate their needs. If the company is trying to market products and services to large companies, globalization will get their attention, showing big clients that the company aggressively pursues growth in foreign markets.

(2) Challenges

On the other hand, although competing in international markets offers important potential benefits, such as access to new customers and the diversification of revenue sources, going to the international market also poses some challenges.

Meeting international rules and regulations is considered the biggest challenge to growth in international markets.

Adapting to a new business environment is also considered a major challenge. Many companies are seeking local partners in an effort to better understand local consumer tastes and needs, effective marketing methods, and other issues such as local business customs.

While the companies succeed in the international market in different ways, they seem to have one characteristic in common. The management of those globalized companies must be ready to make a commitment to the foreign markets. In one word, the key to successful international business for any company is the ability to adapt to an unfamiliar foreign environment.

14.5 The modes of going to the international market

After the decision of going global has been made, the exact mode of operation has to be determined. There are several general ways to develop markets on foreign soil. They include exporting products and services from the country of origin, entering into joint venture arrangements, licensing patent rights and trademark rights, etc. to companies abroad, franchising, contract manufacturing, and establishing subsidiaries in foreign countries. A company can commit itself to one or more of the above arrangements at any time during its efforts to develop foreign markets. Each method has its own distinct advantages and disadvantages.

The risks concerning operating in the international market are often dependent on the level of control a firm has, coupled with the level of capital expenditure outlaid. The principal modes of going global are as follows.

(1) Exporting

New companies, or those that are taking their first steps into the realm of international commerce, often begin to explore international markets through exporting. Export sales can be achieved in numerous ways. Direct exporting involves a firm's shipping goods directly to a foreign market. Sales can be made directly, via mail order, or through offices established abroad. Companies can also undertake indirect exporting. A company employing indirect exporting would utilize a channel or intermediary, who in turn would spread the product in the foreign market. Many companies are able to establish a healthy presence in foreign markets without ever expanding beyond exporting practices.

From a company's standpoint, exporting consists of the least risk. Because in this mode there is no capital expenditure, or spending of company finances on new non-current assets. Thus, the likelihood of sunk costs, or general barriers to exit, is slim. However, a company may have less control when exporting into a foreign market, because it cannot control the supply of the goods within the foreign market.

(2) Licensing and franchising

International licensing occurs when a country grants the right to manufacture and distribute a product or service under the licenser's trade name in a specified country or market. Although large companies often grant licenses, this practice is also frequently used by small and medium-sized companies. Often seen as a supplement to manufacturing and exporting activities, licensing may be the least profitable way of entering a market. Nonetheless, it is sometimes an attractive option when an exporter is short of money, when foreign government import restrictions forbid other ways of entering a market, or when a host country is apprehensive about foreign ownership. A method similar to licensing, called franchising, is also increasingly common. Franchising is an arrangement between two parties. One party grants another party the right to use its trademark or tradename as well as certain business systems and processes, to produce and market a good or service according to certain specifications.

(3) Joint ventures

A joint venture is a combined effort between two or more business entities, with the aim of mutual benefit from a given economic activity. A company trying to enter a foreign market can form a partnership with one or more companies already established in the host country. Often, the local firm provides expertise on the intended market, while the exporting firm tends to general management and marketing tasks. Use of this method of international investing has accelerated dramatically in the past years. The biggest incentive to entering this type of arrangement is that it reduces the company's risk by the amount of investment made by the host-country partner. A joint venture arrangement allows firms with limited capital to expand into international arenas, and provides the marketer with access to its partner's distribution channels. Contract manufacturing, meanwhile, is an arrangement wherein an exporter turns over the production reins to another company, but maintains control of the marketing process. Some countries often mandate that all foreign investment within them should be via joint ventures. By comparison with exporting, more control is exerted; however, the level of risk is also increased.

(4) Direct investment

A company can also expand abroad by setting up its own manufacturing operations in a foreign country. In this mode, a company would directly construct a factory within a foreign country and manufacture a product within the overseas market. But this approach is very costly, and the capital requirements associated with this method generally prevent small companies from pursuing this option. Large corporations are far more likely to use this way, since this mode often allows them to avoid high import taxes, reduce transportation costs, utilize cheap labor, and gain increased access to raw materials.

An example of this is Dell Corporation. Dell possesses plants in countries external to the United States of America, however, it assembles personal computers and does not manufacture them from scratch. In other words, it obtains parts from other firms, and assembles a personal computer's constituent parts (such as a motherboard, monitor, CPU, RAM, wireless card, modem, sound card, etc.) within its factories. Manufacturing concerns the actual forging of a product from scratch. Car manufacturers often construct all parts within their plants. Direct investment has the most control and the most risk attached. As with any capital expenditure, the return on investment (defined by the payback period, net present value, internal rate of return, etc.) has to be ascertained, in addition to appreciating any related sunk costs with the capital expenditure.

Words and Phrases

import quota		进口配额
specialization	n.	分工专业化
comparative advantage		比较优势
economies of scale		规模经济效应
expenditure pattern		消费模式
literacy rate		识字率
trade barrier		贸易壁垒
defensive	adj.	防御性的
proactive	adj.	积极主动的
customize	v.	定制

logistical	*adj.*	物流的；后勤的
opponent	*n.*	对手，敌手
underutilize	*v.*	未充分利用
capital infusion		资本引入
tax exemption		免税
fixed asset		固定资产
brand awareness		品牌意识；品牌知名度
subsidiary	*n.*	子公司
non-current asset		非流动资产
sunk cost		沉没成本
revenue stream		收入来源
afloat	*adv.*	（计划等）尚未定案
host country		所在国；东道国
grant	*n.*	补助金
specification	*n.*	（产品）规格
intended market		目标市场

 **Exercises**

I.   Answer the following questions according to the text.

1. What is the definition of economic globalization?

2. What is the meaning of the globalization of markets?

3. What are the advantages of globalization of production?

4. What key factors are needed to be considered when going into the international market?

5. Why should we understand these factors correctly?

6. What is the most important aspect among the international market environment?

7. How can a company remain competitive according to the passage?

8. What is the biggest challenge for Chinese companies to go global?

9. What are the modes of going to the international market?

10. Which mode of going global is of the greatest risk?

II. Decide whether the following statements are true (T) or false (F) according to the text.

1. The international business is developing rapidly under the background of globalization. (   )

2. The globalization of markets is about the expansion of the world market in size. (   )

3. Although firms marketing abroad face many of the same challenges as firms marketing domestically, international environments present added uncertainties which must be accurately interpreted. (   )

4. Learning foreign languages is considered as the biggest challenge to growth in international markets. (   )

5. Compared with joint ventures and direct investment, exporting consists of the least risk for a company which wants to enter the international market. (   )

III. Read the following passage and fill in the blanks with the words given below. Change the form if necessary.

remain	assess	inherent	resource	familiar
liability	fit	negotiation	feasible	target

The decision to go international must be made with care, as there are many risks and potential obstacles to consider. Cultural and language barriers are among the most obvious of these considerations. Variations in religious beliefs, societal norms, and business 1. _____ styles all have an impact on how business needs to be conducted when dealing with foreign counterparts. Language barriers may present an obstacle when trying to communicate the benefits and advantages of a company's products and services overseas. There are 2. _____ political and economic risks when expanding into foreign markets. Instability of some foreign governments can pose a threat to the security of a business overseas. Even natural disasters happen. Foreign exchange might present a barrier to getting paid when you sell abroad.

The benefits of going international often 3. _____ an advantage, even with all the risks carefully considered. An organization that wants to go overseas needs to be prepared by having developed a specific international marketing plan, and decide how to enter the 4. _____ market. An international marketing plan should outline and define the product or service to be sold and the country or countries in which it will be sold. In doing so, it is essential to consider whether a product that works in one country will work in other countries.

A company that wishes to expand internationally needs to be 5. _____ with the target country's culture and determine the feasibility of marketing its product or service in that environment. Market conditions must be 6. _____ to ensure that a new company can win a share of the foreign market. Tariffs, duties and compliance with a country's export administration regulations are other important issues to consider as well. These considerations require some expertise in the financial and legal aspects of exporting.

Developing the required organizational processes and allocating appropriate 7. _____ to an international effort often requires creating a separate export department within an organization that is responsible for all aspects of dealing with foreign markets. Many companies attempt this by having a single sales manager and his assistants responsible for setting a budget, shipping goods and developing international growth. However, this can be an expensive alternative when overhead and 8. _____ costs are considered.

If a company chooses to go alone, it may need three to five years to develop a sizeable market share. In many cases, assistance from an outside source can dramatically reduce the time it will take to become established in foreign markets.

The use of a consultant or a company with the "Know Who" and the "Know How" is often the most 9. _____ way to break into an international market. In effect, these marketing authorities can manage your entire international sales effort more quickly and efficiently. They can also provide localization services, starting but going beyond, simply translating materials to the desired language. Localization refers to adapting a company's entire image to 10. _____ another culture. Export management companies offer working capital, clearing customs paperwork, and trade insurance for a fee and commission. Beyond the obvious value of intimate know-how and access to extensive overseas contacts that they can provide is the benefit of having after

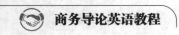

sales support. A good export management consultant has years of specialized experience in knowing or negotiating with governments, freight forwarders and banks.

IV. Translate the following sentences into Chinese.

1. We can take Honda as an example, who is making the spare parts in China, assembling the products in Pakistan and designing the engine in Japan. So, the production is distributed into three places.

2. Bargain is never done by the Dutch, often by Brazilians, and always by the Chinese. The company that does not take the time to understand these differences may have the risk of failing in international marketing.

3. Most foreign customers who seek accessibility to suppliers may request that supply stay local in order to enhance the flow of production. Companies usually follow that request to avoid losing the business.

4. Adapting to a new business environment is also considered a major challenge. Many companies are seeking local partners in an effort to better understand local consumer tastes and needs, effective marketing methods, and other issues such as local business customs.

5. Thus, the likelihood of sunk costs, or general barriers to exit, is slim. However, a company may have less control when exporting into a foreign market, because it cannot control the supply of the goods within the foreign market.

 **Case Study**

Chery in Overseas Markets

Since its early stages, Chery (奇瑞汽车) has paid attention to developing both domestic and international markets. As the first automobile brand in China to "go global", Chery has been expanding overseas markets in various forms including vehicle export, CKD (Completely Knocked Down, (国内组装汽车), joint ventures and localized R&D and production since its first exports in 2001.

Chery has been listed among the "Top 20 Chinese Enterprises with the Best Global Image" five times, and has established four R&D centers, ten production bases and more than

1,500 sales and service outlets overseas. Chery has sold over 1.7 million products in more than 80 countries and regions. From January to December 2020, Chery exported a total of 114,000 vehicles, up by 18.7% year on year, making it the number one exporter among Chinese passenger vehicle manufacturers for 18 consecutive years.

Chery Automobile has been able to maintain its competitiveness overseas for so many years because of its long-term insistence on its international development strategy. In order to build its global competitiveness, Chery formulated a "three-step" strategy: before 2013, Chery took developing markets as the breakthrough point and focused on export trade to make its products "go global" successfully. In 2014, Chery began to "go deeper", actively developing emerging markets such as Brazil and Russia, establishing four major plants, exporting technology, management and culture, and "going deeper" into local markets. From 2020, Chery will push the brand to "go higher" and complete the international layout including mainstream markets such as Europe and America.

In 2020, against the global background of the COVID-19 epidemic, Chery's overseas exports still achieved substantial growth. The high-end brand EXEED entered the Russian market with the TXL model as the pioneer taking a new step in Chery's globalization strategy. The EXEED TXL also won the honor of "Best New Vehicle in 2020" in Russia. Chery's products represented by the new TIGGO 8 are popular in Russia, Saudi Arabia, Chile, Ukraine, Philippines, Peru and other countries, with both sales volume and market share reaching record highs.

At present, Chery is accelerating its global market strategy, including building a global integrated R&D system and sales service system to support the localized operation of Chery products in global mainstream markets. At present, Chery's R&D centers in Europe and North America have been put into operation. The European R&D Center, Chery's "vanguard" for entering the European market, is mainly responsible for three core businesses: first, the design business which supports Chery's European and international projects; second, the R&D business which supports Chery's development of the European market and cooperation with European partners; and third, the market business which makes preparations for Chery's related brands and products to enter the European market in the future. The North American R&D center will focus on the R&D of autonomous driving.

In the future, Chery will further integrate the professional knowledge reserves and development capabilities of major R&D outlets around the world, and introduce global product development processes to further enhance its ability to participate in global market competition.

The severe global epidemic situation and the accelerated reshuffle of the automotive industry have not hindered the pace of Chery's "going higher". Always putting customers first and oriented by customer demands, Chery produces excellent products and satisfactory services with which it wins the trust and support of its customers. In the future, Chery will continue to improve its service experience standards and development quality to bring customers convenient, rapid, sincere, enthusiastic, trustworthy and high-quality services. In 2021, under the double pressure of the global economic downturn and the cyclical adjustment of the automotive industry, Chery is taking great strides towards becoming an international brand with global competitiveness.

Questions for discussion

1. What strategy did Chery take to build its global competitiveness?

2. Why did Chery's overseas exports still achieve substantial growth during the outbreak of the COVID-19 pandemic?

3. How did Chery win the trust and support of its customers?

Assignments

1. Do some research of Chinese products on the international market, and make a list of the products that sell well and the products that have fewer sales. Write a report of about 200 words in English.

2. Prepare a ten-minute presentation to introduce why some companies are very successful in the international market and explain their strategies of going global.

15

E-business

Learning Objectives

After learning this unit, you should be able to:

- explain the concept of e-business;
- know the development process of e-business;
- understand the differences between e-business and e-commerce;
- describe the advantages and disadvantages of e-business;
- know the major considerations and tips of starting your own e-business.

Warm-up Questions

1. Do you often do shopping online? Share some experiences with each other.

2. What is your opinion on e-business?

3. Have you ever thought of starting your own e-business?

Reading

There is no universally accepted definition of the word "e-business". IBM launched a theme activity and built a term called "e-business" in 1997, and it was the first time to use this word. However, e-commerce was a widely used buzzword by then. The change of the term meant a paradigm shift. As the Internet continues to grow and expand, the term "e-business" can be allowed for more types on the web.

15.1 The history of e-business

With the advent of the World Wide Web (WWW), or the web, traditional business organizations that had relied on catalog sales had a new sales vector. Other businesses found that the web was a good place to put customer service information, such as manuals and drivers, and it's also a place to help create a consistent corporate image. As the web developed, a number of Internet-based businesses developed, including companies like eBay and Amazon. The following are some key issues and stages in the history of e-business.

(1) The early use of the web for business

Businesses began using websites for marketing shortly after graphical-based web design became available in the early 1990s. Most of the websites served to provide visitors with basic information about a company's products and services, including contact information, such as phone numbers and email addresses. The purpose is to help consumers contact a company for services. When the marketing departments realized that company websites were available to millions of people, the companies' websites got a new function—attracting business on the web. Online sales began in 1994 with the ability to encrypt credit card and transform it into code data.

(2) The early online sales

When it comes to early online sales, the Secured Socket Layer (SSL) cannot be ignored. This is a technology developed by Netscape in 1994. Owing to it, websites were developed to encrypt sessions, making credit card transactions over the Internet safer. With an encrypted connection between a company's server and a client computer, credit numbers could be masked. So they could not be intercepted by a third party, thus making theft of card information less likely. This security led to an increased number of businesses offering products for sale on the web.

(3) The birth of modern web sales

The online sales in modern times have changed. Developments in server technology, including the ability to build websites from product databases, resulted in the creation of large Internet-only businesses like eBay and Amazon. In previous product-sales websites, each product had to be manually posted on a web page. With database-driven sites, companies could use web-page templates to display tens of thousands of products very quickly. As the number of available products increased, so did traffic and sales on these websites.

(4) The advancement of payment systems

Early SSL implementations were good, but many people still did not trust them to secure credit card payment information. In addition, it was too expensive to process micropayments through traditional credit card systems. The micropayment here means payment of less than a dollar. As a result, a number of micropayment websites came and went. One has remained and done very well because it can transfer money from a variety of funding sources, including credit cards and bank accounts, without revealing the payer's credit card information to the merchant. This company is PayPal. PayPal has enabled credit card processing by many small businesses.

(5) The dot-com bubble of 2001

Problems with customer confidence began in the late 1990s. Throughout this period, online businesses received large capital investments via initial public offerings, and saw their stock selling at prices far above the actual value of their companies. Many companies had good ideas but poor business plans, and speculators bid up the stock prices of Internet companies. The initial blows came as some online companies began reporting large losses and investors began examining the viability of online business plans. Fearful investors started to sell their stocks, causing the overinflated stock prices to drop below their actual value. A number of well-known companies closed. Many other companies that lacked solid business plans failed between 2001 and 2002.

(6) The current state of e-business

Currently, e-business ranges from simple websites providing corporate information to websites offering goods and services for sale online. Innovative uses of new voice and video communication technologies include online language tutoring. Large commercial information websites are growing and the use of the Internet for research is common now. Online sales from web-based storefronts or virtual stores continue to grow. Sales of digital information, in the form of eBooks and digital music files, are more recent offerings by e-businesses like Apple and Amazon.

15.2 The differences between e-business and e-commerce

Many people use e-business and e-commerce interchangeably, because both words apply to businesses using electronic networks to conduct their commerce and other business activities. It is not easy to differentiate the two because they are closely interconnected terms. But actually, they are not the same. E-commerce is nothing but buying and selling of goods on the web. E-business is a little different as it is not limited to commercial transactions, it also provides other services.

(1) The definition of e-business

Electronic business, shortly known as e-business, is the online presence of business. It can also be defined as the business which is done with the help of the Internet or electronic data interchange. E-commerce is just one of the important components of e-business.

E-business is not confined to buying and selling of goods only. It includes other activities that also form part of business, such as providing services to the customers and communicating with employees. Clients or business partners can also contact the company by electronic means if they want to have a word with the company, or if they have any issues regarding the services, etc. All the basic business operations are done using electronic media.

Generally speaking, there are two major types of e-business, which are commonly referred to as click-and-click retailers and brick-and-click retailers. Click-and-click retailers are those companies that sell products only via the website. Amazon.com is a good example, where the company was created specifically to sell products via the Internet. Brick-and-click retailers are those companies that sell products both via a website and via a physical store. Wal-Mart is an example of this. Wal-Mart was a physical store that expanded to create a web presence, so they could also sell via a website.

(2) The definition of e-commerce

E-commerce is an abbreviation used for electronic commerce. It is the process through which buying, selling, dealing, ordering and paying for the goods and services are done over the Internet. In this type of online commercial transaction, the seller can communicate with the buyer without having a face-to-face interaction. Some examples of real-world application of e-commerce are online banking, online shopping, online ticket booking, social networking, etc.

The basic requirement of e-commerce is a website. The marketing, advertising, selling and conducting transaction are done with the help of the Internet. Any monetary transaction, which is done with the help of electronic media, is e-commerce.

E-commerce can generally be categorized into the following categories.

Business-to-Business (B2B)

Website following B2B business model sells its product to an intermediate buyer who then sells the product to the final customer. As an example, a wholesaler places an order from a company's website. After receiving the consignment, it sells the end product to the final customer who comes to buy the product at the wholesaler's retail outlet.

Business-to-Consumer (B2C)

Website following B2C business model sells its product directly to a customer. A customer can view products shown on the website of a business organization. The customer can choose a product and order the same. The website will send a notification to the business organization via email and the organization will dispatch the product/goods to the customer.

Consumer-to-Consumer (C2C)

Website following C2C business model helps consumer to sell their assets like residential property, cars, motorcycles, etc., or rent a room by publishing their information on the website. The website may or may not charge the consumer for its services. Another consumer may opt to buy the product from the first customer by viewing the post/advertisement on the website.

Consumer-to-Business (C2B)

In this model, a consumer approaches website showing multiple business organizations for a particular service. The consumer places an estimate of amount he wants to spend on a particular service, for example, a comparison of interest rates of car loan provided by various banks via the website. The business organization who fulfills the consumer's requirement within a specified budget approaches the customer and provides its services.

Business-to-Government (B2G)

B2G model is a variant of B2B model. Such websites are used by the government to trade and exchange information with various business organizations. Such websites are accredited by the government and provide a medium for businesses to submit application forms to the government.

Government-to-Business (G2B)

The government uses G2B model websites to approach business organizations. Such websites support auctions, tenders, and application submission functionalities.

Government-to-Citizen (G2C)

The government uses G2C model websites to approach citizens in general. Such websites support auctions of vehicles, machinery or any other material. Such websites also provide services like registration for birth, marriage or death certificates. The main objective of G2C websites is to reduce average time for fulfilling people's requests for various government services.

(3) The key differences between e-commerce and e-business

There are four key differences between e-commerce and e-business.

Different focuses

E-commerce focuses on appearance much more than e-business. E-commerce is primarily concerned with transactions, not only with customers but also with online suppliers and distributors. E-business applications strive to give a good idea of their company, promoting the values they use to market their business. As a result, e-commerce is much more concerned with user interface and advertising than e-business.

Different business models

E-commerce typically requires a new or additional business model to govern online sales and services. This new model must include different methods of advertising, system management, security, marketing and the costs involved in maintaining an online website for business transactions. But e-business tends to affect the existing business model more thoroughly, reinventing older processes.

Different management

While e-commerce is concerned more with the outside functions and appearance of the business, e-business is concerned with the inner workings of the company itself. E-business works to apply online solutions to payroll, human resources, internal data management and other systems, which cannot be seen by the customers but can affect every part of the business.

Different benefits

The benefits of e-commerce are mostly market-oriented. It allows businesses to reach markets which they could not reach before and show a new, up-to-date face for the company that may attract potential customers. The main benefit of e-business, on the other hand, is efficiency. While e-business strategies take longer to incorporate and are often more expensive, they create a more fluid, dynamic and efficient business model than before, increasing overall profits and growth.

In one word, e-commerce is a major part of e-business. It can also be said that e-commerce is e-business, but e-business is not necessarily e-commerce. E-commerce is just the online presence of the conventional commerce.

At present, most companies are doing e-business in order to capture the maximum part of the market. More and more e-commerce websites have emerged. They are competing with traditional commercial businesses in the market.

15.3 The advantages and disadvantages of e-business

E-business has transformed the way companies function in today's economic marketplace. The technological advances of the past few decades have given businesses the ability to grow and expand beyond their local market. The Internet allows small businesses to reach national or global consumers with their products and services, increasing their sales and profits. Along with these advantages come some disadvantages, creating higher levels of economic challenges not previously seen.

(1) Advantages

There are four major advantages in using e-business.

Low business costs

E-businesses are becoming famous for their low-cost start-up compared with traditional brick-and-mortar stores once they have increased their working capital. Many of the barriers to opening your own business have been reduced or removed, and many people can operate an e-business while remaining employed in their regular day jobs. As technology gets more advanced, less expensive and more available, it has become even easier to start a business: All you need is a computer and access to the Internet. The Internet gives you access to a much larger customer base than your personal contacts or people in your area.

Speed and efficiency

The design of the World Wide Web intends speed and efficiency, and brings those advantages to small businesses. Online ordering systems can process payments and orders in real time, usually faster, more accurately and cheaper than human workers. You can also store and access any product catalogs and information online, saving the time and money required to print, mail or hand them out. Finally, certain products, such as music, files, e-books, applications, are hosted and downloaded directly from your site, which means no physical inventory or shipping costs and delays.

Competitiveness

The Internet is a great equalizer: Small e-businesses may compete with large companies, and businesses in America and Europe are just as accessible as those in your own backyard. Low start-up costs mean that new businesses can be just as competitive and responsive as those that have been around for years. The online customer is more focused on getting the product or service quickly and accurately rather than what the website looks like or who the business is.

Worldwide presence

A firm engaging in e-business can have a nationwide or a worldwide presence. This is the biggest advantage of conducting business online. E-business allows companies to expand into new markets, both nationally and internationally. Entry barriers to these new markets are relatively low, depending on the type of goods or services sold via the e-business website. Government regulation may also be easier when conducting e-business. Many local and national governments have not imposed heavy regulations on some sectors of e-business.

Besides what we have mentioned here, you can still find some other advantages of e-business. However, just as a famous proverb goes, every sword has two edges, e-business also has its disadvantages.

(2) Disadvantages

There are five major disadvantages in using e-business.

Separation from the customer

The biggest disadvantage of e-business is its inherent separation from the customer. The customer and the product come face to face in a traditional brick-and-mortar business. The faceless nature of an e-business causes an issue of trust, which remains hard to resolve.

Unsuitability in many areas or sectors

Another big disadvantage of e-business is its unsuitability in many areas or sectors. E-business, for instance, cannot treat a patient. Consumers traditionally place high value on customer service in the brick-and-mortar business environment. Creating this same type of positive customer service is difficult for e-businesses, because their customers may be hundreds or thousands of miles away from the e-business' operations.

Unstable service

The third disadvantage of e-business is the unstable service. The success of an e-business depends on robust computer systems, updating and maintaining the website, security of e-commerce transactions, reliability of shipping and delivery, and search engine optimization. Managing such critical components seems easy, but in most cases, such components remain far more unstable and unreliable than the critical components of a traditional brick-and-mortar business. Search engine optimization and other technological components remain in a constant change of flux, with new standards replacing old standards now and then. This requires the e-business to spend considerable time and resources in keeping up with the developments.

The danger from viruses, Trojans, worms, and other malware

A far bigger threat is the danger from viruses, Trojans, worms, and other malware. An e-business needs to invest heavily on SSL certification, antivirus, and other security mechanisms, and even then, the business and its customers are still at risk of various attacks and scams.

Dependence on the delivery channel partner

Finally, the success of an e-business depends largely on the success of the delivery channel partner. Only those e-businesses that can ensure delivery of the product to the customer in a timely and safe manner can survive. Today, most e-businesses rely on third party shipping vendors in this regard.

It is true that e-business does have its own set of pros and cons. However, eventually, every business has to adopt e-business practices in order to ensure survival and success, be it partially or completely.

15.4 Major considerations in e-business

The act of doing business via the Internet—e-business—has exploded in recent years, accounting now for many billions of dollars annually in sales. While many people love the idea of being able to shop without ever leaving their home, e-businesses can offer problems, both for buyers and sellers, which need to be considered.

Generally speaking, there are four important factors that we should bear in mind when conducting e-business.

(1) Security

The biggest concern for both buyers and sellers with e-business is often security; hackers are always looking for unsecured websites, where they can steal credit card information and other data. While improvements have been made in recent years with the advent of complex encryption techniques, there are still many e-businesses out there with gaping holes in their online security.

(2) Connection issues

Traffic on the information superhighway can sometimes be very slow, so shoppers need to wait for a long time as they flip through web pages; a broken connection can lead to orders not getting processed, or a customer accidentally paying for the same item twice. Many e-businesses could solve some of these problems with improvements to their websites or increased bandwidth, but they may not be able to afford to do so.

(3) Delivery services

When a person buys something at a local store, they can often take it home or have it delivered the same day. Items purchased online, however, must be mailed; some businesses process orders quickly and use delivery services that will get items to purchasers the next day. Others, however, may be slow in getting orders out the door, and they may rely on slower delivery methods in order to keep down costs. This may result in delays of several days—and at times, weeks, or items being lost.

(4) Reputation

Developing a good reputation can be a long and tedious process for an e-business, no matter how long they have been doing business in a traditional manner; many customers cannot learn about new e-businesses due to a lack of reviews, so they just do the shopping elsewhere. Such caution is reasonable, because there are many disreputable businesses that have cheated the customers online. The bad reviews will keep customers away from doing business with them.

In summary, e-businesses have changed the very nature of doing business, and have replaced the traditional models of doing business in many industries and sectors. Comparing e-business advantages and disadvantages, we can find that the potential advantages outweigh the disadvantages of e-business, but e-businesses have to overcome challenges related to trust and security before they replace brick-and-mortar stores.

15.5 How to create an e-business enterprise

Electronic business ventures, or e-businesses, are a popular method for starting and running a company. Typically done over the Internet, an e-business can operate as a standalone online storefront, or it can be an additional component to a brick-and-mortar company that operates in the real world. Although it is possible to purchase an existing e-business, it is relatively easy to start one on your own. With a nominal investment and a little time, you can have an e-business up, running and accepting customers.

The following are some tips for running an e-business.

(1) Determine the concept of the business you wish to start

Decide if you would like to have an online storefront to sell products, operate a social network or dating site, or maybe even just report the news and earn revenues from advertising. There are limitless types of e-businesses available. Just choose the type of electronic business you would like to operate.

(2) Write a business plan that will serve as a guide for your e-business

Cover the details about what your business will be and how it will operate. Identify your strengths and weaknesses, your competitors and how you will market your business. Also include a budget that covers your fixed assets, marketing and operational costs.

(3) Secure the investment you need for your e-business

Most start-up companies get their seed capital from cash advances on credit cards or from loans that come from family and friends. You can also take out a small business loan from your bank. If your e-business requires a significant investment, you may require the aid of a private investor or venture capital firm.

(4) Register a company so that a legal entity will own the e-business

Business registration can be done in the city in which you will be conducting business. You can also find the proper paperwork at your local government. Fill out the appropriate forms and pay the related fees to open your company. The amount of the fee will vary depending on where you are and whether your company is a sole proprietorship or a partnership.

(5) Obtain a domain and hosting account

An Internet domain name provides you with a private web address that directs customers to your e-business. The domain is backed by a web hosting account, which provides you with a place to store the files for your e-business. Web hosting is paid on a monthly or annual subscription plan, with the price depending on how much server space and bandwidth you require.

(6) Construct a website for your e-business

The website serves as the primary point of contact between the e-business and its customers. The type of website you build will depend primarily on the primary purpose of your e-business. If you are building a storefront, you will need to build a shopping cart website, while a dating website would require an entirely different design. Consider the purpose of your website and create a design that is specific to those needs.

Words and Phrases

encrypt	v.	加密
micropayment	n.	小额支付
e-commerce	n.	电子商业
e-business	n.	电子商务
brick-and-click		线上和线下
consignment	n.	托付货物；托卖货物
notification	n.	通知，通知书
be accredited by		被认可
market-oriented		以市场为导向的
brick-and-mortar business		实体店

physical inventory		实际库存
flux	*n.*	连续的改变；不稳定的状态
Trojan	*n.*	木马程序
virus	*n.*	病毒
malware	*n.*	恶意软件
antivirus	*n.*	杀毒软件
scam	*n.*	诈骗；诡计
hacker	*n.*	电脑黑客
encryption technique		加密技术
delivery service		送货服务
standalone	*adj.*	独立的
storefront	*n.*	店面
dating site		交友网站
hosting account		托管账户
subscription plan		订阅计划
dot-com bubble		互联网泡沫
bandwidth	*n.*	网络带宽

 **Exercises**

I.   Answer the following questions according to the text.

1.   What is e-business?

2.   When did e-business come to emerge?

3.   What were the functions of the websites at the early stage of e-business?

4.   Why did the company PayPal remain doing very well when so many micropayment sites came and went?

5.   Could you give a brief introduction to "dot-com bubble"?

6.   What are the main advantages and disadvantages of e-business?

7. Why are e-businesses very competitive?

8. What should we pay attention to when shopping online?

9. What are the important factors for an e-business?

10. What can we do when establishing an e-business?

II. Decide whether the following statements are true (T) or false (F) according to the text.

1. E-business is nothing but buying and selling of goods on the web. E-commerce is a little different as it is not limited to commercial transactions, but it also provides other services. (   )

2. Brick-and-click retailers are those companies that sell products both via a website and via a physical store. (   )

3. A website following B2B business model sells its product directly to a customer. (   )

4. Even today the security problem is still one of the biggest concerns for both buyers and sellers in online shopping. (   )

5. The success of an e-business depends largely on the success of the delivery channel partner. (   )

III. Read the following passage and fill in the blanks with the words given below. Change the form if necessary.

air-conditioned	ensure	authorize	contain	access
confidential	location	employee	failover	separate

Despite e-business being business done online, there are still physical security measures that can be taken to protect the business as a whole. Even though business is done online, the building that houses the servers and computers must be protected and have limited 1. _____ to employees and other persons. For example, this room should only allow authorized users to enter, and should 2. _____ that "windows, dropped ceilings, large air ducts, and raised floors" do not allow easy access to unauthorized persons. Preferably, these important items would be kept in a(n) 3. _____ room without any windows.

Protecting against the environment is equally important in physical security as protecting against unauthorized users. The room may protect the equipment against flooding by keeping all equipment raised off of the floor. In addition, the room should 4. _____ a fire extinguisher in case of fire. The organization should have a fire plan in case this situation arises.

In addition to keeping the servers and computers safe, physical security of 5. _____ information is important. This includes client information such as credit card numbers, checks, phone numbers, etc. It also includes any of the organization's private information. Locking physical and electronic copies of this data in a drawer or cabinet is one additional measure of security. Doors and windows leading into this area should also be securely locked. Only 6. _____ that need to use this information as part of their job should be given keys.

Important information can also be kept secure by keeping backups of files and updating them on a regular basis. It is best to keep these backups in a(n) 7. _____ secure location in case there is a natural disaster or breach of security at the main location.

"Failover sites" can be built in case there is a problem with the main location. This site should be just like the main 8. _____ in terms of hardware, software, and security features. It can be used in case of fire or natural disaster at the original site. It is also important to test the " 9. _____ site" to ensure that it will actually work if the need arises.

State of the art security systems, such as the one used at Tidepoint's headquarters, might include access control, alarm systems, and closed-circuit television. One form of access control is face (or another feature) recognition systems. This allows only 10. _____ personnel to enter, and also serves the purpose of convenience for employees who don't have to carry keys or cards. Cameras can also be placed throughout the building and at all points of entry. Alarm systems also serve as an added measure of protection against theft.

IV. Translate the following sentences into Chinese.

1. Most of the websites served to provide visitors with basic information about a company's products and services, including contact information, such as phone numbers and email addresses. The purpose is to help consumers contact a company

for services. When the marketing departments realized that company websites were available to millions of people, the companies' websites got a new function— attracting business on the web.

2. Developments in server technology, including the ability to build websites from product databases, resulted in the creation of large Internet-only businesses like eBay and Amazon. In previous product-sales websites, each product had to be manually posted on a web page. With database-driven sites, companies could use web-page templates to display tens of thousands of products very quickly.

3. Many of the barriers to opening your own business have been reduced or removed, and many people can operate an e-business while remaining employed in their regular day jobs. As technology gets more advanced, less expensive and more available, it has become even easier to start a business: All you need is a computer and access to the Internet. The Internet gives you access to a much larger customer base than your personal contacts or people in your area.

4. Consumers traditionally place high value on customer service in the brick-and-mortar business environment. Creating this same type of positive customer service is difficult for e-businesses, considering that their customers may be hundreds or thousands of miles away from the e-business' operations.

5. Electronic business ventures, or e-businesses, are a popular method for starting and running a company. Typically done over the Internet, an e-business can operate as a standalone online storefront, or it can be an additional component to a brick-and-mortar company that operates in the real world.

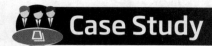 **Case Study**

Light In The Box Provides Value to Consumers Across the World

Shanghai-based, New York-listed cross-border e-commerce platform LightInTheBox (兰亭集势) is now considered a shining example of companies that not only managed to ride out the economic effects of the COVID-19 pandemic but also posted unexpectedly good financial results.

The company, whose name is abbreviated as LITB, released its April-June quarterly results in late August. Its sales revenue rose 96 percent year-on-year to $113.9 million and generated a profit of $8.5 million, the highest quarterly gain since it went public in 2013. It was the fourth consecutive quarter that LITB reported positive financial results.

LITB took off in 2007 as a business-to-consumer cross-border e-commerce platform. It offers made-in-China products to consumers in many countries across the world. In 2013, it became the first Chinese cross-border e-commerce platform to be listed on the New York Stock Exchange. It boasts a global user base of about 10 million in more than 200 countries and regions.

But its NYSE listing did not turn out to be a breakthrough for the company's financial performance. LITB's share price remained between $1 and $3 for years. In late October 2018, it received a delisting warning from the NYSE after reporting losses for five consecutive years since the IPO. Its stock price plunged below $1 for 30 trading days.

Against all COVID-19 odds, LITB survived the first quarter of this year and then turned the corner with impressive second-quarter results. He Jian, LITB's chief executive officer, persuaded himself to discern potential opportunities in the crisis brought about by the pandemic. He knew the European consumers, especially the elderly group, are quite difficult to win over. For, before the epidemic, they hardly shopped online. But, due to lockdowns and social distancing measures that lasted for about three months, online retail became their only option to buy daily necessities and for other kinds of shopping, as brick-and-mortar stores stayed shuttered.

"The online shopping experience turned out to be quite pleasant for them as we offered more products at lower prices. Therefore, our next step in Europe will be to increase the rate of click-throughs to win more consumers," said He.

But the breakthrough in Europe was still more due to circumstance than deliberate strategy. The progress LITB has made over the past quarters, He said, is organic and sustainable. It can be largely attributed to LITB's resolve, since He took office as CEO in 2018, to continue investing in technology, maintain stricter selection of products, restructure management and absorb staff members of Ezbuy, the Singaporean e-commerce platform that the company bought out in late 2018.

Ever since 2018, the company has doubled its investment in research and development, increasing its technical staff strength to 300. "Most of our engineers are based in Shanghai. You can imagine the cost. But only by investing in talent can we become more digitalized, better match clients' demand and increase efficiency," He said.

Products that e-retail on LITB are chosen strategically. Electronic products that sell better on Amazon are not a priority. Instead, LITB features products that showcase China's manufacturing capability. For example, lifestyle and home decor products have pride of place on LITB as they offer a competitive edge, and can be shipped directly to overseas markets without incurring high after-sales expenditure, said He.

Forays into new markets outside of China have played a key role in LITB's growth. Ever since the merger with Ezbuy in 2018, Southeast Asia has become a new growth driver for LITB. In less than two years, the region now weighs as much as the United States, Europe and the Middle East in terms of contribution to LITB's turnover. He explained that while the penetration rate of e-commerce was only about 2 percent in Southeast Asia three years ago, the figure has since more than doubled. The higher birthrate in the region will be translated into a larger group of younger consumers. Therefore, it is quite likely that the e-commerce penetration rate in Southeast Asia will be on a par with that of China's in about five years, He said.

He further observed China is internationally competitive now in terms of cross-border e-commerce. While cheaper mass-market products defined China's manufacturing prowess 20 years ago, the scene is very different now. Flexible manufacturing, which is required by e-commerce platforms, has emerged as the key strength of China's supply chain. "We have witnessed China leapfrogging, in terms of its capacity to make consumer goods as well as the high efficiency reached by the entire ecosystem," he said.

That was possible because of the supportive policies of the Chinese government. The State Council announced on April 7 that 46 more cross-border e-commerce comprehensive pilot zones will be set up across the country. When they materialize, their total number will surpass 150 in 30 provinces, municipalities and autonomous regions of China. Data from the China E-commerce Research Center showed that the total trading volume of China's cross-border e-commerce industry exceeded 10 trillion yuan ($1.5 trillion) last year. The compound annual growth rate of the industry topped 20 percent between 2014 and 2019, significantly overtaking the 3.61 percent annual growth rate of China's foreign trade during the same period.

Questions for discussion

1. What's He Jian's attitude toward e-commerce in Southeast Asia and why?

2. Why does He Jian believe China is internationally competitive now in terms of cross-border e-commerce?

3. What can other e-commerce companies learn from strategies taken by LITB to maintain competitiveness?

Assignments

1. Interview some people who have online shopping experiences. Ask about their opinions of the e-business and the trouble they have met in online shopping. Write a report of about 200 words in English.

2. Prepare a ten-minute presentation to introduce the development process of three famous e-commerce companies of the world and analyze the reasons of their success.

教师服务

　　感谢您选用清华大学出版社的教材！为了更好地服务教学，我们为授课教师提供本学科重点教材信息及样书，请您扫码获取。

》 最新书目

扫码获取 2024 **外语类**重点教材信息

》 样书赠送

教师扫码即可获取样书